WITHDRAWN

Treating Chronic Juvenile Offenders

The LAW AND PUBLIC POLICY: PSYCHOLOGY AND THE SOCIAL SCIENCES series includes books in three domains:

Legal Studies—writings by legal scholars about issues of relevance to psychology and the other social sciences, or that employ social science information to advance the legal analysis;

Social Science Studies—writings by scientists from psychology and the other social sciences about issues of relevance to law and public policy; and

Forensic Studies—writings by psychologists and other mental health scientists and professionals about issues relevant to forensic mental health science and practice.

The series is guided by its editor, Bruce D. Sales, PhD, JD, ScD(*hc*), University of Arizona; and coeditors, Bruce J. Winick, JD, University of Miami; Norman J. Finkel, PhD, Georgetown University; and Valerie P. Hans, PhD, University of Delaware.

* * *

Treating Chronic Juvenile Offenders

ADVANCES MADE THROUGH THE
OREGON MULTIDIMENSIONAL
TREATMENT FOSTER CARE MODEL

Patricia Chamberlain

American Psychological Association • Washington, DC

Published by
American Psychological Association
750 First Street, NE
Washington, DC 20002
www.apa.org

To order
APA Order Department
P.O. Box 92984
Washington, DC 20090-2984
Tel: (800) 374-2721; Direct: (202) 336-5510
Fax: (202) 336-5502; TDD/TTY: (202) 336-6123
Online: www.apa.org/books/
E-mail: order@apa.org

In the U.K., Europe, Africa, and the Middle East, copies may be ordered from
American Psychological Association
3 Henrietta Street
Covent Garden, London
WC2E 8LU England

Typeset in Goudy by Stephen McDougal, Mechanicsville, MD
Printer: Port City Press, Baltimore, MD
Cover Designer: Berg design, Albany, NY
Technical/Production Editor: Jennifer L. Zale

The opinions and statements published are the responsibility of the authors, and such opinions and statements do not necessarily represent the policies of the American Psychological Association.

Library of Congress Cataloging-in-Publication Data

Chamberlain, Patricia.
   Treating chronic juvenile offenders : advances made through the Oregon multidimensional treatment foster care model / Patricia Chamberlain.—1st ed.
      p. cm. — (Law and public policy)
   Includes bibliographical references and index.
   ISBN 1-55798-996-6 (alk. paper)
      1. Multidimensional Treatment Foster Care Program. 2. Juvenile delinquents—Rehabilitation—United States. 3. Foster home care—United states. 4. Juvenile ecidivists—United States. I. Title. II. Series.

RJ506.J88C455 2003
618.92'858206—dc21   2003001930

British Library Cataloguing-in-Publication Data
A CIP record is available from the British Library.

Printed in the United States of America
First Edition

To John Reid, mentor, colleague, and friend.

CONTENTS

ACKNOWLEDGMENTS

The development of the treatment model described in this volume has been the result of a collaborative effort that has included help from numerous professional colleagues and dedicated community members who have volunteered to be foster parents. In particular, for getting us started, I thank Irma August, Karla and Bob Antione, Kate Kavanagh, John Reid, and Marion Forgatch. In recent years, when we have held our feet to the fire and looked critically at outcomes, we sometimes have had to change our favorite ways of thinking and acting because they did not work. For this flexibility, leadership, and innovation I thank JP Davis and Phil Fisher. JP, Phil, Leslie Leve, and Mark Eddy have played key roles in pushing theory development forward.

Recognition and success have brought a new set of challenges that include coming through with quality programming on a day-in and day-out basis in our own community. I thank Kevin Moore, Dana Smith, Peter Sprengelmeyer, and Kim Bronz for their hard work, dedication, and exceptionally good clinical skills that make the theories actually translate into something that matters for kids and families. Finally, thanks to Gerry Bouwman, who keeps all manner of bad things from happening and who figures out how to spread the word, and to Judy Boler, for her help with this manuscript and with numerous other projects and details.

INTRODUCTION

Juvenile delinquency is a legally defined status and not a psychiatric condition. The issue of whether juvenile delinquents should receive treatment or punishment is a long-standing debate subject to political considerations and public perceptions of the threat that juvenile crime presents in local communities. In most locales, juvenile justice systems deal with conflicting missions. The community needs to be protected. Children need to be cared for. Should the juvenile offender be considered an individual who committed a conscious act that he or she should be held accountable for regardless of age or cognitive ability? Will he or she respond to rehabilitation? Can community-based programs be designed and implemented to counteract the effects of poor prior socialization, negative societal influences, mental health problems, and inept skills?

In this volume I consider these questions and then present a conceptual framework and practical methods for treating chronic juvenile offenders in community-based settings. I discuss treatment considerations in the context of research on the developmental course of antisocial behavior during the childhood and adolescent years. The primary aim of the book, however, is to describe the development, effects, and implementation of the Oregon Multidimensional Treatment Foster Care (MTFC) model. The MTFC model has been used with serious, chronic juvenile offenders as an alternative to placement in locked settings or placement in residential or group care. I describe clinical methods, outcomes, and mediators of outcomes as well as adaptations of the model for special populations.

The book is intended for clinicians, community program administrators, researchers, policymakers, judges, and attorneys. Although trying to write a book that has relevance for such a broad audience is a daunting task that potentially sets the stage for disappointment all around, too often research has little influence on or relevance to practice, and what happens in "real-world" programs rarely filters back into research designs. This disconnect has impeded the progress of both practitioners and researchers on producing positive results for youths and their families. The overall aim of this book is to provide "take-away" messages for key players from multiple disciplines that can be used to stimulate thinking about how to grapple with the complex set of theoretical and practical issues one faces when designing and implementing programming for delinquent adolescents in community settings.

In chapter 1, I review the research-based underpinnings of the MTFC model with a focus on how research has informed what we know about the development of antisocial behavior during childhood and adolescence. The studies discussed summarize the work on risk and protective factors for antisocial behavior. How multiple factors at the individual, contextual, and social interaction levels contribute to and shape the development of delinquency has relevance for how program developers, administrators, and clinicians conceptualize program and treatment goals for participating youths and their families. The review is intended to be free of jargon and succinct so as to be relevant to policymakers and juvenile justice authorities as well.

Chapter 2 deals with how the research base relates to intervention methods that are currently widely practiced, including group-based and residential models of service delivery. I make the case for designing interventions that target multiple systems and studies on the roles of key systems, including the family, peers, and schools. Chapter 2 is intended to set the stage for understanding how the complex task of focusing on simultaneous treatment goals within multiple systems can be integrated into a clearly conceptualized program model that integrates several different considerations that research has shown to be important to outcomes.

In chapter 3, I present the rationale and evidence base for efficacious community-based interventions along with research on barriers to positive outcomes. The MTFC model builds on previous work in the area of family-based interventions that have produced positive outcomes for children and youths with conduct problems and on community-based prevention and intervention models that target multiple settings and systems, including the family. In chapter 3, I draw attention to theory, evidence, and practice considerations that are relevant for program design and implementation. Policy can potentially be informed by what has worked (and not worked) in previous attempts to influence short- and long-term outcomes.

Chapter 4 describes the development of the MTFC model, including a brief history, the evidence supporting the effectiveness of MTFC compared with standard practice, an overview of the treatment components that constitute the model, and a description of how staff roles work. This chapter gets to the specifics of the model and how the parts work together.

In chapter 5, I describe the "nuts and bolts" of the MTFC model, including methods for recruiting, training, and supervising foster parents; treatment components; and staff roles. I also describe the way staff members work as a team. Chapter 5 ends with a case study that is intended to illustrate the principles and practices of MTFC.

In chapter 6, I present evidence on why MTFC works. I review and discuss the specific factors within the model that have been shown to influence youth outcomes. My hope is that program developers and clinicians who are working with antisocial youths in a variety of settings will find the data on what factors mediate specific treatment effects informative. I describe the interplay of science, clinical, and service system considerations in this and the previous chapter. In particular, the first part of chapter 6 is an attempt to explain to clinicians and policymakers the relevance and steps of the science of treatment development and validation.

In chapter 7, I discuss adaptation of the MTFC model for working with girls with severe problems with antisocial behavior. I provide a background of research that highlights the unique problems of girls and present the implications for long-term outcomes. This chapter also includes the preliminary results from a study in progress with girls referred from juvenile justice because of chronic problems with delinquency. Although girls have traditionally received less attention from juvenile justice than boys, they represent the fastest growing segment of the adolescent offender population as of 1999. Although there is much discussion about gender-specific programming, there is relatively little research to inform it. In this chapter, I attempt to discuss some of the key issues relative to girls and their families.

Chapter 8 is coauthored by Philip A. Fisher, a colleague at the Oregon Social Learning Center (OSLC) who developed an adaptation of the MTFC model for preschoolers in foster care called Early Intervention Foster Care (EIFC). The EIFC model reconceptualizes intervention targets to fit the needs of the population being served. We present the components of EIFC and data on the efficacy of the EIFC model. In addition to highlighting several innovations incorporated into EIFC, we also demonstrate how the MTFC approach can be tailored to fit additional populations.

In chapter 9, also coauthored with Fisher, we discuss our experiences in disseminating MTFC. This chapter is of interest to those considering this approach for use in their own communities. We describe our attempts to bridge the gap between establishing and testing a program model in a research-based setting and getting it out into the "real world." It is hoped that this chapter will be helpful to researchers, practitioners, and policymakers.

Throughout this volume runs a theme that has been identified in both research and practice: Effective programs for chronic juvenile offenders must provide both accountability (including discipline) and treatment (including skills training and support). I present a conceptual framework and practical methods for treating chronic and serious juvenile offenders in community-based settings. I also review community safety and treatment considerations in the context of research on the developmental course of antisocial behavior during childhood and adolescence. Because the general emphasis of this volume is on treatment, rehabilitation, and prevention of continued delinquency, I do not attend in detail to predictors of juvenile crime that are currently outside of our ability to directly influence (e.g., genetic contributions to antisocial behavior and neuropsychological factors). Because the specific focus of the book is on the MTFC model and its theoretical underpinnings, I do not include reviews of other theoretical approaches and instead emphasize the work that has been conducted by the group of researchers at the OSLC.

Throughout this volume, I draw on the rich history of research on the development and treatment of antisocial behavior in children and adolescents that has paved the way for the articulation of intervention models aimed at working with some of society's most troublesome youngsters.

Treating Chronic Juvenile Offenders

1

THE DEVELOPMENT OF
ANTISOCIAL BEHAVIOR

One summer afternoon, Ronny and his buddy were bored. They were playing near a construction site where a new house was being built. Ronny's friend threw a piece of wood at him. Ronny threw some dirt back at his friend's face. A worker chased the boys off. They circled around the block and came back to the site. Ronny picked up a tile that was on the ground and scratched it across the surface of a parked truck. Then both boys urinated on the truck. Again, a construction worker observed the boys' antics, and this time the police were called. Both boys were charged with criminal mischief. Ronny and his parents were sent a letter of warning. At the time, Ronny was 14 years old.

Two months later, Ronny's status with the Juvenile Department was formalized when he and some friends were caught kicking in the door of an empty house and stealing beer. He was charged with burglary and detained overnight, and his parents were called to appear before the judge the following day. At that time Ronny was placed on probation and released to the custody of his mother and stepfather, who were warned to carefully supervise him. Two days later, Ronny broke out the window of a bakery and ran off with some cookies. He was spotted by a security guard and chased down. The police were called, and he was charged with a second burglary and detained for a week.

Over the next 7 months, Ronny had 10 additional charges filed against him, including 3 burglaries, 3 criminal mischief charges, furnishing liquor to a minor, minor in possession of a controlled substance, a theft II, and a disorderly conduct. Ronny was detained several times and participated in a drug treatment program. The court report referring him for placement in out-of-home care described Ronny as a boy with few internal controls who used extensive thinking errors in excusing his crimes ("I don't see why I was charged with stealing the cookies—I dropped them when the guard chased me." "What's the big deal with breaking into an empty house?"). His mother and stepfather had experience with the juvenile court system. Both of their older daughters were on parole. The parents were described as being close and caring for each other and Ronny, but "they just don't get it." Ronny's mother was very much against Ronny being placed outside of her home and felt that the system was picking on her boy.

How does a boy like Ronny get to the point at which he thinks it is OK to break rules, violate private space, and take things that are not his? During the past 20 years there have been significant breakthroughs in the understanding of how youngsters become engaged in antisocial behavior and, once engaged, what the process looks like as they grow and develop. These breakthroughs have come as the result of several large-scale, longitudinal studies conducted in the United States and Europe. Although the specifics of these longitudinal studies varied, they all possessed the same basic set of goals: to be able to look at the causes of antisocial behavior and delinquency; what made the process start; what kept it going; and what could be done to prevent it, or failing that, turn it around. As a result of this fine body of meticulously conducted research, the prospects for designing effective interventions to prevent and treat antisocial behavior and delinquency improved more during the 1990s than they had for the previous 80 years.

These rapid breakthroughs came about because research designs and ways of collecting and analyzing data had become more sophisticated. Investigative teams became more multidisciplinary, and major studies of the development and prediction of antisocial behavior and delinquency examined individual, environmental, and social interaction factors within the same studies. The introduction of the concept of developmental progressions was another positive factor. Longitudinal studies have been extremely useful in finding out about developmental sequences and patterns starting in the prenatal period and extending through late adolescence.

Even for those interested in developing interventions for adolescents who are already seriously embroiled in the antisocial process, information on the identification of early risk factors, and how they unfold over time and are exacerbated or diminished, is tremendously useful. Depressingly, both epidemiological and developmental studies have found that the normal course of male antisocial behavior tends to be highly stable over decades, beginning as early as age 2 (Cummings, Iannotti, & Zahn-Waxler, 1989; Olweus, 1979). In Ronny's case, the early signs were first seen in the school setting. He had been suspended in Grade 2 for fighting and was so far behind in Grade 3 that he was retained. Even though the overall frequency, seriousness, and prevalence of antisocial behavior is likely to shift over time, the relative rank ordering of individuals within a given cohort tends to be constant. Yet data show that the specific manifestations of antisocial behavior vary tremendously depending on the individual's developmental stage.

Uninterrupted progression along an antisocial trajectory moves toward increasingly serious and multifaceted manifestations, including both covert and overt acts. In early childhood, antisocial behavior typically begins with problems such as excessive temper tantrums and noncompliance. In the toddler stage, high rates of defiance, irritable crying, and whining ensue. Preschool brings rejection by nonaggressive peers and negative attention from teachers. By grade school, as academic and compliance demands increase, failure at school and exclusion from normal socializing influences such as participation in sports or clubs occurs. Middle school leads to association with delinquent peers and substance use. This process escalates rapidly for some youngsters like Ronny, who quickly become involved in committing large numbers of property and some person-to-person crimes.

At each juncture in their development, the presence of antisocial patterns limits youths' successful transition to the next stage. As they grow and develop, their skills for dealing with the increasingly complex demands made by their teachers, coaches, and peers become less and less adequate. By the time an early-starting antisocial boy reaches adolescence, his decision to engage in deviant behavior is not only a motivational problem. He also has missed out on enough socialization that he has little idea how to make it in the key settings in his life: with normal peers, in school, or in work. This process describes (in a simplified way) the progression for the majority of chronically delinquent boys. A smaller but significant number of boys who become chronic delinquents first initiate serious antisocial behavior when they become teenagers. For them the process looks different.

Longitudinal studies have given us precise information that incorporates data on how individual characteristics, the environment, and the social interactions that occur in daily life influence the development of antisocial behavior. These studies have found that factors at all of these levels are influential and interplay with each other in lawful ways. For example, it is now well recognized that exposure to a given risk factor at one point in development usually increases the risk of being exposed to or affected by other risk factors at later points in development (Reid & Eddy, 1997).

Beginning in the 1980s, theories of intervention began to incorporate data on individuals and their environment or context. Developmental psychologists influenced the field to incorporate information on normal child and family development. Studies begun in the 1960s on the power of daily social interactions to shape the escalation or decrease of antisocial behavior were strongly influential. Social learning influences on antisocial behavior in children and families had been demonstrated to be powerful predictors of change. This resulted in a reconceptualization of intervention strategies that involved attending to how the child or adolescent functioned in multiple settings (e.g., family, school, and among peers) and how functioning in one setting influenced functioning in others.

Obviously, antisocial behavior is not typically an inert act. The negative or coercive nature of most antisocial acts virtually guarantees that they will not be ignored. In most instances there will be a reaction, one that often escalates negativity. Recent conceptualizations of theories and treatments for antisocial behavior take into account the concurrent and long-term effects that people engaging in such behaviors have on each other (e.g., how the parents' behavior influences the child's subsequent behavior and how the child's behavior influences the parents' subsequent behavior) and how interactions characterized by antisocial behavior shape the escalation or decrease of problems over time (Patterson, Reid, & Dishion, 1992).

Rapidly expanding knowledge during the past two decades has set the stage for major advances in community-based treatment models for dealing with chronically offending youths. However, there are still huge gaps in our understanding. Two of the most prominent are that studies on the development (or treatment) of antisocial behavior in girls have been virtually nonexistent; and we know much less about the late-adolescent to early-adult stage of development than we do about earlier periods of development. Both topics recently have received more attention. Subsequent chapters discuss these neglected areas.

In the 1990s, two groups of experienced scientists, policymakers, and advocates highlighted the necessity for interventions to be carefully informed by data-driven, life-course models: the Institute on Medicine (Mrazek & Haggerty, 1994) and the National Institute of Mental Health (National Institute of Mental Health, Prevention Research Steering Committee, 1993). Both groups also recommended that interventions map out the relationships between developmental antecedents and maladaptive outcomes and that key variables thought to predict outcomes be measured in intervention studies.

Interventions for people who are chronically delinquent have the benefit of several well-documented life-course studies that have clearly identified three constellations of factors that are influential in understanding the development, maintenance, and escalation or desistance of the antisocial trajectory: individual factors, contextual factors, and social interaction or transactional factors. I discuss these groups of factors in the remainder of the chapter.

INDIVIDUAL FACTORS

In the young child, individual factors that have been identified as being predictive of antisocial behavior and later delinquency include difficult temperament in infancy (Bates, Maslin, & Frankel, 1985); early attachment problems (Erickson, Sroufe, & Egeland, 1985); and problems with emotional regulation, including the inability to inhibit one's own impulses, self soothe, or focus attention (Katz & Gottman, 1991). Other individual factors include low intelligence (Moffitt, 1990), the presence of attention deficit hyperactivity disorder (ADHD; Lahey & Loeber, 1997), and a tendency to overattribute hostile intentions of others (Dodge, 1980). In Ronny's case, the diagnosis of ADHD had been made when he was 9 years old, at which time doctors prescribed Ritalin.

Although evidence supports correlations between each of these and other factors (e.g., genes and biology) and antisocial tendencies, it is a fallacy to think of any single individual characteristic or constellation of characteristics as the cause of delinquency. The vast majority of children having a single or a subset of these characteristics do not have problems with antisocial behavior (see Dishion & Patterson, 1997, for a discussion).

To the extent that these individual characteristics occur, they may increase the child's risk of being vulnerable to other risk factors that increase the probability of antisocial behavior. For example, difficult early temperament in infancy may trigger processes in the parent–child relationship that have implications for future development of child antisocial behavior. Difficult infant temperament coupled with parental stress and lack of social support has been found to relate to low parental responsiveness to the child, low parental involvement with the child, and harsh disciplinary practices. These factors, in turn, relate to higher levels of child disruptive behavior, aggression, and noncompliance later in toddlerhood (Shaw & Winslow, 1997). Having an infant with a difficult temperament makes it harder for the parent to be responsive to the infant's needs, which in turn makes it more likely that the parent will be less involved with the infant and use harsher disciplinary practices as the child becomes a toddler. Low parental involvement and harsh discipline have been shown in several studies to relate to increases in childhood disruptive behavior (Gardner, 1987; Patterson, 1982). High levels of child disruptive behavior (e.g., noncompliance, temper tantrums, and defiance) put the child at further risk when he or she is later exposed to regular interactions in the peer group, typically in the preschool setting. Shaw and Winslow (1997) reviewed several studies that provide strong support for the relationship between child disruptive behavior in preschool and peer rejection.

The importance of the presence of individual or constellations of characteristics in the determination of antisocial behavior is not that they operate as direct causes. Over time, they add to the child's vulnerability to engagement in processes that create a cascading set of events that push the child toward increasingly serious forms of antisocial behavior.

CONTEXTUAL FACTORS

Social disorganization theory emphasizes the role that communities play in disrupting basic social processes in families and peer groups. Sampson and Laub (1994) found that the presence of a "toxic environment" has an undermining influence across cultural groups. Living in communities with high levels of violence and poverty makes everyday tasks such as going to and from school or work more stressful, difficult, and dangerous. Neighborhood characteristics and exposure to violence have been reported in several studies as being critical factors in predicting adolescent outcomes (Bank & Noursi, 2001; Duncan, Brooks-Gunn, & Klebanov, 1994).

Researchers have examined contextual factors in terms of their direct and indirect effects on child and family outcomes. Negative or toxic contexts may indirectly affect the individual by amplifying existing patterns. For example, Patterson (1993) examined the amplification hypothesis with families referred for treatment because of child antisocial behavior. He found that on days when the mother experienced increased levels of stress, she was more irritable and used harsher discipline methods when interacting with her child. Snyder (1991) replicated and extended the finding. He found that daily variations in stress influenced parent's mood, which in turn related to ineffective discipline and negative child outcomes.

Key social settings for the child create contexts for amplification or dampening of antisocial tendencies. School atmosphere, including factors such as behavioral expectations, rules, policies, and procedures for monitoring playground violence, has been shown to affect levels of child antisocial behavior (Walker, Stieber, Ramsey, & O'Neill, 1993). Variation in school contexts can significantly affect antisocial trajectories (Rutter, 1978).

The number of family moves or transitions has been found to contribute to exacerbation of antisocial tendencies. Capaldi and Patterson (1991) examined the relation between the number of parenting transitions that boys experienced and their adjustment in multiple areas (e.g., drug use, antisocial behavior, academic achievement, self-esteem, depression, and arrest records). A linear relation was found such that boys who had experienced multiple transitions in parent figures showed the poorest adjustment compared with those from intact or once-separated families.

Like individual characteristics that are implicated in the development of antisocial behavior, negative contexts in and of themselves cannot be seen as causal but rather as mechanisms that facilitate or amplify participation in the antisocial process. Also like individual characteristics, to the extent that contextual factors are malleable to change, they become candidates as targets for interventions.

SOCIAL INTERACTION PROCESSES

Family, peer group, and school are the three key settings in which studies on social interaction processes have contributed to understanding the development of antisocial behavior. I discuss studies on each of these settings in this section.

Studies on the Role of Family Processes

Daily interactions between family members have been shown to shape and influence both prosocial and antisocial patterns of behavior that children develop and carry with them to their interactions with others outside of the family (peers, teachers, and coaches). Researchers have identified specific family processes or interaction patterns that predict the development of behavior problems in children and adolescents. For example, parental use of harsh punishment, poor monitoring of the child's activities, low parental engagement, and failure to set limits are all processes that have been shown to relate to the development of aggressive patterns of child behavior (Patterson, 1982).

Observational studies in family homes have shown that not only do families with behavior problem youngsters have more negative interactions, but also the parents do not notice when their child is behaving appropriately. In this way, the child is not only "taught" to be coercive, but he or she does not develop the skills necessary to have positive behaviors that could be of use in making friends or in relating positively to teachers, coaches, or other adults (Patterson, 1982).

At the microsocial interaction level, children referred for problems with antisocial behavior are likely to have learned strategies of behaving that, in the short run, are effective for getting their needs met but that may have long-term negative effects. For example, because they may work in the short term, parents and children may have gradually shaped each other to use more and more negative control strategies over time. Unfortunately, the evidence is that there are damaging long-term effects. The child's reduced behavioral and social competencies set him or her up for school failure. There is evidence that such children are likely to be rejected by their peers and that rejected children are more likely to associate with other aggressive, rejected children who tend to reward negative behavior in their interactions with each other (Dishion, French, & Patterson, 1995; Parker, Rubin, Price, & DeRosier, 1995).

Over time, without effective intervention, these processes continue and become amplified. The youth's experience of early parental negativity, failure in school, rejection by peers, and exclusion from clubs and sports activities sets the stage for associating with delinquent peers, dropping out of school, using drugs, and being delinquent in adolescence. I review interventions that are aimed at teaching and supporting parents and that have shown promise in altering childhood negative trajectories in chapter 3.

Longitudinal studies examining the development of antisocial behavior have highlighted the contribution of parenting practices to the later development of problems in childhood and adolescence. For example, in their reanalysis of data from several longitudinal studies, Loeber and Dishion (1983) found that composite measures of parental family management practices were the most powerful predictors of subsequent delinquency when compared with other variables such as ratings of earlier child behavior, criminality of the parents, separation from parents, and socioeconomic status. Laub and Sampson (1988) reported that family process variables (supervision and discipline) mediated 80% of the variance in contextual factors such as household overcrowding, father's drunkenness and criminality, and economic dependence.

Several studies have implicated poor discipline and especially inconsistent, overly harsh punishment in the development of child antisocial behavior (e.g., Dumas, Gibson, & Albin, 1989). For example, in a study in the St. Louis Ecological Catchment Area, Holmes and Robins (1988) found that reports of harsh and unfair parental discipline during the childhood years of ages 6 to 13 were strongly related to later adult diagnoses of depression for women and alcoholism for men.

These findings have obvious implications for intervention studies. If key parenting practices can be identified as contributing to later poor adjustment, they become logical targets for theory driven intervention studies.

In Ronny's family, his mother was described as running a chaotic household. His stepfather was uninvolved with the kids. The mother cared deeply for her children but was so busy with life that she was not able to focus. She routinely missed appointments with the probation officer and with the court-referred family counselor. There were always "good reasons" why she was unable to follow through, and by the time the family was referred to our program, she was feeling like the system had abused and misunderstood her and that they "had it in for" her children.

Studies on the Role of Peer Processes

Several studies have found that the nature and quality of peer relationships, particularly in adolescence, are an important determinant of antisocial outcomes, including delinquency and substance use (Elliott, Huizinga, & Ageton, 1985; Fergusson & Horwood, 1999). As discussed previously, children who have high levels of disruptive or aggressive behaviors tend to be rejected by peers during their early school years. Once rejected by peers, the child becomes a target for further aggression (Asher & Dodge, 1986). Although there is some controversy about how school-aged youngsters who are rejected by peers come to be affiliated with other rejected youths as they reach adolescence, there is strong evidence that aggressive children form friendships with others who are aggressive. This process of selective affiliation appears to happen in both childhood and adolescence (Cairns & Cairns, 1994; Dishion, 1990).

Association with deviant peers has been shown to be a strong predictor of both initial involvement in and escalation of aggressive and delinquent behavior. Research in sociology and developmental psychology over the past 25 years supports the notion that youngsters who have strong bonds with delinquent peers are at far greater risk for becoming delinquent—and for escalating in delinquency over time—than those who associate with nondelinquent peers (Dishion, McCord, & Poulin, 1999; Elliott et al., 1985; Patterson et al., 1992).

There is less research on identifying the specific processes or mechanisms that place the youth at risk for forming affiliations with delinquent peers. An exception is the work of Dishion and colleagues who have conducted observational studies of peer interactions with antisocial and non-antisocial boys. Dishion and Andrews (1995) showed that boys with a history of early arrest were more likely to reinforce each other's antisocial or rule-breaking talk with laughter than were nonarrested boys. Deviant peers were also more likely to *not* react positively to normative (non–rule-breaking) talk. These investigators also found that laughter in response to rule-breaking talk resulted in longer discussions of deviancy (Dishion, Spracklen, Andrews, & Patterson, 1996). Dishion labeled these types of interactions as a "deviancy training process" (Dishion & Patterson, 1997, p. 208) that predicted adolescent initiation into delinquency and escalation of delinquent behavior.

Research has shown that peer support for aggressive behavior in the classroom increases aggression (Guerra, Huesmann, Tolan, Van Acker, & Eron, 1995), and interaction with negative peers has been shown to predict later substance use (Dishion & Andrews, 1995; O'Donnell, Hawkins, & Abbott, 1995). McCord's (1997) reanalysis of the Cambridge–Somerville Youth Study data showed that youths who attended summer camp with other antisocial boys were more likely to become adult offenders than youths who did not attend summer camp.

Ronny convinced his parents that who he picked for friends was his right and that they had nothing to say about it. His mother believed this to be true and further she felt helpless to influence his choices because "that's just not the kind of thing that a parent can dictate."

AGE OF ONSET AND SEVERITY OF DELINQUENT BEHAVIOR

Numerous studies show that the severity of antisocial behavior during childhood predicts the early age of onset for juvenile offending for boys (e.g., Lahey & Loeber, 1994). Several studies have also shown that early onset predicts greater seriousness and persistence of antisocial behavior (Farrington, Loeber, & Van Kammen, 1990; Tolan & Thomas, 1995). In a review of categories of antisocial behavior, Rutter (1997) noted that twin studies show that adult crime has a stronger genetic component than juvenile crime. Taken together with the findings on early onset predicting increased seriousness and persistence, this finding implies that adolescent-onset delinquency is largely environmentally determined and is less likely to persist into adult life. Rutter contended that early-onset antisocial behavior is likely to involve a stronger genetic component and is more likely to persist into adult life. In accord with the genetic hypothesis, some studies have found that children with early-onset antisocial behavior are also more likely to have problems with hyperactivity (see review by Lahey & Loeber, 1997). From an intervention perspective, these distinctions raise several questions. Are early-onset offenders more difficult to treat and less likely to have good outcomes? Are there essential differences in the interventions that should be delivered to early- versus late-onset offenders?

Findings from the Oregon Youth Study (OYS; Capaldi & Patterson, 1994) support the idea that early onset predicts chronicity and seriousness and provide some implications for treatment. OYS is a prospective longitudinal study with 200 boys and their families from high-risk neighborhoods who are followed with intensive yearly assessments. The study began in 1984 and is ongoing. Boys who scored above the median on antisocial behavior at age 10 had a .46 probability of being arrested by age 14, and 72% had been arrested by age 18. From the childhood onset group (i.e., those who scored high on measures of antisocial behavior at age 10), 75% became chronic offenders, and 86% of the boys in the OYS sample who eventually committed a violent crime came from the chronic group. The odds of arrest by age 14 were 13 times greater for children scoring above the median on antisocial behavior at age 10. Given that the child was arrested by age 14, the odds were 16 times greater that he would become a chronic offender.

Capaldi and Patterson (1994) compared nonoffenders, early-onset offenders, and late-onset offenders in the OYS sample on two sets of variables: contextual (i.e., income, social disadvantage, parent employment, family transitions, and parent's antisocial behavior), and family management practices (supervision and discipline). On the contextual variables, families of early-onset boys ranked the lowest (i.e., low income, high social disadvantage, low employment, high transition, and high parent antisocial), next lowest were families in the late-onset group, and highest were those in the nonoffending group. On family management practices, families of late-onset boys practiced stronger discipline and better supervision of children than did families of early-onset boys. No differences were found in parenting practices between the late-onset and nonoffending groups. Other analyses conducted by these investigators suggest that most of the training in delinquency for the late-onset boys comes from their interactions with delinquent peers (Dishion, Patterson, & Griesler, 1994).

These findings raise several questions for intervention studies. To what extent are the differences in outcomes for early- and late-onset offenders amenable to intervention? Studies that examined differences in early versus late onset were longitudinal designs, and no intervention was included. Although it might be the case that individual characteristics, such as having ADHD, and contextual factors, such as having antisocial parents, contribute to the likelihood of early-onset antisocial behavior in boys, can interventions lessen the negative impact of these factors? These studies strongly implicate parenting practices in the development of antisocial behavior. Can interventions aimed at improving parenting impact delinquency outcomes?

HOW DO WE DETERMINE WHICH FACTORS TO TARGET FOR INTERVENTION?

A complex array of individual, contextual, and social interactional factors contribute to the development and escalation of antisocial behavior over time. How does one combine all of this rich information to design an intervention to prevent the development of problems in the first place or to treat them once they have occurred? Examination of the timing, sequence, and settings in which the antisocial process unfolds provides some guidance.

A developmental model of antisocial behavior was described by Reid and Eddy (1997) and is shown in Figure 1.1. The model, which depicts antisocial behavior from preinfancy through adolescence, highlights some important considerations for selection of interventions. First, some of the risk factors are active for only a short time (e.g., maternal smoking and substance use during pregnancy), whereas others are active for years (e.g., lack of parent involvement, supervision, and discipline). Information about when risk factors are relevant is crucial for the timing of intervention programs. Second, the settings in which proximal risk factors exert their influence vary across development. For example, comprehensive interventions could be designed for the preschool child that focused only on the child and his or her parents (and siblings, if applicable). By the time the youth has reached adolescence, if serious problems with antisocial behavior exist, powerful risk factors can be found in at least three settings: home, school, and peer group. Unless there is a clear reason for predicting that an intervention in one setting would have an impact in the other settings where risks are occurring, a multisetting intervention is likely to be required.

As can be seen in Figure 1.1, parents and the parent–child relationship play a pivotal role in the development and evolution of antisocial behavior throughout the life-course model. A good deal of research has been conducted on family-based interventions for children and adolescents

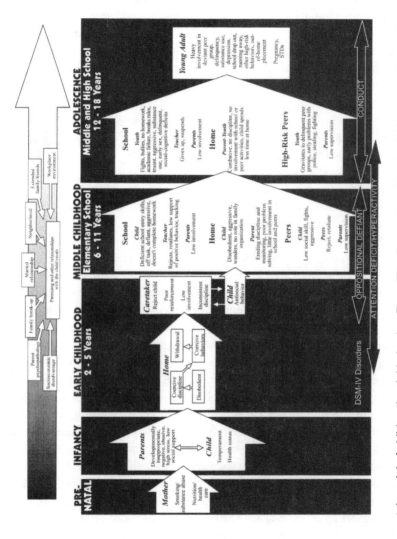

Figure 1.1. Developmental model of child antisocial behavior. From "The Prevention of Antisocial Behavior: Some Considerations in the Search for Effective Interventions" (p. 346) by J. B. Reid and J. M. Eddy, 1997, in *Handbook of Antisocial Behavior,* edited by D. M. Stoff, J. Breiling, and J. D. Maser. New York: Wiley. Copyright 1997 by Wiley. Reprinted with permission. DSM-IV = *Diagnostic and Statistical Manual of Mental Disorders, 4th Edition.*

with problems with antisocial behavior and delinquency. I review this work in chapter 2.

RONNY, ONE YEAR LATER . . .

Despite his mother's objections, Ronny was enrolled in the Oregon Social Learning Center's Multidimensional Treatment Foster Care (MTFC) Program and placed in the home of Sharon and Jim Stamm. Ronny had a smooth adjustment to both the foster home and the program. Sharon described him as a boy who had a good heart and who could be sweet. The Stamm's major complaint was that Ronny tended to always want the last word and continually attempted to draw adults into discussions or debates. Because of this, in addition to focusing on compliance with household and school rules, the daily behavior management system designed for Ronny that was implemented in the MTFC home included an emphasis on accepting "No" for an answer without arguing. Predictably, Ronny argued about whether he really was arguing and tried to explain that he was simply trying to express his point of view. Rather than getting drawn into these debates, the Stamms ignored Ronny's verbal behavior and took points (a procedure explained in chapter 5). The point loss emphasized actions rather than words. The MTFC program staff, the Stamms, and Ronny's parents all agreed that Ronny needed to gain a better understanding of the idea that actions are more meaningful than words if he was going to be successful at avoiding participation in criminal behavior once he returned home. "It matters more what you do than what you say about what you do" was a consistent theme used in the foster home, individual therapy, family therapy, and skills-training components of the program.

Ronny made significant positive changes during his 7-month placement in the program. He developed age-appropriate social skills and interactions and responded well to the structure and controls imposed by the program, such as intensive supervision at home and at school. He successfully completed all treatment goals and did not reoffend. He developed the capacity and motivation to associate with prosocial peers. Ronny's biggest accomplishment was at school. He went from a boy who did not attend school to being on the honor roll and ending the program with a 3.5 grade point average.

Initially, Ronny's mother and stepfather were difficult to engage. During the first phase of family therapy, Diane, the MTFC therapist, worked hard to show Ronny's mother that program staff were not going to blame her but rather were there to act as consultants to her with the aim of figuring out how to set things up so Ronny could be successful when he returned home. After a rocky start with several missed appointments and no-shows during home visits, Diane and Ronny's mom and stepdad got down to working on some rather specific parenting skills. They needed help in identifying problem behaviors, giving clear directions, not engaging in debates, setting limits, and following through with negative consequences for misbehavior and incentives for compliance and cooperation. The parents were taught to use the same daily behavior management system with Ronny that the MTFC parents used in the foster home. These topics were covered in weekly family therapy sessions, and Ronny had frequent home visits during the course of the placement so he and his parents could practice these new ways of relating.

Ronny returned home in early summer. He had a part-time job as a day camp "counselor in training." Weekly family therapy and individual skills training sessions continued through the fall until his transfer back to his home school was well established. The schedule was then changed to monthly family therapy and twice-monthly skills training. Ronny's mother talks to his former MTFC program supervisor[1] weekly to check in and troubleshoot problems (arguing is still an issue). Although time will tell, at this point, it seems like things have turned around for Ronny. He has been offense free for more than a year.

In many ways, Ronny is typical of the youth who have participated in MTFC. Because he did not respond to the sanctions delivered by the juvenile justice authorities, and because his delinquency continued to escalate, he was referred to out-of-home care. In most communities, this would mean placement in a group care facility of some type. Although group treatment is widely used in the U.S., is it effective? In the next chapter, I review the research on group care and make a case for designing interventions that target multiple factors.

---

[1]The role of the program supervisor is to supervise all of the activities and personnel involved with the youth and family, including the MTFC parents, the family and individual therapists, and the skills trainer. In previous publications, this position was referred to as *case manager*, but this title was changed because it was confusing to many agency and community partners who use case management as a lower level function.

2

HOW IS THEORY RELATED
TO INTERVENTION?

The studies reviewed in chapter 1 implicate multiple factors in the development of severe antisocial behavior in children and adolescents. Examples are individual factors such as cognitive processing styles (Dodge, 1980), contextual factors such as school environment (Felner et al., 1993), social interactional processes such as coercive parent–child interactions (Dishion & Patterson, 1997), and negative peer associations (Elliott, Huizinga, & Ageton, 1985). Studies indicate that this complex web of factors drives the development of antisocial behavior. Given that research shows serious antisocial behavior to be highly stable over time, and developmental studies show that multiple layers of risk factors influence its development and escalation, how might we design effective interventions?

Although studies in family therapy have shown that positive changes in parenting relate to improved child outcomes (e.g., Forgatch & DeGarmo, 1999), research on developmental progressions show that, by adolescence, severely antisocial youngsters are also heavily influenced by extrafamily forces that increase pressure on them to escalate their antisocial behavior. These progressions, coupled with the skill deficits that most chronically delinquent youths have accumulated over the years, combine to create substantial challenges for treatment models intended to alter antisocial trajectories for these youngsters.

In many communities, placement in group residential care is the most common form of treatment for severely antisocial children and adolescents. In 1983, estimates were that more than 19,000 such youngsters were in residential care. By 1986, the number had increased by 32% to more than 25,000 (Select Committee on Children, Youth, and Families, 1990). This is an underestimate of the true numbers because these data exclude youths placed in for-profit residential treatment centers. The American Public Welfare Association (cited in Kutash & Rivera, 1996) estimated that approximately 70% of the total funding for children's mental health services was used for residential services. Yet little research exists on either the short-term effectiveness or long-term benefits of these placements (Burns & Friedman, 1990). In commenting on the effectiveness of various types of treatment models available for children and adolescents, Burns, Hoagwood, and Maultsby (1997) noted, "A dominant observation is that the least evidence of effectiveness exists for residential services, where the majority of dollars are spent" (p. 8). There is evidence in the literature on group care that children and adolescents who have problems with antisocial and aggressive behavior are the most difficult population to treat in those settings and that they tend to benefit the least from residential care in comparison with their non-antisocial counterparts (Zoccolillo & Rogers, 1991).

A range of placement types characterize contemporary approaches to group residential care (Wells, 1991); the most prevalent of these include community-based, family-style group homes, cottages within larger institutional settings, and large group living situations with shift staff. The theoretical foundations that underpin these programs vary as widely as their physical characteristics. Commonly used treatment modalities include psychoanalytic (Bettelheim, 1982), psychoeducational (Hobbs, 1982), behavioral (Fixsen et al., 1978), and peer cultural (Vorrath & Brendtro, 1985). However, systematic studies examining the application of various theories that use well-controlled designs are few and far between.

The empirical gap in research on residential care is difficult to explain, especially for the treatment of children and adolescents with severe and antisocial problems, given the large body of research on the development of and interventions for these problems. Considering the growing use of residential placements and the proportion of mental health dollars spent on this form of care, increased emphasis is long overdue on studies devoted to examination of their effectiveness.

OVERVIEW OF STUDIES ON GROUP RESIDENTIAL CARE

In reviewing studies on residential group care, it would be desirable to focus on studies that had sound research designs; however, the lack of systematic work in this area precludes that approach. Several previous reviews of the state of research on residential treatment have identified various residential program models (e.g., Curry, 1991; Quay, 1986; Whittaker & Pecora, 1984). In my own research (Chamberlain, 1999), I have reviewed two types of studies on residential care: (a) those with single samples and without comparison or control groups (these represent the majority of studies conducted) and (b) studies that compared residential treatment with no treatment, that compared residential treatment with other forms of treatment, or that compared different forms of residential treatment. In this section I describe studies on residential care that identify key processes relating to program effectiveness.

Two major reviews have looked at factors that predicted positive outcomes in residential care. Blotcky, Dimperio, and Gossett (1984) found that, in 24 studies conducted from 1936 to 1982, the following child factors predicted relatively successful outcomes: (a) higher intelligence, (b) nonpsychotic diagnosis, (c) no neurological dysfunction, (d) absence of antisocial behavior, (e) healthy family functioning, (f) adequate time in the program, and (g) adequate aftercare services. Pfeiffer and Strzelecki (1990) summarized results from studies on residential treatment and hospitalization from 1975 to 1990. Because only 2 of the 34 studies they examined reported means and standard deviations for outcome scores, they devised a system of rating program effects as negative, neutral, or positive and then adjusted this value according to sample size. In their analysis, less severe dysfunction (in both child and family), the presence of a specialized treatment regime, and availability of aftercare services were all related to positive outcomes. Higher child or adolescent intelligence and length of stay were moderately related to positive outcomes; age and gender were unrelated to outcomes.

Both of these reviews called for more scientific rigor in the design and conduct of future studies on residential care. For example, Pfeiffer and Strzelecki (1990) suggested that the field adopt four concepts in future studies: (a) identification of the necessary and sufficient dimensions of the treatment to be examined, (b) use of multiple measures and perspectives to define success or adjustment, (c) use of statistical techniques and experimental designs to test specific hypotheses, and (d) use of both micro- (e.g., small, observable behaviors) and macro-level indicators (e.g., broad-based traits) of outcomes.

In a study reviewed by Dalton, Muller, and Forman (1989), 26 children with antisocial behavior were found to have no significant change in behavior at 3 months follow-up from discharge from an inpatient unit. Curry (1991) reviewed three studies of residential treatment and found that 71% of the youngsters were functioning "adequately" at follow-up but that their progress while in care was not predictive of good adjustment in follow-up. Curry and others (e.g., Durkin & Durkin, 1975; Quay, 1979; Whittaker & Pecora, 1984) have concluded that several key factors are important in determining positive postdischarge adjustment. These include the degree of support provided to the youngster in aftercare, the need to work with his or her family, and the need to include in residential programming opportunities for learning that can be generalized to the community environment to which he or she will return.

Other studies have endorsed the notion that support for the youth, on returning to his or her home community, is crucial for long-term success. Day, Pal, and Goldberg (1994) examined the postdischarge functioning of children treated for antisocial behavior within a residential setting that emphasized family involvement and treatment. The children's parents participated in mealtime and bedtime activities and attended weekly family therapy sessions and parent training groups. At 6 months postdischarge, improvements were found on Child Behavior Checklist scores (Achenbach & Edelbrock, 1983) with significantly fewer children being in the clinical range at 6 months postdischarge than they had been at admission on both externalizing and internalizing scales.

Hoagwood and Cunningham (1992) examined outcomes for 114 children and adolescents who had been placed in residential care by school districts in a large southwestern state. All participants had been identified as seriously emotionally disturbed, which includes symptoms of antisocial behavior. The average length of stay in residential care for these youngsters was 18.2 months. In 63% of the cases, participants were rated as having made either no or minimal progress at the time of discharge. More positive outcomes were associated with shorter lengths of stay. However, participants with positive outcomes and shorter lengths of stay were not less disturbed than their less-successful counterparts according to preplacement ratings of severity of problems. In fact, they were rated as being significantly more disturbed on the severity of impairment of functioning measure used. Availability of community-based services during the transition from residential care to home was the most likely reason reported for positive discharge. Services that were mentioned as being important included family support, respite care, crisis intervention, and day treatment.

Residential models reviewed here that seemed to have the most positive impact included components that attempted to strengthen the youth's postresidential environment (e.g., increased family skills and support, and community support) and that included family treatment.

STUDIES ON RESIDENTIAL CARE WITH CONTROL OR COMPARISON GROUPS

A few studies have been conducted since 1990 that have examined specific components of residential care or that have focused on outcomes in residential care in comparison to other alternatives. These studies have fo-

cused on the Teaching Family Model (TFM) that uses a family-style placement setting with from 4 to 8 youths and a Teaching Parent couple. Teaching Parents are trained in operant learning theory and social learning theory
and are closely supervised in the TFM approach (Chamberlain & Friman,
1997).

Friman et al. (1996) compared measures of quality of life in residential
care using the Teaching Family Model at Boys' Town to "treatments as usual"
for youngsters referred to Boys' Town but not admitted due to lack of a program opening or quicker availability of a placement in another program. The
two groups were comparable on age, gender, and ethnicity at baseline. Participants were assessed every 3 months for up to 4 years. The variables studied were (a) delivery of helpful treatment, (b) satisfaction with supervising
adults, (c) isolation from family, and (d) sense of personal control. Several
differences favoring the TFM treatment were found. Participants rated the
TFM program higher than other programs on the amount of helpful treatment delivered after admission.

Youngsters in TFM reported being more satisfied with supervising adults
than those in the comparison condition. Furthermore, the high level of satisfaction with adults generalized to their postplacement settings. Feelings of
isolation from family and friends decreased from baseline more for the TFM
group than for the comparison group. No reliable differences were found between groups for sense of personal control, but a trend favored participants in
the TFM condition. This carefully conducted study challenged some of the
negative beliefs about residential care and documented the fact that a good
deal of variability exists in the quality of daily life in residential care.

Thompson and colleagues (1996) examined the short- and long-term
educational outcomes for adolescents who had participated in TFM homes
at Boys' Town compared with a group of youngsters who had been admitted
to that program but never attended. The comparison group was similar to the
Boys' Town group in terms of demographic characteristics. Participants in
the comparison group received treatment in alternative settings. The study
followed youngsters after admission for up to 4 years. There was an initial
increase in academic grade point average after the initial interview for the
TFM but not for the comparison group. Although the grade point average for
the TFM group decreased at 6 months after discharge, it was still higher than
that obtained for the comparison group after discharge.

The TFM group completed years of school at a faster rate than did those
in the comparison group. Eighty-three percent of the TFM group and 69% of
the comparison group completed high school; this difference was statistically
significant. Participants in the TFM group rated the importance of college as
being higher in assessments conducted after the initial interview than did
those in the comparison group. Although this score decreased after discharge,
the study reported that the TFM group believed college was more important
than did participants in the comparison group at follow-up. Finally, Thomp-

son and colleagues assessed the amount of help the child was given with homework during residential placement and after discharge. Like the other measures, the TFM group reported a significantly greater amount of help with homework than did comparison cases during their placements. This score decreased for both groups after discharge, but the TFM group mean remained statistically higher than the mean for the comparison group. It was unclear from the report on this study if there was more parental involvement in the homes of TFM graduates, or if TFM graduates sought out more help from parents, or both.

This study demonstrated a carryover of positive treatment effects into follow-up, an unfortunately rare finding for outcome studies on residential care. The TFM program model specifically targets school achievement during placement and apparently produces lasting gains that are evident once the placement is ended. More research needs to be conducted on interventions such as these that can facilitate turning points that are likely to have a positive effect on the trajectory of the youth's long-term adjustment in the community.

RATIONALE FOR INTERVENTIONS THAT TARGET MULTIPLE SYSTEMS

Once a youngster has become severely antisocial, it is entirely possible that residential treatment that focuses on individual factors, family treatment, or for that matter any one treatment modality alone will lack sufficient strength to turn the tide. In their review of treatment for antisocial youths, Southam-Gerow and Kendall (1997) concluded that parent training or cognitive–behavioral approaches alone will rarely be sufficiently strong to treat severely antisocial youths. These authors recommend the integration of family- and child-focused interventions along with interventions in the school and in other areas, as indicated (e.g., substance abuse, parental or child depression). Multimodal interventions that simultaneously target multiple settings and systems, although more expensive, complex, intensive, and restrictive than single-focused approaches to outpatient family therapy, show promise for the treatment of such youths.

These multimodal treatment approaches share several characteristics. They operate under the assumption that there are multiple causes and correlates of delinquency and that youths' antisocial behavior is related to important processes occurring in multiple settings, including their families, peer systems, schools, and communities. Interventions are simultaneously conducted in these multiple settings. These approaches emphasize promoting behavior change in youths' natural environments, and treatment is structured, task oriented, and focused on the present. Individual treatment plans are flexible, and treatment varies depending on the individual's identified problems that are targeted for change. Family interventions are seen as being central to amelioration of the child's or adolescent's problems.

Family interventions can be designed to focus on increasing parenting skills and empowering parents with resources to sustain positive changes made during treatment. Increasing parental expressions of encouragement, positive reinforcement and affection, use of effective nonviolent discipline, and effective monitoring of their youngster are frequently targets of treatment. Another shared goal of these approaches is to decrease the youth's association with and influence by deviant peers and to increase contact and affiliation with a prosocial peer group. Studies that guide the identification of the specific family and peer variables to target in these interventions allowed for the development of theory-based intervention models during the 1990s.

THE ROLE OF THE FAMILY

Two parenting processes in particular have been implicated in the development and escalation of severe antisocial behavior: discipline and monitoring or supervision. Poor parental discipline typically takes one of two forms (Capaldi, Chamberlain, Fetrow, & Wilson, 1997): Parents are overly indulgent or are overly harsh. Combinations of these patterns are common as well. It is typical for a parent to ignore many episodes of garden-variety misbehavior, such as noncompliance and whining, to become increasingly fed up but not to act, and finally to react harshly to a fairly low level of child misbehavior that is the "final straw." The child is inadvertently taught two things: that noncompliance and whining "works" most of the time and that discipline is unpredictable.

Observational studies in the homes of families with children referred to treatment for antisocial behavior show that relative to families with non-antisocial children, coercive child behavior is often reinforced by the parent giving in and by positive behavior being ignored. These types of findings have been reconfirmed numerous times beginning in the early 1960s in a series of studies at the Oregon Social Learning Center and by other researchers (e.g., Wahler in Tennessee [Wahler & Dumas, 1986]; Forehand in Georgia [Forehand & McMahon, 1981]; and Conger in Iowa [Ge, Best, Conger, & Simons, 1996]). Results from these studies have shown that, typically, it is the accumulation of such banal family processes, rather than some cataclysmic event, that trains children to be aggressive.

Treatment studies, such as the one by Forgatch and DeGarmo (1999) reviewed in chapter 3, have shown that altering discipline practices results in improvements in child antisocial outcomes. Interventions should be structured to teach the adolescent that coercive strategies and defiant behavior do not work and to decrease the reinforcement and incentives for such behavior. At the same time, parents should teach and consistently reinforce alternative behaviors and skills. The idea of providing the adolescent with a clear and consistent set of such contingencies, day in and day out, forms part of the basis for designing effective interventions for antisocial adolescents. In addition, it is also critical to limit the adolescent's exposure to other well-documented risks such as exposure to delinquent peers and school failure.

Supervision of the youth's whereabouts and associations is a key variable in reducing the likelihood of criminal activity in adolescence. Stoolmiller (1994) studied the relationships among the amount of unsupervised time in the community, exposure to delinquent peers, and detainment in lockup for 206 boys from high-risk neighborhoods (i.e., those with high rates of juvenile crime). Boys participated in the Oregon Youth Study and were assessed when they were ages 10, 12, 14, and 16 years. Figure 2.1 shows the trivariate relationship between unsupervised time, delinquent peers, and the average number of days in detainment per 2-year period. As can be seen, there is a significant interaction between the number of delinquent peers and the amount of unsupervised time in the prediction of days spent in lockup. The importance of supervising adolescents at risk for association with delinquent peers is high as evidenced by this analysis and the fact that more than 80% of all juvenile crime is committed in the presence of two or more youths. Juvenile crime is a social activity, unlike adult crime of which 90% is committed alone (Zimring, 1981). The challenges of providing good supervision increase in the presence of other risk factors such as high-crime neighborhoods; few parental resources, including time and money; the youth's previous affiliation with antisocial peers; a negative child–parent relationship; and other factors that interfere with the adults' ability to know about and regulate their youngster's whereabouts and associations. Effective interventions for severely antisocial youths must provide high levels of supervision not only to protect them from increased exposure to deviant peers but also to protect the community from their criminal behavior.

THE ROLE OF THE DEVIANT PEER GROUP ASSOCIATION

In their review of the role that peers play in the development of delinquency and drug use, Thornberry and Krohn (1997) pointed out that, as far back as the 1920s, research has demonstrated a strong correlation between delinquency and association with negative peers. More recently, studies have elevated to causal status the influence of negative peers on the development and escalation of delinquent behavior (e.g., Dishion, McCord, & Poulin, 1999; Eddy & Chamberlain, 2000; Elliott & Menard, 1992).

However, currently most widely used treatments for delinquency, such as Positive Peer Culture, attempt to use the group process to gain a therapeutic effect. The assumption is that the peer group can best motivate and influence youths to change their behaviors and attitudes. However, it seems un-

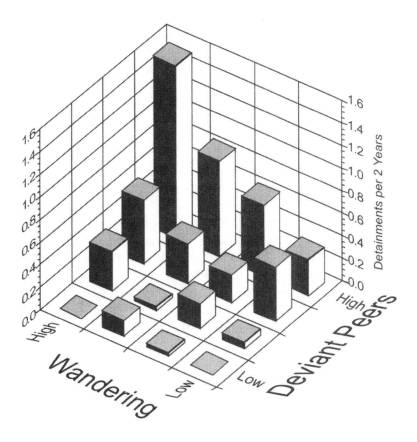

Figure 2.1. Deviant peer association, wandering, and detainment of at-risk boys (from ages 10 to 16 years). From "The Prevention of Antisocial Behavior: Some Considerations in the Search for Effective Interventions" (p. 349) by J. B. Reid and J. M. Eddy, 1997, in *Handbook of Antisocial Behavior,* edited by D. M. Stoff, J. Breiling, and J. D. Maser. New York: Wiley. Copyright 1997 by Wiley. Reprinted with permission.

reasonable to expect youngsters with histories of serious delinquent behaviors to function as a group and somehow become good influences on each other or establish prosocial norms or values. It may be that these approaches vastly underestimate the influence that adult-initiated norms and rules of conduct can have in the face of day-to-day involvement in a peer-dominated culture.

Dishion and Andrews (1995) found iatrogenic effects of group work in their study aimed at the prevention of conduct problems and substance use. They compared the effectiveness of five conditions (parent groups, adolescent groups, parents and adolescents combined, and two control groups). A total of 158 families with young adolescents participated. The parent-only group was superior to all of the others in producing reduced family conflict, teacher ratings of reduced externalizing behaviors, and reduced tobacco use.

Conversely, teachers reported significantly higher externalizing scores for those in the adolescent-only group than for youths in any other condition. These findings suggest that strategies that aggregate high-risk youths in intervention conditions should be reassessed in that in this study the group treatments produced the highest escalation in tobacco use and problem behaviors in school beginning at termination and persisting during the one-year follow-up period. Other studies also report iatrogenic effects for association with negative peers (Chamberlain & Reid, 1998; McCord, 1997).

The National Youth Survey (Elliott et al., 1985) sampled more than 1,000 adolescents using a longitudinal design. They found that association with delinquent peers strongly contributed to continued and escalated patterns of criminal behavior. Without the variable of "association with delinquent peers," the growth in delinquency over time was virtually nonexistent. These investigators commented that given the negative effects of becoming involved in a delinquent subculture, it is ironic that most delinquency treatment and prevention programs aggregate high-risk adolescents to implement their programs.

Yet the popularity of group-based intervention models continues to grow. "Boot camps" are a good example. Despite information about the potential for negative peer modeling and conversely of positive influence and modeling by caring adults, boot camps typically involve little or no contact with parents, no attempts to work with parents or other supportive adults, and extended incarceration with other delinquent youths. Stays in boot camps are characterized by a variety of work and military-type experiences intended to provide a corrective experience for the youths. Although boot camps are a politically satisfying remedy, they are not grounded in developmental theory, and there is no research to indicate that lack of such daily rigor leads to the commission of delinquent offenses. Indeed, the Office of Juvenile Justice and Delinquency Prevention (1997) reported that youths who participated in boot camps were equally likely to reoffend as were youths in the control conditions.

If we take the results of these studies seriously, they have broad implications for interventions. First, treatment models that aggregate delinquent peers should be avoided. Second, given that relationships with delinquent peers are interrupted, and that the severely antisocial youngster has been rejected early on by the normal (positive) peer group, how can affiliations with non-problem peers be initiated and supported? Again, we turn to the literature on the development of antisocial behavior and, in this instance, to the literature on the development of friendships, social rejection, and delinquent peer affiliation.

Why is it that the same youngsters who are identified in research studies as being socially rejected in their early elementary school years are at risk for affiliation with delinquent peers in early adolescence? Cairns, Cadwallader, Estell, and Neckerman (1997) reviewed two lines of developmental data relevant to this question. They looked at the types of social friendship groupings that children and adolescents tend to form, and the quality of social friendship relationships established by aggressive youngsters in childhood and adolescence.

Social network data indicate that antisocial children may have as many reciprocated friendships as non-antisocial children, but they are less likely to be named by the majority of the children as being liked and are more likely to be named as hostile and disliked. Although such "rejected" children may be feared and disliked by their classmates, they are no more likely to be isolated from friendships. Rather, they affiliate with others who are disliked. There is selective affiliation and selective choice on the basis of antisocial behavior, particularly acting-out, aggressive behaviors (Cairns & Cairns, 1994).

By Grades 3 or 4, groups of both non-antisocial and antisocial youngsters begin to form tight social networks. Once antisocial friendship networks are established, they begin to challenge conventional norms in their schools and communities. These friendships, although they may be as close and long lasting as friendships among non-antisocial youths, are by no means protective. In fact, for children and adolescents in general, Cairns and colleagues asserted that there is a strong bias toward synchrony in friendships beginning at ages 10 or younger. That is, individuals in the friendship group readily enmesh actions and attitudes of friends. Friends gravitate toward mutual similarity and together develop norms and values. In the case of antisocial youngsters, these norms and values tend to challenge other social units, such as the school and the family.

Observational studies conducted by Dishion and colleagues (Dishion, Andrews, & Crosby, 1995) demonstrated some of the social interactional processes that occur in friendships between antisocial (vs. non-antisocial) boys. In antisocial dyads, rule-breaking talk is reinforced by laughter, and normative talk is ignored. This pattern of "deviance training" results in longer episodes of deviant talk and is likely to promote conformity and escalation over time in antisocial behaviors and attitudes.

Cairns and colleagues (1997) stated that, "For many youths, the problem is to escape from synchrony with deviant peers. Hence, social isolation is often a buffer from delinquency" (p. 197).

Research in sociology and developmental psychology over the past 25 years supports the notion that youngsters who have strong bonds with delinquent peers are at far greater risk for becoming delinquent—and for escalating in delinquency over time—than are those who associate with nondelinquent peers (Dishion et al., 1999; Elliott et al., 1985; Patterson, Reid, & Dishion, 1992). In spite of this evidence, most community-based treatment models put youngsters with conduct problems or criminal histories together in groups that have the potential to facilitate further bonding and development of common social identities among group members.

THE ROLE OF THE SCHOOL

As pointed out by Reid and Eddy (1997), risk factors in the school setting are in many ways similar to those in family and peer group settings. Teachers see antisocial youngsters as being negative and coercive, and rightly so, as studies show that their rate of disruptive, defiant behavior is elevated both on the playground and in the classroom (Walker, Stieber, Ramsey, & O'Neill, 1993). Not surprisingly, there is also evidence that both teachers and peers tend to react coercively in retaliation to these youngsters (Trachenberg & Viken, 1994). Providing clear rules, consistent consequences, and an organizational climate that includes good supervision and reinforcement for positive behavior in the classroom and in ancillary settings (playground, cafeteria, or school bus) is crucial in school settings to minimize antisocial behavior. Several interventions have been used that target reducing aggressiveness in school environments and that attempt to improve academic organization and success and teach positive peer social skills (see Walker, Colvin, & Ramsey, 1995, for a review).

One of the best designed of these efforts was conducted by Kellam and colleagues (Kellam, Rebok, Ialongo, & Mayer, 1994). They compared the effects of two low-cost interventions (the Good Behavior Game [GBG]; and Mastery Learning [ML]) in a large-scale, epidemiologically based, randomized trial. GBG is a classroom-based behavior management system that rewards prosocial behavior by rewarding groups of youngsters who keep their negative behaviors to a minimum. ML targets academic achievement and requires that the majority of children demonstrate mastery in reading and math tasks before moving onto the next set of tasks. Compared with control students, students in both the GBG and the ML conditions showed lower rates of aggressive behavior and better academic achievement.

IMPLICATIONS AND DIRECTIONS FOR INTERVENTIONS

Taken together, the results from developmental studies and single-setting intervention studies set the stage for the design of multisetting collaborative interventions. These interventions, designed to take place in multiple settings or systems, should involve the coordinated use of theory-driven approaches aimed at addressing the difficult and complex problems and sets of factors contributing to antisocial and delinquent behavior in youths. In addition to including key treatment elements, it is important to recognize that some treatments or structural conditions (i.e., placing delinquent peers together) might have iatrogenic effects.

3

EVIDENCE FOR POSITIVE
EFFECTS AND BARRIERS TO
SUCCESSFUL TREATMENT

In the 1970s, reviews of treatment programs for serious and chronic juvenile offenders concluded that nothing worked (e.g., Martinson, 1974). There are several possible explanations for this failure to find positive results. Until the mid-1980s, delinquency treatments were, in general, individually focused. They were often delivered in institutional or residential care settings that had little resemblance to the communities where the youth's problems occurred in the first place or to where the youth would return after treatment. These treatments also typically failed to address the complex interplay between multiple factors and settings that have been shown to contribute to the development and escalation of antisocial behavior.

By the early 1990s, meta-analysis of delinquency treatment programs provided more sophisticated analyses of program effects and were more optimistic. For example, after reviewing almost 500 programs that evaluated interventions for juvenile delinquents, Lipsey (1992) and Lipsey and Wilson (1998) concluded that there were relatively more favorable outcomes for programs with certain characteristics. The relatively successful programs used structured treatments, taught and practiced skills, worked on improving family relationships, and worked on improving school performance. The strongest evidence for success was found for programs that focused on both improving parenting skills and on improving management of youths in naturally occurring community settings such as in school. Programs that combined individual skills development in youths, teaching parent management skills, and building parent–teacher relationships outperformed single-focus interventions.

In this chapter I review evidence that supports the use of family-focused interventions that are delivered in community-based settings. I also examine barriers to successful treatment, including family isolation, stress, and resistance to treatment. Finally, I describe a prevention program that is a school-based intervention designed to decrease the rates of occurrence of child conduct problems.

FAMILY-BASED INTERVENTIONS

Studies examining the life-course development of antisocial behavior have highlighted the contribution of problems with parenting to the later development of difficulties in childhood and adolescence. For example, in their reanalysis of data from several longitudinal studies, Loeber and Dishion (1983) found that composite measures of parental family management practices were the most powerful predictors of subsequent delinquency when compared with other well-known predictors such as ratings of earlier child disruptive behavior, criminality of the parents, separation from parents, and socioeconomic status. Laub and Sampson (1988) reported that family process variables such as supervision and discipline mediated 80% of the variance in environmental factors such as household overcrowding, father's drunkenness and criminality, and economic dependence. Patterson and Forgatch (1995) came to the same conclusion. They found that changes in parenting practices from pre- to posttreatment and into follow-up predicted future rates of child out-of-home placements and arrests for a sample of 69 cases in which children and families were referred to treatment because of the child's severe antisocial behavior. If parenting practices predict later poor child adjustment, they become logical targets for theory-driven intervention studies.

In a comprehensive review of treatment research, Kazdin (1987) identified that interventions targeting change in the family were the most promising methods for the treatment of child and adolescent conduct disorders, relative to other treatment approaches. This general conclusion received support from a meta-analysis conducted by Shadish et al. (1993), who examined results from 163 studies, including journal articles, book chapters, dissertations, and unpublished manuscripts. Studies included in the meta-analysis met three criteria: Participants had been randomly assigned to treatment groups, participants had been clinically distressed at intake, and the study included an examination of a marital therapy (n = 62) or a family therapy (n = 101) approach.

Within the 163 family therapy studies, 18 dealt specifically with families who were being treated because their children or adolescents were having conduct problems. In these studies the family therapy had a significant effect size (d = .53, n = 18). Shadish and colleagues divided these studies into those focusing on treating cases where aggression was the primary referral complaint (d = .61, n = 5) and those focusing on delinquency symptoms (d = .34, n = 3). In terms of theoretical orientation within the family therapy approach, behaviorally oriented treatments yielded an effect size of d = .55 (n = 13), and systemic approaches yielded an effect size of d = .26 (n = 8). The effect size for humanistic treatments for conduct disorder was d = −.15 (n = 1), and eclectic was d = .57 (n = 7). The researchers also reviewed other subsets of relevant studies. Eleven studies examined parent management training yielding an effect size of .41, and 11 looked at effect size for studies using multiple behavioral strategies yielding an effect size of .83.

Other meta-analyses (e.g., Hazelrigg, Cooper, & Borduin, 1987) and reviews (e.g., Loeber & Hay, 1994; Tolan, Cromwell, & Brasswell, 1986) have emphasized the family's role in the development and maintenance of conduct disorders and delinquency. They have also endorsed the use of family therapy as a well-validated treatment approach for working with families with antisocial youngsters (Dumas, 1989; Patterson, Dishion, & Chamberlain, 1993).

Some evidence suggests that family therapy has a positive influence on posttreatment adjustment for youths who have been placed in residential care. Garrett (1985) conducted a meta-analysis on the components of treatment within residential care settings for juvenile offenders. That study found that, whereas individual and group therapies had no impact on subsequent recidivism, family therapy appeared to be more effective. Borduin and colleagues (1995) found that recidivism for institutionalized delinquents after release from the institution was significantly less for those who received family therapy than for those who did not (60% vs. 93%).

Whether or not family treatment should be a routine part of residential treatment programs for antisocial children and adolescents is a controversial issue within the residential care field. As many providers of residential services point out, logistical barriers interfere with including families in treatment. Youths are often placed far away from their home communities. However, given the demonstrated influence of parenting factors on antisocial behavior, it is not reasonable to expect that in-placement changes in child behavior will maintain postplacement without consistent adult support. Ideally, parents or other aftercare parent substitutes can be helped to provide consistent daily structure and support for a youngster similar to what he or she received in the residential care setting. This would include similar levels of supervision, discipline, and expectations and encouragement for academic and work skills.

Failure to include parents in youngsters' treatment may represent the single largest barrier to generalization of treatment effects from residential care to living at home (Chamberlain, 1999). On their return home, children and adolescents are likely to gravitate toward like-minded peers. Parents or other community caregivers need the resources and skills to prevent this drift, which has been shown to be a key part of the progression toward delinquency and drug use (e.g., Elliott, Huizinga, & Ageton, 1985). For youths whose parents or relatives are not available to provide support and guidance, communities may find that efforts to establish alternative surrogate parental relationships are worthwhile and cost effective in terms of producing positive outcomes for youngsters and for society in general.

A BRIEF OVERVIEW OF SELECTED THEORIES OF FAMILY TREATMENT

Much of the published research on the effectiveness of family-oriented treatments for child and adolescent conduct disorders has its roots in two major theoretical approaches: behavioral social learning orientations (Social Learning Family Therapy; SLFT); and structural–systemic family therapy (SFT) approaches. More recently, interventions have been used that target multiple systems in addition to the family (e.g., school and peer group) and that use a combination of these theoretical approaches. In addition to Multidimensional Treatment Foster Care (MTFC), the two most prominent examples include Multisystemic Therapy and Functional Family Therapy.

Studies using SLFT approaches have been examined in numerous tightly controlled research trials, whereas SFT has been researched to a lesser extent, and what studies exist were less rigorous. However, the SFT approach has a well-articulated theoretical basis (e.g., Haley, 1976; Johnson, 1973, 1974, 1975a, 1975b, 1977, 1978) and is widely used in clinical practice.

Although the intervention strategies used in SLFT and SFT overlap, they are distinct in terms of their theories about the relation of family change to antisocial and delinquent behavior and in terms of their assumptions about how family processes mediate adolescent problem behaviors and attitudes. In this section I review the underlying assumptions and mechanisms of change for each of the approaches.

Social Learning Family Therapy

SLFT is founded on the notion that antisocial behavior is inadvertently developed and sustained through daily maladaptive parent–child interactions in the home. An extensive body of research involving observations in family homes confirms that, compared with normal control parents, parents of children and adolescents referred for antisocial behavior engage in several processes that promote aggression and suppress prosocial behavior (see Patterson, 1982, for review). Coercive interaction patterns are chief among these processes. Coercive interaction refers to instances where the deviant behavior of one family member (e.g., the child when he tantrums) is directly reinforced or supported by another (e.g., the mother when she gives in). Positive child behavior is likely to be ignored or punished in referred (vs. normal) families, gradually shaping the child into producing aversive behaviors that gain parental attention and fulfill the child's immediate needs. SLFT is designed to alter the pattern of dysfunctional interchanges by building parental skills in identifying problem and prosocial child behaviors, delivering reinforcement contingent on positive behavior, delivering mild forms of discipline, and negotiating compromises.

Structural Family Therapy

SFT addresses issues related to poor family organization, cohesion, and structure. This approach views antisocial behavior as a logical outcome of a malfunctioning system. SFT also views the family system as having an equilibrium that it attempts to maintain so that forces of change are met with internal shifts toward self-stabilization. These efforts to self-stabilize will tend to lead to a reorganization of the family system along hierarchical lines (Sameroff, 1989). In addition to attempting to alter family interactions, SFT targets mechanisms of emotional engagement and distancing, shared family beliefs, and reorganization of family subsystems and hierarchies. With regard to the treatment of antisocial behavior problems, this approach has been adapted to fit culturally specific values and beliefs (e.g., Szapocznik, Kurtines, & Fernandez, 1980; Szapocznik, Scopetta, Kurtines, & Aranalde, 1978).

EVIDENCE SUPPORTING THE EFFICACY OF INTERVENTIONS USING SOCIAL LEARNING FAMILY THERAPY

Social learning–based approaches are the best-researched therapy techniques for antisocial youngsters and hold the most promise for achieving positive changes (Kazdin & Weisz, 1998). Social Learning Theory underlies Parent Management Training (PMT) interventions that include procedures that train, support, and supervise parents as they alter their child's problem behavior and build positive socialization skills in their home. PMT has been used in many studies on child and adolescent problems in addition to antisocial behavior, including eating disorders, enuresis, autism, attention deficit hyperactivity disorder, learning disabilities, and adherence to medical regimens. A central idea in the PMT approach is that parents have a major impact on their youth's day-to-day functioning and are in an ideal position to powerfully influence their child's adjustment.

Studies have shown that, for problems with child antisocial behavior, PMT has a more potent effect than does individually based treatments that focus on having a therapist work one-on-one with the child or adolescent (Kazdin & Weisz, 1998; Miller & Prinz, 1990). Research has indicated that treatment effects from PMT persist into follow-up for from 1 to 14 years posttreatment (Long, Forehand, Wierson, & Morgan, 1994). Treatment effects have been shown in multiple domains, including parent and teacher reports of child problems; direct observations of children and parents' behavior at home, at school, and with peers; and on child self-reports and official reports of criminal activities (see review by Patterson, Dishion, & Chamberlain, 1993). Studies have also found that PMT has a positive impact on aspects of family adjustment that are not the direct focus of the treatment, such as maternal depression, and improvement in sibling behavior (Kazdin, 1995).

There are numerous variations of PMT designed to focus on specific groups of children and families referred to treatment for conduct problems, including families of preschoolers (Webster-Stratton, 1994, 1996) and school-age children (McMahon & Wells, 1989; Patterson, Chamberlain, & Reid, 1982).

PMT has been used as a central component in prevention studies in which the goal is to decrease the number of children in the population who develop conduct problems (e.g., Reid & Eddy, 1997; Sanders, Dadds, Johnston, & Cash, 1992). PMT has also been used as a component in interventions that target adolescents at risk for antisocial behavior and substance abuse (Dishion & Andrews, 1995) and for those who are already involved in serious and chronic delinquency (e.g., Borduin et al., 1995; Chamberlain & Reid, 1998).

A recent advance in research on PMT has demonstrated that changes in specific parenting variables are causally related to changes in child outcomes. Forgatch and DeGarmo (1999) conducted a PMT intervention with mothers who were recently divorced (Parenting Through Change; Forgatch, 1994). The aim of the study was to prevent the development of negative outcomes for the young sons of these mothers who had been shown in previous studies to be at risk for problems with antisocial behavior, poor academic performance and peer relations, and depression and anxiety. The intervention was delivered in 14 sessions with groups of divorcing mothers and covered topics such as encouraging child cooperation, setting effective limits, developing communication skills, solving problems, managing conflict, and monitoring children's activities away from home. The assessment and analysis of treatment effects used a sophisticated, state-of-the-art, multiple-informant, multiple-method strategy that included interviews, questionnaires, and observations with mothers and children and measures of school adjustment conducted by teachers. Results showed that sons in the intervention group had more positive functioning at home and at school in follow-up than did boys whose mothers had not received the intervention. The key contribution of this study was that two specific parenting practices were identified as accounting for positive changes in the boy's behavior as reported by the mothers, the boys themselves, and the boy's teachers.

The first and most powerful parenting practice examined included two types of parent–child interaction: negative reinforcement and negative reciprocity. Negative reinforcement was defined as the frequency of conflict episodes initiated by the mother that were ended by the boy. For example, mother asks the child to do something, the child shouts "no way," and the mother fails to follow up or withdraws. The mother's backing down after his noncompliance has reinforced the child's use of coercive behavior. Negative reciprocity was defined as the conditional likelihood that the mother reciprocated the boy's negative behavior with a negative behavior of her own. These two scores, both taken from coded videotaped interactions of mothers and sons, were combined to form a coercive discipline score. One year after treatment, coercive discipline diminished in families that underwent the intervention, and it increased in those that did not. Further, the change in coercive discipline accounted for the change in the boy's school adjustment and adjustment at home according to both the boy and his mother.

Mother's positive parenting also benefited from the intervention. Positive parenting was defined as mother's positive involvement in the boy's life, mother's encouragement of the boy's skills development, and mother's use of problem-solving techniques. Mothers of boys in the intervention condition had higher scores on this variable than did control families, and like the discipline score, positive parenting was shown to account for better boy adjustment in school and at home in follow-up.

Studies such as this that pinpoint specific family processes related to prevention or treatment of antisocial behavior and are founded on theoretically and developmentally relevant variables advance the science of intervention and pave the way for development and implementation of effective, community-based programs. Eddy and Chamberlain (2000) described a similar measurement and analysis strategy in a study with chronic juvenile offenders reported in chapter 6.

RESEARCH ON THE EFFICACY OF FAMILY-BASED INTERVENTIONS FOR DELINQUENT YOUTHS

During the late 1980s and early 1990s, three empirically based program models emerged that have been shown to reduce rates of delinquency. These are Multidimensional Treatment Foster Care (MTFC; which is the primary focus of this book and is described in detail in chapter 5), Multisystemic Therapy (MST), and Functional Family Therapy (FFT). These three models have been the focus of national attention during the past 5 years, have been widely disseminated, and have been selected as interventions that are models of violence prevention (Blueprints for Violence Prevention, Elliott, 1998; Strengthening America's Families, Alvarado, Kendall, Beesley, & Lee-Cavaness, 2000). I briefly describe research on the MST and FFT models next.

A Brief Overview of Research on Multisystemic Therapy

After a series of promising pilot studies (e.g., Henggeler et al., 1986), Henggeler examined the efficacy of MST for a population of youths from Simpsonville, South Carolina, who had at least three nonviolent arrests or one violent arrest and who were living with at least one parent figure. Goals of the MST intervention were to reduce criminal behavior and out-of-home placement at a relatively low cost. The Simpsonville MST study included 84 youths, with an average of 3.5 arrests before treatment. Youths had spent an average of 9.5 weeks in lockup in a correctional facility prior to their entry into the study. Participating youths were an average of 15.2 years old, 77% were male, and 56% were African American. Youths were randomly assigned to participation in MST or to "usual services," which consisted of court-ordered curfew, school attendance, and referral to other community agencies for treatment. Results showed that at 59 weeks after referral to the study, MST youths had significantly fewer arrests (an average of .87 for MST youths and 1.52 for control youths) and had spent approximately 66% fewer days in lockup. In addition, families in MST reported improvement in family cohesion and that their youngsters were less aggressive with peers than were those in the control group. These lower rates of arrest held at a 2.4-year follow-up (Henggeler, Melton, Smith, Schoenwald, & Hanley, 1993).

In a more comprehensive test of MST, Borduin and colleagues (1995) compared the effectiveness of the approach with that of individual therapy. Participants were 200 12–17-year-olds referred from local juvenile justice departments and randomly assigned to MST or individual therapy (IT). Participants had a history of an average of 4.2 previous arrests, and 63% had previously been incarcerated. They were 14.8 years old when they entered the study, and 67% were male. Results from a 4-year follow-up showed that MST youths were significantly less likely to be arrested than were IT youths. Twenty-two percent of MST participants who completed treatment (77 of 92 cases) were rearrested compared with 46.6% of MST dropouts (15 of 92 cases), whereas 71.4% of IT completers were rearrested (63 of 84 cases) compared with 71.4% of IT dropouts (21 of 84 cases). In addition, significantly fewer MST participants were arrested for violent crimes in follow-up.

In addition to these two studies, MST has been examined in a multisite study in South Carolina (Henggeler, Brondino, Melton, Scherer, & Hanley, 1997), where it was found that therapist adherence to the MST protocol was significantly associated with decreased rates of arrest and incarceration at follow-up. In that study, the overall arrest rate for MST youths was 26% lower than for control youths, but the difference did not meet the criteria for statistical significance. Researchers in Charleston, South Carolina, are also examining MST as an alternative for youths with substance use problems in a randomized trial (Henggeler et al., 1997). Preliminary results from that study look promising in terms of reduced rates of out-of-home placement for youths in the MST condition compared with control youths. Recent work of Henggeler and colleagues has focused on understanding factors that relate to promoting treatment fidelity in replications of the MST model and how treatment fidelity relates to client outcomes (e.g., Henggeler et al., 1997).

A Brief Overview of Research on Functional Family Therapy

The theory for the FFT model is strongly influenced by the structural family therapies. In a series of studies conducted in the late 1970s and early 1980s, Alexander and his colleagues focused on court-referred adolescents and used a variation of the SFT approach. Their FFT model was aimed at "instituting reciprocity" in families and incorporated aspects of structural and systemic theory such as promoting family engagement through reframing focus and blame on one family member (e.g., "He is a rotten kid") to characteristics with positive attributions that can be endorsed by the entire family (e.g., "We are upset about his behavior because we care so much about him"). The FFT model also incorporates aspects addressed by PMT interventions, such as behavioral contracting and focusing on parental supervision and discipline (e.g., Alexander et al., 1998; Alexander & Parsons, 1973, 1982; Klein, Alexander, & Parsons, 1977).

Research on FFT includes eight studies using experimental designs and indicates that FFT produces significantly better outcomes than client-centered, psychodynamic, or no-treatment control groups, both in terms of youth recidivism and on measures of family interaction. In one study, long-term effects were found in that 3 years after intervention, siblings of FFT cases had significantly fewer court contacts than siblings in the control groups. These findings suggest FFT provides positive outcomes for adolescents with behavioral problems and may have positive implications for the siblings of these adolescents.

These two treatment approaches have much in common with MTFC. Both see association with delinquent peers as a major risk factor that must be avoided, and an essential component is to increase association with positive peers. Both focus their interventions in the context of family settings. Both models concentrate on improving the youth's school adjustment and emphasize participation in prosocial community activities. Both are pragmatic approaches that focus on the here and now and promote behavior change in the youth's natural environment. Theoretical similarities exist as well. Both

MST and FFT developers designed their interventions on the basis of research on causes and correlates of delinquency reviewed in chapters 1 and 2. Both approaches design interventions to target key systems in which the youth interacts, as well as the interplay between those systems (e.g., improving communication between parents and school). Both rely on empirically based treatments to form the core of their interventions. Both support the social–ecological view (Bronfenbrenner, 1979) that youth behavior is multidetermined through the interplay of the individual and his or her social systems, including family, peers, school, and work.

There are also differences between these two approaches and MTFC. In MST, participants are youths who are at risk of being removed from their family homes because of repeated arrests. MST treatment takes place in family homes or other community settings selected by the family. FFT has been most effective with first-time offenders. The average number of offenses for participants in MST is between 2.9 and 4.2, depending on the study (Henggeler, Mihalic, Rone, Thomas, & Timmons-Mitchell, 1998). FFT has been shown to be effective with first-time and less-serious offenders. For MTFC participants, the average number of offenses before enrollment ranges from 10 to 14. In MTFC, youths have already been removed from their family homes by the juvenile authorities due to severe and chronic delinquency and are slated for placement in institutional or residential care settings. MTFC creates family foster care placements for such youths and works with them and their families of origin (parents, relatives, or other adult aftercare resource) while they are placed in MTFC.

Compared with other treatment approaches for youths with problems with delinquency, the evidence for the efficacy of MTFC, MST, and FFT is strong. All three models incorporate a clear set of theoretical and developmental factors. These factors strengthen community-based treatment models and should be part of conceptualizations for new intervention models. Information on common barriers to success in treatment should be added to the mix so that intervention models can avoid problems that interfere with positive outcomes.

BARRIERS TO SUCCESSFUL TREATMENT

Several studies have shown that multiple personal and environmental stressors experienced by family members, particularly parents, derail their efforts to benefit from treatment and make implementation problems more likely (e.g., Dumas & Wahler, 1983; McMahon, Forehand, Griest, & Wells, 1981; Patterson, 1982). Differential effectiveness has been associated with two family-related factors: (a) attrition and (b) family stress and lack of social support.

Attrition

Families who drop out during treatment have been found to have higher rates of certain characteristics such as lower socioeconomic status and mothers who were more depressed (e.g., McMahon et al., 1981) and to be agency- (vs. self-) referred (Chamberlain, Patterson, Reid, Kavanagh, & Forgatch, 1984). Kazdin (1990) assessed parent, child, and family characteristics of treatment completers and dropouts. Families who dropped out had children and adolescents with a greater number of symptoms of conduct disorders and delinquency, lower educational and occupational status, and lower income. Mothers in dropout families reported more depression and higher life event stress scores. Dropout rates of over 50% have been reported in some treatment studies with families of youngsters with conduct disorders (e.g., Hawkins & Nederhood, 1987; Johnson & Kaplan, 1988).

Losing clients after initial contact but prior to the first treatment session has been identified as a problem. Szapocznik and his colleagues (Szapocznik et al., 1988) have examined this problem as a significant barrier to providing services. For example, in their study of 650 families, all of whom made the initial contact requesting treatment, only 250 came in for a screening interview, and 145 completed the intake. They found that the application of strategic and structural family systems engagement strategies significantly improved initial engagement rates.

Family Stress and Lack of Social Support

Wahler and his colleagues (e.g., Dumas & Wahler, 1983; Wahler, 1980; Wahler & Dumas, 1986) have conducted a series of studies that examined the relationships among family socioeconomic disadvantage, social isolation, and outcomes. They found that at follow-up (i.e., 1 year), the probability of treatment failure, judged on the basis of home observations of child behavior, steadily increased as a function of low socioeconomic status, social isolation, or both. This finding has been replicated in other studies (e.g., Webster-Stratton, 1985).

The impact of stress seems to be somewhat ameliorated if the parent has a relative or close friend from whom they can seek social support. For example, in their study with single parents and antisocial children, Dadds and McHugh (1992) found that maternal perception of social support was the best predictor of treatment responsiveness. Several studies have suggested that inclusion of specific components designed to enhance social support increases the effectiveness of family treatments (e.g., Dadds, Sanders, Behrens, & James, 1987; Dadds, Schwartz, & Sanders, 1987; Griest et al., 1982; Miller & Prinz, 1990), but these have been conducted with families of younger children with conduct problems and may not be generalizable to adolescent populations.

In addition to family factors, specific child factors have also been found to influence treatment efficacy. Researchers have found family therapy interventions to be less effective for older (over 12.5 years) versus younger cases (Patterson et al., 1993) and for adolescents who engage in both overt (e.g., aggression) and covert (e.g., stealing) conduct problems (Reid & Hendricks, 1973). In general, family therapy, although shown to be effective, is more difficult to implement for adolescent populations from multistressed families. In more difficult cases, family therapy may be a necessary component of treatment but perhaps is not a sufficient strategy for producing clinically significant behavior change. In addition, parental resistance to treatment has also been studied as a barrier to improvement in child and adolescent outcomes.

Resistance to Treatment

Participation in family therapy makes obvious demands on parents, such as implementing procedures at home and attending weekly sessions often in the face of multiple stressors and lack of sufficient resources. Parents of antisocial youngsters are also often extremely discouraged about the prospects of making meaningful changes with their children and do not welcome the idea that their efforts will be instrumental in making those changes.

In an attempt to gain a better understanding of how client resistance influences change in family treatment and how therapist behavior interacts to exacerbate or lessen resistance, a group of colleagues at the Oregon Social Learning Center (OSLC; Forgatch, Patterson, Reid, Kavanagh, & Chamberlain) conducted a series of studies in the mid-1980s. The aim of this research was first to see if we could reliably measure client resistance as it occurred in treatment sessions. We defined resistance as the parent making a statement expressing disagreement with the therapist, or saying that what the therapist was suggesting that they do was impossible or not relevant. The second goal of the research was determining whether there was a "typical" pattern of resistance that could be observed, and whether this varied in successful versus nonsuccessful cases. The third, and more complex, set of questions we sought to answer involved the relationship between what the therapist did in the treatment sessions and the parent's resistance (or lack of resistance) and how this interaction between therapist and parent affected case outcomes. In the first in a series of studies on this topic, we found that it was possible to code and measure the occurrence of client resistance in treatment sessions on a moment-by-moment or microsocial level (Chamberlain et al., 1984). In addition, we found that there were systematic changes in levels of client resistance at different stages of treatment (see Figure 3.1).

Parents tended to show the highest level of resistance during midtreatment. This made sense because it is at this phase of treatment that we broach the topic of improving discipline strategies and practicing new

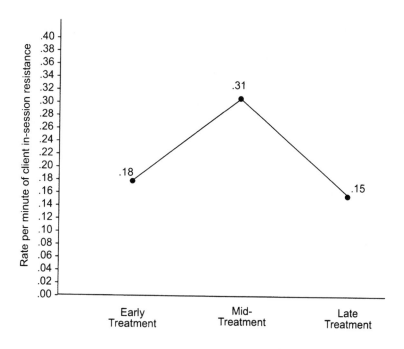

Figure 3.1. Average observed rate per minute of client resistance at three phases of treatment. From "Observation of Client Resistance," by P. Chamberlain, G. R. Patterson, J. B. Reid, K. Kavanagh, and M. S. Forgatch, 1984, *Behavior Therapy,* p. 150. Copyright 1984 by the Association for Advancement of Behavior Therapy. Adapted with permission.

methods for using discipline at home. We also found that parents who dropped out of treatment early had higher initial resistance scores than those who completed treatment. Parents who had self-referred to treatment were less resistant in early sessions than those who were referred by a public agency, such as child welfare or juvenile justice.

Next we examined the relationship between parent resistance and therapist behavior. A Therapy Process Code was developed (described in Chamberlain & Ray, 1988) that categorized therapist behavior into seven mutually exclusive codes. We found that, like parent resistance, therapist behavior varied systematically during different phases of treatment. OSLC therapists tended to do more teaching during the mid-phase of treatment.

Patterson and Forgatch (1985) examined the relationship between teaching and resistance in two studies. In the first study they tested the hypothesis that within-session levels of parent resistance would be correlated with levels of therapist teaching and confronting. In the second study, they actually manipulated the levels of therapist teaching and confronting during a series of single sessions and found that parent resistance levels went up and down in kind. Therapist behaviors such as supporting and facilitating were found to decrease parent resistance. These findings helped to clarify that therapists who conduct parent management treatments have a dual challenge. To position parents to help their child change his or her antisocial behavior patterns, therapists must teach and support parents to use more effective, contingent family management practices. At the same time, the therapist's efforts to teach are likely to elicit resistance from parents. Skilled therapists must learn how to use a combination of teaching and support to help parents change how they interact with their child.

Another strategy for dealing with the development of serious child conduct problems and chronic delinquency is to implement interventions that target the predictable antecedents along developmental pathways in early childhood. Such early intervention studies are grounded in the notion that preventing the development of antisocial behavior in the first place, and preventing its spread to more generalized forms in the school, with peers, and in the community, will decrease the disorder's rate of prevalence in the general population.

PREVENTATIVE INTERVENTIONS AS AN APPROACH TO REDUCING CONDUCT PROBLEMS AND DELINQUENCY

Prevention studies aim to interrupt the accumulation of risk factors that have been shown to increase the risk of antisocial behavior at subsequent stages of development. Reid and Eddy (1997) reviewed research on prevention theory and on several illustrative interventions that targeted both proximal, or near-term, and distal, or long-term, outcomes for youngsters at risk for antisocial behavior. They defined preventative interventions as those that attempt to effect positive changes in the trajectories of youngsters as evidenced by three variables: (a) reduction of antecedents of antisocial behavior targeted during the intervention, (b) reduction in the probability that a subsequent antecedent risk factor or set of risk factor antecedents will occur, and (c) reduction in the risk of long-term socially significant outcomes (e.g., delinquency, violence, or incarceration). Reid and Eddy described several preventative interventions that met these criteria (e.g., the Nurse Home Visiting program, Olds, Henderson, Chamberlin, & Tatelbaum, 1986; the FAST Track program, Coie, 1996). Here I describe the outcomes for one such intervention, the LIFT program (Linking Interests of Families and Teachers).

AN ILLUSTRATIVE MULTISETTING PREVENTIVE INTERVENTION

Like much early delinquency treatment, most early prevention efforts did not have a demonstrable impact (Berleman & Steinburn, 1969). By the mid-1980s, several theoretically based, multisetting prevention programs that targeted child antisocial behavior were being instituted around the United States (e.g., Conduct Problems Prevention Research Group, 1992; Tremblay, Pagani-Kurtz, Vitaro, Masse, & Pihl, 1995). Most of these programs combined interventions focused on the child, school setting, and family.

LIFT is a multisetting intervention designed by John Reid and his colleagues (Eddy, Fetrow, and Mayne) at the OSLC for use in an elementary school context (Reid, 1995). It has three components: (a) a 10-week classroom child problem-solving and social skills curriculum, (b) a playground behavior management protocol modeled after the Good Behavior Game (Barrish, Saunders, & Wolfe, 1969) described in chapter 2, and (c) a 6-week parent management training course. These three components were selected because they were thought to be the most relevant to the subsequent development of adolescent delinquency and violence (i.e., the distal outcome) for children who are in elementary school. The immediate or proximal outcomes targeted by LIFT were selected because they were hypothesized to predict subsequent distal outcomes. Proximal outcomes included antisocial, aggressive, and socially unskilled behavior in children, and parent discipline and monitoring.

The LIFT intervention was delivered to all elementary students in the first and fifth grades at randomly selected schools in lower socioeconomic neighborhoods. Control schools did not receive any intervention, but teachers, students, and parents took part in the assessment portion of the study, and control schools received $2,000 in unrestricted funds. The elementary school setting was selected as a point of focus because elementary school is the first place where the majority of children come together to make up a broad cross section of the population. The overall aim of the LIFT project was to decrease the prevalence of delinquency and violence in a population at a cost that most states could afford. Therefore, LIFT was designed to be a low-intensity, low-cost intervention.

In the classroom component, teachers gave students a brief lesson and then role-played a set of social or problem-solving skills. On the playground, children were rewarded with colored armbands if they were observed engaging in positive behavior toward their peers. Students could earn rewards for themselves, their entire class, and for a small group to which they were assigned. If teachers observed a child behaving in a negative manner, they noted this in a logbook. After recess the total number of negative points earned by the group was subtracted from a preset number of "good-faith" points each group received at the beginning of the recess period. Parent sessions were conducted for groups of 10–15 families and included lecture, discussion, and role-plays on topics typically covered in parent management training interventions. Group facilitators who were trained in parent management also used videotaped scenarios to demonstrate skills and generate discussion. At the end of each session, parents were given a "home practice assignment." The idea was to implement a specific technique that would be covered in the group session with their child during the coming week. The content of all three components of the intervention were modified to be developmentally appropriate for first and fifth graders.

The LIFT program did several things to maximize parent participation. Parents received weekly newsletters describing LIFT activities at school and providing suggestions for complementary activities at home. A telephone and answering machine was installed in each classroom to facilitate communication between parents and teachers. Teachers were encouraged to leave a brief message about the class activities each day and about homework assignments. Parents were encouraged to listen to these messages and to leave messages for the teacher. Parents used the "LIFT Line" frequently and reported that they appreciated having easy access to such information. During the 6 weeks that facilitators conducted parent groups, they telephoned parents once per week to check in and address questions or concerns about the home practice assignment. If parents missed the group session, they were invited to attend another group being conducted that week. If this was inconvenient, facilitators arranged for a home visit. If that was not possible, materials from the group session were mailed to the parents. For any given LIFT parent session, an average of 59% of the families attended the scheduled group, 13% had a home visit, 23% received the materials by mail, and 5% refused to participate. Due to the use of these multiple modes of service delivery, the rate of parents who dropped out of the LIFT program was low (7%).

Researchers measured the immediate or proximal impact of the LIFT intervention in three domains: the child's level of physical aggression toward classmates on the playground, the level of parent–child negative behavior during videotaped problem-solving discussions, and teacher reports of his or her impressions of child positive behavior with classmates. These outcomes were measured in the spring following the intervention. Compared with children in the control condition, LIFT children were less aggressive on the playground and were perceived as being more positive toward peers. Parents in the LIFT condition were less negative toward their children during problem solving than were control parents. The effects were strongest for children who scored the highest on level of behavior problem prior to the intervention. Of the three domains, the effects for aggression on the playground were the strongest. During the spring following the intervention, the LIFT youngsters averaged 4.8 aversive behaviors per day on the playground versus an average of 6.6 per day for control youngsters. This difference, although seemingly trivial, meant that, during the spring term, LIFT participants were exposed to 1,700 fewer physically aversive events on the playground than were their control counterparts.

The long-term or distal impact was measured 3 years later. By that time, study participants who were in Grade 5 at the time of participation were in middle school, and the first graders were in Grade 4. Outcomes of interest for middle school youths included association with delinquent peers, police arrests, and drug and alcohol use. Compared with LIFT participants, youngsters in the control condition were 2.2 times more likely to affiliate with misbehaving peers, 1.8 times more likely to be involved in patterned alcohol use, and 1.5 times more likely to have tried marijuana. Control group youths were also 2.4 times more likely to be arrested during middle school than were LIFT youths (Eddy, Reid, Stoolmiller, & Fetrow, 2002). For fourth graders, teachers of LIFT participants reported that they exhibited fewer problems with inattention, impulsivity, and hyperactive behaviors.

This intervention demonstrated that a combined approach targeting multiple facets of the child's world had the potential to change the child's social milieu as a whole, which was then, in turn, thought to have effects on individuals within the milieu, rather than vice versa (Eddy, Reid, & Fetrow, 2000). Communities are becoming increasingly committed to implementing prevention programs such as LIFT in an effort to stem the tide of youths coming into the juvenile justice and mental health systems. With the advent of accountability-based movements such as managed care there is an increased emphasis on tracking short- and long-term outcomes of such efforts. The focus on producing meaningful and long-lasting outcomes for treatment programs for older severely delinquent youths has created increased pressure for communities to be more accountable in terms of how they spend public dollars to fund their local programs.

CONCLUSION

Theory, attention to developmental considerations, and knowledge of barriers to treatment success can all be used to inform the development of interventions. In the next two chapters, I present the "nuts and bolts" of the MTFC model. The model was designed on the basis of previous research conducted at OSLC and elsewhere that highlighted the potential of caring, well-trained, and supervised adults to make an impact on youths with severe behavioral and emotional problems.

4

AN OVERVIEW OF THE HISTORY AND DEVELOPMENT OF THE MULTIDIMENSIONAL TREATMENT FOSTER CARE MODEL AND THE SUPPORTING RESEARCH

In the early 1980s, the clinical research group at the Oregon Social Learning Center (OSLC) tested the efficacy of a Parent Management Training (PMT) intervention with teenagers who had multiple police offenses (Bank, Marlowe, Reid, Patterson, & Weinrott, 1991). To qualify for inclusion in the study, youths had to have three or more officially recorded offenses, one of which had to be a nonstatus offense (i.e., crimes that adults could be charged for, not, e.g., minor in possession or runaway). The aim of treatment was to help parents increase their skills in dealing with day-to-day issues that typically included problems with youths' criminal behavior in the community, skipping school, and defiance at home. However, accomplishing the PMT goals was difficult because these families were beset by frequent crises generated from within and outside of the immediate family. The teenager was often at the hub of an array of problems and thwarted the parents' attempts to influence or control him or her. In an attempt to deal with this, the clinical treatment team adopted the PMT treatment protocol to focus additional emphasis on teaching family problem-solving skills.

Results from this study were mixed. Statistically, we found that, compared with the control group, where adolescents received individual therapy, PMT cases demonstrated reliably fewer arrests and lower incarceration rates over a 3-year period. But clinically, we found that these cases were extraordinarily difficult to treat, especially the most serious and chronic cases. It became obvious to the clinical treatment team conducting this study that parents in these families were embroiled in escalating conflict with their youngsters and had little capacity to provide a supportive or corrective influence on their sons or daughters.

The youngster became increasingly committed to and influenced by delinquent peers. The delinquent peer group, in turn, reinforced the teen's alienation from adult influence. As delinquency escalated, the youth's behavior began to compromise community safety to the point where courts intervened and required that the youth be held accountable. At this point in the youth's development, where close parental supervision and guidance are absolutely critical, parents were typically distressed, demoralized, defeated, and cynical. The challenge was to come up with an intervention to provide corrective or therapeutic parenting for antisocial adolescents whose parents, for one reason or another, are unable to rise to the occasion. Because of the number of disruptions occurring in these families, interventionists using the PMT approach found it difficult to work on improving specific family management skills, which are at the core of the approach.

This motivated us to rethink the model for treating such families. We examined existing programs and found that most aggregated delinquent youths were in residential settings such as group homes. Many of these programs relied on theoretical approaches, such as Positive Peer culture (PPC; Vorrath & Brendtro, 1985), that assume that the peer group is the best vehicle for influencing and motivating youths to change their problem behaviors and attitudes. This change is thought to take place through therapeutic group work. Although this approach is logically appealing, we were aware of the findings from longitudinal research that implicated association with delinquent peers in the development and escalation of delinquency. Could severely antisocial youngsters placed in group settings be directed and supervised so that they could become positive socializing influences on one another? The empirical support for such models was absent (Burns & Friedman, 1990; U.S. Department of Health and Human Services, 1999), but belief in the approach was widespread among community treatment providers and those funding juvenile justice services.

We were skeptical about the usefulness of PPC-type approaches and were, despite difficulties, still hopeful about the possibility of caring adults being in the best position to be a strong socializing force for delinquent teenagers. We developed a family-based model for teenagers who were severely delinquent to the point where they had been removed from their homes by the juvenile authorities. Community families were recruited and trained to provide placements for such youths. One youth was placed in each home so as to minimize the influence of delinquent peers and capitalize on adult influence. A brief history of the development of this approach follows.

DEVELOPMENT OF THE MULTIDIMENSIONAL TREATMENT FOSTER CARE MODEL

OSLC began providing Multidimensional Treatment Foster Care (MTFC) services in 1983 when we received funding from the State of Oregon, Children's Services Division, to develop a program that could serve as an alternative to incarceration. At that time, Oregon's rate for incarcerating juvenile offenders was relatively high compared to other states. They wanted to support the development of community-based alternatives to locking youths up in the state training schools. We began with a small program: five youths at any one time. One of the first challenges was to recruit and train suitable treatment foster parents to provide placements and to work as part of our treatment team. Other team members included a program supervisor to coordinate all aspects of the intervention; a family therapist to work with the youth's biological, relative, adoptive, or other aftercare resource; an individual therapist to work with the youth; and a foster parent trainer and PDR (Parent Daily Report) caller who could have daily contact with the MTFC parents. Other staff included administrative and secretarial support. In subsequent sections of this chapter, I describe the roles of these team members and how they interact with each other and with outside agencies, such as juvenile justice parole and probation officers and school personnel.

In 1986, after having run the juvenile justice program for 3 years, the director of the Child and Adolescent Treatment Program (CATP) at the Oregon State Hospital asked us to consider adapting the approach for use with children and adolescents leaving that setting. These youngsters had been hospitalized due to severe emotional and mental disorders and had spent an average of 1 year in the CATP, and the program was having difficulty finding appropriate aftercare placements. This request coincided with an opportunity to apply for federal funding from the Children's Bureau to develop community demonstration programs for severely emotionally disturbed youths. From 1987 to 1989, we treated 10 children and adolescents using a variation of the MTFC model that focused less on controlling antisocial behavior and more on providing mental health–oriented treatments. Adding a psychiatric consultant to our clinical team provided this focus.

At the completion of the federal funding for that program, referrals from the State Hospital continued, and referrals from the local child welfare branch (i.e., child protective services) increased. We applied for and obtained eligibility to provide Medicaid-funded mental health services through the county mental health authority, which subsequently evolved into the local managed care organization. Now MTFC cases could be referred to us locally or from around the state by child welfare or mental health. We did not accept referrals if parents or other key adult caretakers lived too far away to have regular contact with the program because we maintained a strong interest in working with the families to which the youths would return after the program.

In 1996, after completing the randomized trial (results described in chapter 6) with male juvenile offenders, we began to focus our research and clinical efforts on girls referred from juvenile justice. We treated several girls throughout the tenure of the program and came to realize that there were gender-related issues not being well addressed in the program model, which had been mostly developed and implemented with boys. We applied for and received funding from the National Institute of Mental Health (Violence and Traumatic Stress Branch) to conduct a 5-year, randomized trial with girls and their families. That study, which is currently under way, I describe in detail in chapter 7.

As our work with child welfare and mental health agencies increased, we were getting referrals for younger children. Our MTFC model had been developed for adolescents and did not address the appropriate developmental or behavioral targets for preschool children. In addition, the outcomes that we were used to measuring were not relevant for this group. In 1989, Phil Fisher joined our team and revised the clinical and research aspects of the MTFC model to be applicable to this population. We describe this adaptation in chapter 8.

Another population for whom we received frequent referrals were youths who were developmentally delayed and who had a range of difficult behaviors (including inappropriate sexual behavior) that made them very challenging to place in community settings. Kevin Moore developed a version of the MTFC program specifically designed for this population (Moore, 2001).

Throughout the years that we have been conducting Treatment Foster Care programs, we have been impressed by the applicability of the model to diverse populations of youths with complex and challenging problems. Because only one youth is placed in each MTFC home, the program can be highly individualized to fit unique needs and capitalize on individual strengths. MTFC does not require any of the compromises or concerns about the "good of the group" that need to be considered in aggregate care settings. The MTFC model is also inexpensive compared to group care. I describe a cost analysis at the end of this chapter. In addition to costing less, because no funds are required to build or maintain the facility in MTFC, more of the program dollar can go into direct treatment-related activities than in most other residential options.

We have focused our initial research efforts on evaluating program efficacy for juvenile offenders. More recently we have focused on studying the effects of selected components of MTFC on improving outcomes for youngsters in "regular foster care." Clearly, additional studies are needed to understand the limits and benefits of this approach for use with other populations of children, teenagers, and families. Across all adaptations of the MTFC approach implemented at OSLC, we have attempted to adhere to three general principles of practice. These include providing a supportive environment for MTFC parents, creating and maintaining a reinforcing environment for youths, and having clearly described and understood staff roles that promote client engagement and support. Specific elements of the MTFC model, including a description of the program components, staff roles, and relationships with other community agencies (e.g., juvenile justice and schools), I describe in chapter 5 (see also Chamberlain, 1994; Chamberlain & Mihalic, 1998).

RESEARCH ON MULTIDIMENSIONAL TREATMENT FOSTER CARE

So far, four studies have been conducted on the effectiveness of the OSLC MTFC approach (see Table 4.1). Three additional randomized trials are currently under way. In 1990, we examined the rates of incarceration for boys and girls who participated in MTFC compared to those who had received treatment in other community-based programs (Chamberlain, 1990). All participants had been committed to the state training school but were placed in community-based programs as an alternative to incarceration. This first study used a matched comparison design where youths were matched on age, sex, and date of commitment to the state training school. Youths who participated in this study were girls and boys from ages 12 to 17 years (average 14.56 years), and 15% were ethnic minorities. Other demographic and risk factors are shown in Table 4.2.

The outcomes we examined were the number of days spent incarcerated during the first 2 years posttreatment and program completion rates (vs. expulsion or running away). Results showed that youngsters in MTFC spent significantly fewer days in lockup during follow-up, a difference in cost of $122,000 over a 2-year period (estimating incarceration costs at $100 a day). In addition, significantly fewer MTFC youths than matched comparison youths were incarcerated following treatment. Although, on the average, youths in both groups spent the same amount of time in treatment, more MTFC participants completed their treatment programs. There was a significant relationship between the number of days in treatment and the number of days of subsequent incarceration for youths in the MTFC (but not in the comparison) group. In this study, the community comparison condition in-

TABLE 4.1
Four Studies Using the Multidimensional Treatment Foster Care Model (MTFC)

Location	Participants	Comparison/control group	Assignment procedure	Follow-up period	Risk/protective factors	Outcome	Reference
Eugene, OR	32 youths committed to state training school; ages 12–18	2 groups: MTFC and other residential	Matched on age, gender, and date of commitment	2 years	Supervision Family processes	MTFC < days incarcerated	Chamberlain, 1990
Eugene, OR	20 youths from Oregon State Hospital	2 groups: MTFC and treatment as usual in community	Random	1 year	Family support	MTFC > days out of hospital. More MTFC youths placed in family homes	Chamberlain & Reid, 1991
Eugene, OR	70 foster care families	3 groups: Enhanced Treatment Services (ETS) > payment (IP) Assessment only (AO)	Random	7 months	Behavior management training for foster parents	ETS < disrupts than IP and AO ETS > foster parent retention than IP and AO	Chamberlain, Moreland, & Reid, 1992
Eugene, OR	79 boys; ages 12–18 M = 13 offenses	2 groups: MTFC and other residential	Random	1 year (so far)	Delinquent peers Supervision Discipline Relationship with caretaking adult	MTFC arrested < 1/2 the time in follow-up Fewer days incarcerated Higher rates of program completion	Chamberlain & Reid, 1998

TABLE 4.2
Demographic and Risk Factors Comparison Between
Experimental and Traditional Studies

Demographic and risk factors	Experimental studies	Control studies
Age (years)	14.56	14.56
Sex	10 male, 6 female	10 male, 6 female
Mean no. of prior out-of-home placements	1.75 (range 0–8)	1.31 (range 0–5)
Family risk factors		
Family income below poverty level	8 (50%)	10 (63%)
Divorce between natural parents*	16 (100%)	12 (75%)
Three or more siblings	6 (38%)	10 (63%)
Adopted*	5 (31%)	0 (0%)
Parent hospitalized (current or previous)	1 (6%)	1 (6%)
Parent convicted of felony (current or previous)	2 (13%)	1 (6%)
Siblings institutionalized (current or previous)	2 (13%)	2 (13%)
Family available for aftercare	10 (63%)	11 (69%)
Child risk factors		
Physically abused (reported)	6 (38%)	7 (44%)
Sexually abused (reported)	2 (13%)	2 (13%)
Chronic runaway (>3 priors)	7 (44%)	8 (50%)
Suicide attempts	4 (25%)	3 (19%)
Child dangerousness		
Sexually abusive (adjudicated)	3 (19%)	3 (19%)
Previous felony charge	11 (69%)	10 (63%)
Dangerous to others	4 (25%)	5 (31%)
Dangerous to self	6 (38%)	4 (25%)
Child school adjustment		
Chronic truancy	12 (75%)	12 (75%)
Below grade level (at year 1)	9 (56%)	10 (63%)

*$p < .02$.

cluded placement in group homes, residential care, or drug and alcohol treatment facilities.

MULTIDIMENSIONAL TREATMENT FOSTER CARE FOR CHILDREN AND TEENAGERS WITH SEVERE BEHAVIORAL AND EMOTIONAL PROBLEMS

In a second study, we compared the effectiveness of MTFC with treatment as usual in the community for children (ages 9–18 years) leaving the state mental hospital (Chamberlain & Reid, 1991). Demographics, risk, and clinical variables are shown in Table 4.3. Participants had been hospitalized for an average of 245 days during the year prior to referral. Participants were randomly assigned to MTFC or "treatment as usual" in the community. Cases were referred by the hospital community outreach team as being ready for

TABLE 4.3
Oregon Social Learning Center Transitions Program: Characteristics of Participating Youths, January 1987 to August 1988

Characteristic	Treatment group	Control group
Youths admitted to date	10 (5 male, 5 female)	10 (3 male, 7 female)
Average age (years)	13.9 (range 9–18)	15.1 (range 12–17)
Average no. of out-of-home placements	5.1 (range 1–10)	5.0 (range 1–12)
Family makeup		
Divorced[a]	7 (78%)	8 (89%)
Failed adoptions	3 (30%)	
Siblings institutionalized	2 (20%)	3 (30%)
Siblings in foster care	5 (50%)	4 (40%)
History of family mental illness or in institutions	8 (80%)	9 (90%)
Family as aftercare resource	0 (0%)	2 (20%)
Risk variables		
Family at poverty level	5 (50%)	6 (60%)
Family violence	8 (80%)	9 (90%)
Three or more siblings	5 (50%)	4 (40%)
Youths with record of felonies (documented)	3 (30%)	3 (30%)
Youths with physical attacks on others (documented)	6 (60%)	5 (50%)
Sexually abusive	4 (40%)	2 (20%)
Fire setting	1 (10%)	1 (10%)
History of law violations (adjudicated)	5 (50%)	4 (40%)
Special clinical concerns		
Suicide attempts	6 (60%)	2 (20%)
Drug or alcohol dependency	3 (30%)	5 (50%)
Multiple runaways	6 (60%)	8 (80%)
Chronic truancy	4 (40%)	7 (70%)
Sexually abused	8 (80%)	7 (70%)

[a]$N = 9$.

placement in the community. Measures included the Parent Daily Report (PDR) Checklist, a daily parent report of child problem behaviors (described in detail in chapter 5) that examined rates of problem behaviors, the Behavior Symptom Inventory to examine the presence or absence of psychiatric symptoms, and tracking of rehospitalizations. Results showed that youngsters in the MTFC group were placed out of the hospital significantly more quickly than were those in the control condition. In fact, during the 7-month follow-up period, 33% of the control youngsters remained in the hospital the entire time because no appropriate aftercare resource was identified. Given that the child was placed in the community, more MTFC youngsters were placed in family settings, whereas control youths tended to be placed in institutional settings.

ADAPTING MULTIDIMENSIONAL TREATMENT FOSTER CARE FOR USE WITH CHILDREN IN "REGULAR" FOSTER CARE

In a third study, we examined the impact of conducting weekly foster parent groups, based on those used in the MTFC program, on placement disruption rates for children in "regular" foster care (Chamberlain, Moreland, & Reid, 1992). These were state foster homes where children were placed due to severe parental abuse or neglect. Seventy foster families from three Oregon counties were randomly assigned to one of three conditions: assessment only, payment only, or enhanced training and support groups. In the enhanced training and support group, foster parents were taught to use a version of the MTFC behavior management system with their children to help them reinforce positive child behaviors and deal with behavior problems on a daily basis. Foster parents in the enhanced training and support condition were also paid a monthly stipend ($70) for participating in the study. In the payment-only group, foster parents did not participate in the enhanced services but did receive the monthly stipend. In the assessment-only group, foster parents did not receive the extra services, and they did not receive the monthly stipend.

Three major outcomes were assessed: (a) the daily rates of child behavioral problems using the PDR Checklist, (b) the rate of children who were moved to another home due to problems between the child and foster parent (i.e., disruptions in foster care), and (c) the percentage of foster parents who dropped out of providing care during the course of the study. This last variable was measured because foster parent retention is a major concern for child welfare agencies due to the chronic shortage of qualified foster parents that we face in this country. We hypothesized that given increased support and training, foster parents would be more willing to remain providers, and the number of foster parents who dropped out of the system could be decreased.

In the enhanced training and support (ETS) condition, there was a significantly higher retention rate for foster parents. In terms of child outcomes, children whose foster parents participated in the enhanced condition had significantly fewer disruptions in their placements. In addition, children in the ETS group showed the largest drop in rate of problem behaviors at 3-months follow-up. See Figure 4.1 for data on specific outcomes.

EFFICACY OF MULTIDIMENSIONAL TREATMENT FOSTER CARE FOR ADOLESCENTS REFERRED FROM JUVENILE JUSTICE

In the largest and most comprehensive test of the MTFC model, we randomly assigned 79 12- to 18-year-old male offenders referred from the juvenile justice system to treatment in MTFC or group care (GC). Group

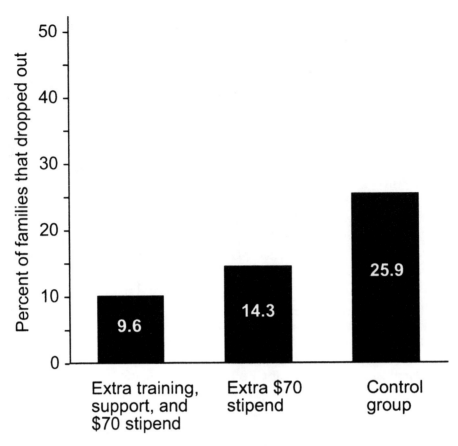

Figure 4.1. Training, support, and small stipend increased foster parents' willingness to provide care.

care was selected as a comparison condition because placement in group homes or group residential settings is the standard practice used in communities for the treatment and management of chronic juvenile offenders. Participating boys had an average of 13 previous arrests and 4.6 felonies prior to entering the study. Table 4.4 shows demographic characteristics of the participants and a description of their risk factors.

This study included evaluations of both treatment processes and outcomes. In addition to evaluating whether MTFC had an impact, the aim was to examine key factors that we thought would predict successful and unsuccessful outcomes for study participants regardless of the condition to which they were assigned. These factors were selected from those processes that had been identified by longitudinal studies (reviewed in chapters 1 and 2) as contributing to the development, maintenance, and escalation of delinquency in early adolescence. The study design is shown in Figure 4.2. Participating boys and their parents (or other adult caretakers) were assessed at baseline, 3 months after placement in MTFC or GC, and then every subsequent 6 months for 2 years.

TABLE 4.4

Characteristics of the Sample (*N* = 79) and Risk Factors

Characteristic	GC	MTFC
Mean age *(SD)* at referral (years)	15.1 (.96)	14.8 (1.5)
Mean age *(SD)* at first criminal referral (years)	12.5 (1.8)	12.8 (1.8)
Mean no. of *(SD)* previous charges	14.6 (7.5)	12.6 (10.1)
Mean no. of *(SD)* lockup days, 1 year prereferral	89 (103)	71 (59)
Risk factors		
Single-parent family	54%	59%
Target youths adopted	5%	9%
Parent hospitalized	7%	9%
Parent convicted of crime	30%	25%
Siblings institutionalized	22%	16%
Perpetrator of sexual abuse	7%	13%
Drug or alcohol abuse	15%	3%
Chronic truancy	69%	61%
Fire setting	22%	13%
Had runaway from placement	78%	75%
Two or more of above factors	85%	87%
Three or more of above factors	63%	56%

Note. GC = group care; MTFC = Multidimensional Treatment Foster Care Model.

The purpose of the 3-month assessment was to examine the strength of four factors that we hypothesized would predict treatment outcomes (specifically, subsequent arrests) regardless of the boy's placement setting (MTFC or GC). In other words, we hypothesized that to the extent that these four factors were operating well, boys would commit fewer crimes and report engaging in less criminal behavior in follow-up. The four factors examined were (a) the extent to which the boy was closely supervised, (b) whether he received fair and consistent discipline, (c) whether he had a positive relationship with a caretaking adult, and (d) the extent to which he was associating with deviant peers. We measured each of these factors from multiple perspectives (e.g., boy, caretaking adult, parole officer, and interviewer ratings) using multiple modes of measurement (e.g., telephone and in-person interviews, questionnaires, and diary). In chapter 6, I discuss the relationship between each of these factors and criminal behavior in follow-up. Here in this chapter, I review outcomes including youth participation, incarceration rates, reunification with family, and criminal and delinquent activity.

Youth Participation

A primary question faced by communities that are considering using the MTFC model is, "Is it feasible and safe to place chronic and serious juvenile offenders in community families?" To address this question, we compared runaway and program completion rates for boys in MTFC with those

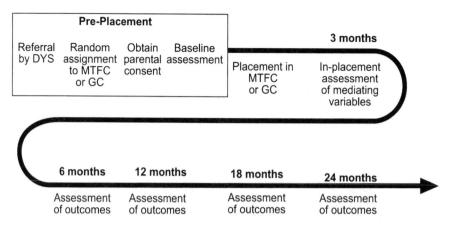

Figure 4.2. Study design and timeline for placement in either Multidimensional Treatment Foster Care Model (MTFC) or group care (GC). DYS = delinquent youth services.

in GC. Data on the number of days that boys spent in various settings after referral to the study were collected by coding each boy's individual records and by then verifying those data with parole or probation officer reports, which were obtained every 2 months. These data are shown in Figure 4.3.

Fewer boys ran away from MTFC than from GC (30.5% vs. 57.8%, respectively; $p = 02$). More boys completed the MTFC program than completed GC (73% vs. 36%, respectively; $p = .001$). During the year following referral to the study, boys in MTFC spent fewer days in lockup than did boys in GC ($p = .02$), which included fewer days in local detention (MTFC $M = 32$, GC $M = 70$) and fewer days in the state training schools (MTFC $M = 21$, GC $M = 59$). Overall, boys in MTFC spent 60% fewer days in detention than did GC boys during the year after referral.

The goal of both MTFC and GC programs was to have boys return to live with family members after their out-of-home placements. During the 1-year period after enrollment in the study, MTFC boys spent nearly twice as much time living with parents or relatives compared with GC boys.

Criminal and Delinquent Activity

The data on the rates of criminal activity for study boys were analyzed using two methods. First, two-by-two mixed analyses of variance (ANOVAs; group by time) were conducted to examine potential differences in rates of official criminal offenses and in rates of self-reported criminal activities. Second, because the sample consisted of boys who varied substantially on key variables that are known to have strong effects on rates of delinquency and suspected to affect amenability to interventions (e.g., current age, age at first criminal referral, and prereferral rates of delinquency), a series of multiple regression analyses were conducted. We used the multiple regression analy-

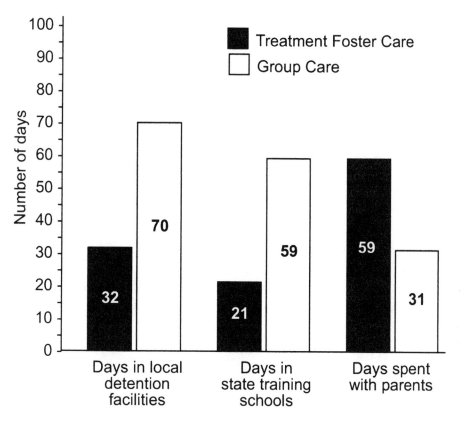

Figure 4.3. Foster care resulted in less time in jail and more time with parents.

ses both to control for these factors and to examine their influence, if any, on the response to the interventions. The regression analyses allowed for the examination of developmental and offense history issues that the ANOVAs alone did not address. For example, 84% of the sample had their first criminal referral before age 14 (M = 12.6 years; range, 5.9–16.3 years) and could be classified as "early-onset" delinquents who are at extremely high risk for continued patterns of chronic offending. Most of the youngsters, however, had their first criminal referral at a far earlier age. A consistent body of research findings indicate that early starters not only commit the most, and most serious, offenses, they may also have significant cognitive impairments that would reduce their response to intervention (e.g., Moffitt, 1993). Therefore, we examined whether or not age at onset would relate to criminal referral rates after program placement.

Second, the sample varied quite a bit on the age at referral to the program (M = 15.0 years; range 12.1–17.9 years). Because of the general consensus that early treatment is more effective than later treatment (e.g., Kazdin, 1993), we examined the relation of age at referral to continued criminal activity thereafter. Third, although all boys had more than one criminal referral before baseline (M = 13.6 prior criminal offenses), the range of the number of referrals was

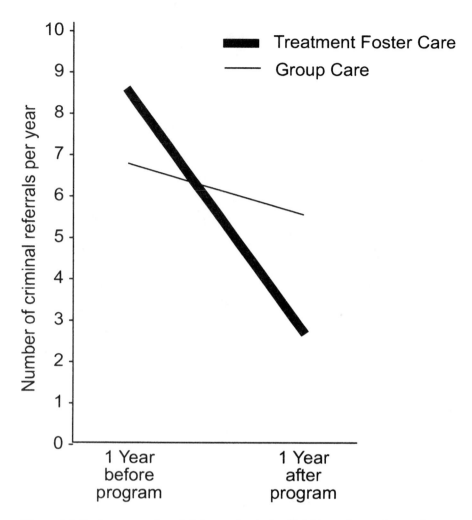

Figure 4.4. Foster care reduced delinquent acts in official juvenile court records.

considerable (5–55 prior criminal offenses). Therefore, we also examined the number of prior criminal offenses and how they related to the effectiveness that the programs had on subsequent police referrals.

Criminal Referral Data

We conducted a two-by-two mixed ANOVA (group by time) to examine potential differences between MTFC and GC criminal referral rates from baseline to placement plus 12 months posttermination from GC or MTFC. The group-by-time interaction was significant: p = .003, with MTFC boys showing larger drops in official criminal referral rates. The mean rates for criminal offenses are shown in Figure 4.4. The rate of criminal offenses

TABLE 4.5
Multiple Regressions for Official Criminal Referrals

Variable entered	Beta	R	R²	F	p
Step 1: Age at first criminal referral	.044	.044	.002	.155	.70
Step 2: Age at baseline	.202	.185	.034	1.34	.27
Step 3: Annual rate of criminal referrals prior to referral	238	.282	.079	2.16	.10
Step 4: Group assignment	−2.129	.438	.192	−3.22	.01
Zero-order corrections with postcriminal referrals					
Age at first referral	$r = .04$				
Age at baseline	$r = .18$				
Annual criminal referral rate	$r = .04$				
Group (MTFC or GC)	$r = .34$				

Note. MTFC = Multidimensional Treatment Foster Care Model; GC = group care.

postplacement was not correlated with the amount of time that boys spent in treatment for participants in either condition.

We conducted a series of multiple regression analyses to examine several factors, in addition to type of intervention that would likely affect the continued rate of criminal offenses after enrollment in the program. To account for the contribution of these three variables (i.e., age at first criminal referral, age at baseline, and number of prior offenses), we used a hierarchical multiple regression analysis in which the variables were entered first, before the dichotomized intervention variable (i.e., MTFC or GC), to predict the total number of criminal offenses during the period from placement to 1-year posttreatment. The results of those analyses are shown in Table 4.5. The only significant univariate predictors of postplacement, officially recorded, criminal activity were age at first referral and group assignment ($p = .002$), with the MTFC youngsters showing significantly fewer criminal offenses.

After accounting for these individual differences, MTFC was significantly more effective than GC programs in reducing officially recorded delinquent activity. Although, in a statistical sense, this study showed that the effect for MTFC was greater on criminal offenses, many researchers have pointed out that such a finding may have little "real-world" meaning (e.g., Jacobson & Truax, 1991; Kendall & Grove, 1988).

To examine the clinical significance of the difference in changes in criminal offenses for the two groups, we compared these changes with a "normative" population of boys in the same geographic area. We used the population-based sample of high-risk boys who have participated in the Oregon Youth Study (OYS; Patterson, Reid, & Dishion, 1992).

The OYS has followed the lives of 206 boys since they were attending fourth grade in 1983–1984. The sample was chosen solely on the basis of an elevated risk of delinquency in neighborhoods (i.e., greater than the urban area average) in which the boys' schools were located. Thus, while the OYS is not truly "normative" in the sense that participating boys were drawn only from the highest-risk schools in the community, the existence of the OYS does provide the opportunity to compare MTFC and GC boys against the norms of an at-risk population from the same area.

Computing clinical significance traditionally involves comparison of the mean and standard deviation of a normative group on a variable of interest with the mean and standard deviation of a treatment group following discharge. In the case of criminal offenses, however, the use of these simple summary statistics is not justified due to the extreme distribution of referrals. Even in the at-risk OYS sample, the "distribution" of referrals at any given age generally consisted of outlier and extreme values, with the vast majority of boys having no referrals. Across ages 12 to 18 years, on average, 81.5% (range 72.3–89.8%) of the OYS boys had no referrals in a given year. Thus, here we make only simple comparisons between the proportions of MTFC or GC boys with no referrals and the proportion of boys with no referrals in our "normative" group.

Prior to placement, boys in MTFC or GC had an average of 7.6 referrals in the prior year (SD = 5.5, mode = 5, median = 5, 0% had no referrals) compared to OYS boys, who averaged .32 referrals in any given year (SD = .98, mode = 0, median = 0, 81.5% had no referrals). Clearly, at baseline the MTFC and GC groups were deviant in terms of the number of referrals. From placement through the year after discharge from treatment, 41% (n = 15) of MTFC boys had no referrals. In contrast, only 7% (n = 3) of GC boys had no referrals. Although these values are obviously quite discrepant from the average of 81.5% of boys in OYS who had no referrals in any given year, the MTFC group had moved halfway to the normative OYS value, whereas the GC group had moved little.

Self-Reports of Criminal Behavior

Another question addressed by this study was whether or not MTFC would be effective, compared to GC, in reducing boys' self-reported involvement in criminal behavior. Self-reports are considered an important indicator of delinquency because, despite their importance as an indicator of general criminality, official reports of criminal activities provide a biased underestimate of the volume or seriousness of delinquent activity.

There are several possible reasons for this. The police detect only a small fraction of delinquent acts. Of those detected, only a fraction of the acts result in official reports, and different precincts and communities vary widely as to which offenses are actually written up (Elliott & Voss, 1974). Particularly for chronic offenders, police may record serious offenses only as technical or parole violations to avoid paperwork and court procedures, with the parole officer handling the offense informally (DiJulio, 1995). In fact,

TABLE 4.6
Average Numbers of Items Endorsed on the Elliott Self-Report Scales

Subscale/Group	M	SD	F	p
General delinquency				
Group home	28.9	32.4		
MTFC	12.8	20.5	6.5	.01
Index offenses				
Group home	8.6	11.9	5.3	.03
MTFC	3.2	7.2		
Felony assaults				
Group home	2.7	3.8	4.1	.05
MTFC	1.2	2.7		

Note. $N = 79$; group home, $n = 42$; Multidimensional Treatment Foster Care Model (MTFC), $n = 37$.

official records underestimate serious criminal activity by the most chronic offenders (DiJulio, 1995). Several investigators agree in concluding that, compared with arrest records, self-reports better capture the actual nature, incidence, and frequency of juvenile offending (Blumstein & Cohen, 1979; Capaldi & Patterson, 1996; Elliott & Voss, 1974; Erickson & Empey, 1963; Gold, 1963).

Therefore, all study boys completed the Elliott Behavior Checklist (EBC; Elliott, Ageton, Huizinga, Knowles, & Canter, 1983), a confidential self-report of delinquency. The respondent is asked how many times he has engaged in any criminal behaviors during a specific time frame. We examined three subscales: General Delinquency, Index Offenses, and Felony Assaults. We chose the General Delinquency subscale as an additional measure of overall criminal activity and the other two scales to measure the rates of more serious and person crimes. The checklist has demonstrated good content and construct validity (Elliott, Huizinga, & Ageton, 1985).

Three subscales of the EBC (Elliott et al., 1985) were examined: General Delinquency, Index Offenses, and Felony Assaults. On all three subscales, EBC scores for 1 year postbaseline showed significant differences between the groups, with boys in MTFC reporting significantly fewer criminal activities. The means, standard deviations, and significance levels for the EBC subscales are shown in Table 4.6.

In a hierarchical regression analysis we entered the boy's age at first criminal referral, then age at baseline, then number of delinquent acts self-reported before referral, and finally intervention condition (MTFC or GC) to predict the number of acts self-reported during the year after baseline. First, we examined the General Delinquency subscale, which included 22 items with a range of property and person crimes. The results of this analysis replicated those found in the analysis of total criminal offenses referrals in that the intervention condition accounted for significant variance over and above the contributions made by age at first criminal referral, age at baseline, and previous rates of general delinquency (see Table 4.7).

TABLE 4.7
Multiple Regressions for Self-Reports of Criminal Behavior

Subscale/Variables	Beta	R	R²	F	p
General delinquency					
Age at first criminal referral	.096	.096	.009	.66	.42
Age at baseline	.121	.142	.020	.73	.49
Prereferral rate of general delinquency	.418	.436	.190	5.41	.002
Group assignment (MTFC or GC)	−.234	.491	.241	−2.14	.036
Index crimes					
Age at first criminal referral	.028	.028	.008	.056	.813
Age at baseline	.121	.109	.012	.425	.655
Prereferral rate of index crimes	.303	.318	.101	2.60	.059
Group assignment (MTFC or GC)	−.238	.392	.154	−2.05	.044
Felony assaults					
Age at first criminal referral	.032	.032	.001	.073	.788
Age at baseline	.025	.038	.002	.053	.949
Prereferral rate of felony assault	.361	.363	.135	3.48	.020
Group assignment (MTFC or GC)	−.265	.442	.196	−2.33	.022

Note. MTFC = Multidimensional Treatment Foster Care Model; GC = group care.

Next, as shown in Table 4.6, we examined self-reported rates of index offenses, including nine items describing serious property offenses (e.g., stole motor vehicle) and person offenses (e.g., aggravated assault). Again, group assignment (i.e., MTFC or GC) contributed significantly to the prediction of the rate of postreferral index crimes over and above age at first criminal referral, age at baseline, and previous rates of index offenses (see Table 4.5).

Finally, to assess the effect of the intervention on person crimes we examined pre- and postintervention rates of the Felony Assaults subscale, which includes aggravated assault, sexual assault, and gang fights. The group assignment variable was a significant predictor of postreferral reports of felony assault rates, even in the context of age at first official offense, age at baseline, and previous rates of felony assault.

For all three self-report subscales, boys' reports of previous rates of criminal activities (i.e., general delinquency, index crimes, and felony assaults) also significantly predicted postreferral rates on those same subscales (see Table 4.6).

DIFFERENCES BETWEEN MULTIDIMENSIONAL TREATMENT FOSTER CARE AND GROUP CARE MODELS

Results from this study showed that participation in MTFC produced more favorable outcomes than participation in GC. Boys ran away less frequently from MTFC than from GC, completed their programs more often, and were locked up in detention or training schools less frequently. MTFC boys had fewer criminal offenses than did boys in GC from the time they were placed through the year following discharge from the programs, and they reported that they committed fewer delinquent acts and fewer violent or serious crimes. Given the high proportion of GC boys who failed to complete their programs (64%) in this sample, traditional group care appears not to provide the community with good protection from the criminal behavior of program participants.

What are the implications of this study for the treatment of chronic offenders in community programs? The two models of treatment compared were different on several dimensions. In the group care condition, boys went to one of 11 community-based group care programs located throughout the state. Group care programs had from 6 to 15 youths in residence, and all GC programs used shift staff. Although programs differed somewhat in terms of their theoretical orientations, variations of the Positive Peer Culture (PPC) approach (Vorrath & Brendtro, 1985) were most often used (i.e., in 66% of GC placements). The PPC approach assumes that the peer group can best influence and motivate youngsters to change their problem behaviors and attitudes. This takes place through therapeutic group work during which youngsters are expected to establish prosocial norms, confront each other on negative behavior, and participate in the discipline and decision making (Craft, Stevenson, & Granger, 1964; Vorrath & Brendtro, 1985). Other theoretical orientations identified by GC programs were social–cognitive (5% of placements), eclectic–behavior management (5% of placements), and reality therapy (24% of placements). Sixty-seven percent of GC youths participated in individual therapy; 14% participated monthly or less than monthly, 64% participated weekly, and 21% participated in 2 to 4 sessions per week. Seventy-seven percent of GC youths participated in group therapy; 13% monthly, 25% weekly, 6% in 2 to 4 sessions per week, and 56% in 1 or more group therapy sessions each day. They most often attended in-house schools (i.e., 83% of cases). Family contact was encouraged, and when families could commute to program sites (i.e., 55% of cases), family therapy was typically provided. For those families who received family therapy, sessions occurred monthly or less than monthly in 83% of the cases. For the other 17% of the cases, family therapy sessions occurred weekly.

Prior to placing boys into program settings, we interviewed senior line staff (in GC) or foster parents (in MTFC) to examine assumptions about change mechanisms and to assess daily program practices, including discipline strategies, supervision rules and restrictions, and the roles of peers and adults in the treatment process. On the basis of the theoretical and intervention models, we expected to find differences in daily treatment methods with the MTFC foster parents relying primarily on direct adult interventions in dealing with the youngsters and GC staff using peer-mediated interventions. To examine treatment fidelity for the two approaches, we conducted an interview examining program practices at each placement site after boys had been there for 3 months. We found significant differences between programs in the two treatment conditions in several areas (Chamberlain, Ray, & Moore, 1996). For example, group therapy was conducted at least weekly in 77% of the GC placements, and it was not offered at all in MTFC. Adults in GC and MTFC differed in terms of who they thought had the most influence on boys' success (i.e., significantly more adult vs. peer influence in MTFC than in GC). In GC, adults spent less one-on-one time with boys than they did in MTFC. In GC, peers had more influence on deciding house rules and discipline than in MTFC. Finally, GC boys spent more time with peers than did their counterparts in MTFC.

In MTFC, several steps were taken to ensure treatment integrity. MTFC parents were telephoned every weekday and asked to report on the number of points the boy earned and lost within the past 24 hours. In addition, during weekly supervision meetings MTFC parents handed in boys' weekly school and point cards to program supervisors. MTFC parents participated in weekly 2-hour supervision and support meetings with program supervisors. Program supervisors and individual and family therapists were supervised in weekly 2-hour meetings with the project director (Chamberlain) and clinical consultant (Reid). We videotaped and reviewed individual and family therapy sessions in these meetings. A book describing the MTFC approach (Chamberlain, 1994) was used as a guide to train new clinical personnel along with other materials developed on parent management training interventions conducted at our center and elsewhere (e.g., Patterson, Chamberlain, & Reid, 1982; Wahler & Fox, 1980). What factors accounted for these differences in the two models? I address that topic in chapter 6.

CONCLUSION

In this chapter, findings from the four outcome studies that have been conducted so far support the notion that MTFC is a viable and relatively effective alternative to placement in traditional forms of care, such as group homes or residential centers. Clearly, these studies are only a start in providing information on the potential and limits of the MTFC model. Currently, three additional randomized trials are under way that will add to the body of research on this model. Preliminary findings from a study that began in 1996 are presented in chapter 7. That effort focuses on girls who have problems with chronic delinquency and are referred by the juvenile justice system. In 2002, the National Institute on Drug Abuse funded an extension of that work to examine the effects of the MTFC approach on girls' participation in health-risking behaviors such as drug and alcohol use and risky sexual behavior. The second ongoing study focuses on the application of MTFC to preschoolers in the foster care system and is called Early Intervention Foster Care. Phillip Fisher from OSLC conducted this adaptation, and he and I describe it in chapter 8. The third ongoing study examines the effects of applying a less intense version of MTFC to children in regular foster care. This is the largest scale test of the model so far and extends the intervention to both kinship and foster families in an ethnically diverse population in an urban setting. Over a 5-year period, 700 foster families in San Diego County will participate. Half of the participants will participate in selected components of MTFC with the aim of improving rates of placement stability for children in the San Diego County foster care system. In addition, we are examining rates of foster parent retention and system outcomes, including use of mental health services. This study is a collaboration between researchers at the Center for Child and Adolescent Services Research (Joe Price and John Landsverk), the San Diego County Department of Health and Human Services (Yvonne Campbell), and OSLC (myself and John Reid).

In the next two chapters I outline the nuts and bolts for running an MTFC program. In chapter 5, I review core program components, staffing patterns, and principles of practice. In chapter 6, research that examines how specific program components contribute to youth outcomes is presented, along with implications for training foster parents and program staff.

5

MULTIDIMENSIONAL TREATMENT FOSTER CARE PROGRAM COMPONENTS AND PRINCIPLES OF PRACTICE

As described in chapter 4, we began to develop the Multidimensional Treatment Foster Care (MTFC) model by examining previous research and theory, pilot testing program components, collecting data on program effects, and then revising and adapting program components in an attempt to increase efficacy or to fit certain populations of youngsters and families. At this point, we have a very specific set of program components and principles of practice for working with youths referred from juvenile justice. This is not to imply that there is no room for improvement or change. As can be seen in chapter 7, where I discuss treatment of girls referred from juvenile justice, the model is still evolving. Nonetheless, we have thoroughly tested core components of MTFC in several clinical trials with a large number of youths and families. In this chapter, I discuss these components along with three core principles of practice: (a) providing a supportive environment for MTFC parents, (b) creating and maintaining a reinforcing environment for youths, and (c) having clearly defined staff roles that promote client engagement and support. I include a case example at the end of this chapter that illustrates how staff roles can be used to further clinical goals in the face of client resistance.

RECRUITING MULTIDIMENSIONAL TREATMENT FOSTER CARE FAMILIES

The importance of recruiting capable and willing foster parents cannot be overstated. We have found that recruitment takes hard work and persistence but that it can be done successfully in 2 to 3 months, especially in communities where the concept of Treatment Foster Care is new. We recruit MTFC parents through a variety of methods. Word-of-mouth and newspaper advertising have been our most successful methods. We pay existing MTFC parents a "finder's fee" of $100 for recommending interested families that we later train and with whom we place youngsters. Newspaper ads are most successful if they are eye-catching, include the age and gender of the child to be placed, and state the amount of the monthly stipend MTFC parents will receive. Figure 5.1 shows some sample ads developed by Kathy Reid, our foster parent recruiter.

Potential foster parents who call as a result of an ad are screened over the telephone for basic eligibility (e.g., adequate space in their home, no previous criminal history) and then sent an application. After the application is returned, the recruiter conducts a home visit. During the home visit, the recruiter explains program goals, how program staff and foster parents work together, and training and certification requirements. The purpose of the home visit is to meet the prospective family, see if their home atmosphere is conducive to caring for a disturbed or delinquent youngster, and give them more information about the program. Many families who are suitable for "regular" foster care are not good MTFC parents. In MTFC, the parents must be willing to take an active treatment approach and work as team members with program staff in implementing a daily structured program for the youngster.

Since the program's inception in 1983, we have had MTFC families from all walks of life. Single parents and married couples, with and without children of their own, have been successful MTFC parents. In two studies, we attempted to systematically identify a set of selection factors, such as individual and family characteristics, that predict who will be successful as a foster parent working in the MTFC model. This research effort has yielded no better results than using clinical judgment to select prospective foster parents. Qualities that seem related to success in working with challenging children and adolescents include an ability to take another person's perspective, a good knowledge of child and adolescent development (often acquired through raising one's own children), and a healthy sense of humor. The recruiter makes an informal assessment of these characteristics during the home

Figure 5.1. Foster parent want ads.

visit. We refer families that appear to be unsuitable to the local child welfare office to participate in providing "regular" foster care, or we simply discourage the family from continuing in the process.

PRESERVICE TRAINING OF MULTIDIMENSIONAL TREATMENT FOSTER CARE PARENTS

MTFC parents participate in a 20-hour preservice training. During the preservice training, we provide an overview of the model, review policies and procedures, and emphasize specific training on dealing with challenging youth behavior. MTFC parents are taught a four-step approach to analyzing behavior and the basic procedures for implementing an individualized daily behavior management program for youths. The training methods are both didactic and experiential and include a lot of role-plays. During training we place a great deal of emphasis on methods and techniques for reinforcing and encouraging youths. Prospective MTFC parents resistant to the idea of giving youngsters extra support and attention for doing what they are supposed to do are encouraged not to continue. Many well-intentioned people feel that providing daily incentives for achievement undermines the individual's basic motivation. Because daily encouragement is such an important component of our MTFC programs, we insist that families share, or at least do not oppose, this philosophy.

Following preservice training, the program matches prospective MTFC parents with referred youths. MTFC parents are given all of the information the program has on the youth, including all files and anecdotal information, so they are fully informed about the youth's history. After a youth and family are matched, the program supervisor meets with the MTFC family to work out details of the youth's initial daily behavior management program. The daily program specifies the schedule of activities and behavioral expectations and assigns the number of points the youth can earn for satisfactorily performing each activity. Points are a concrete way for MTFC parents to provide youths with positive feedback about their progress. The goal of the point program is to give MTFC parents a vehicle for providing youngsters with frequent positive reinforcement for normative and prosocial behavior and to give youngsters a clear message about how they are doing.

The daily behavior management program implemented in the MTFC home provides youths with structured daily feedback by means of a three-level point system. Youths earn points throughout the day for expected activities, including going to class on school days. Points are lost for rule infractions, including small "violations" such as not minding or having a surly attitude. The economy of the point system is set up to emphasize positive achievements, including participating in developmental tasks appropriate for youngsters in the relevant age group. MTFC foster parents are trained to take points in a matter-of-fact or even slightly sympathetic way. They are specifically taught to refrain from lecturing or arguing and are taught methods for disengaging if the youngster initiates an argument.

OVERVIEW OF THE DAILY BEHAVIOR MANAGEMENT SYSTEM

Youths begin the program on Level 1, where they earn points for routine daily activities such as getting out of bed on time in the morning, getting ready for school, doing a short chore, doing homework, having a mature attitude, attending classes and having a cooperative attitude in school, and other behaviors designated by the MTFC parents and program staff. Youths trade points earned one day for privileges on the following day. On Level 1, daily point totals are also tracked to determine when the youth is eligible for advancing to Level 2. Typically, youths are on Level 1 for about 3 weeks or until they earn a total of 2,100 points.

On Level 2, youths accumulate points over a week and apply them to an expanded list of privileges that can be earned during the following week. On Level 3, privileges are expanded further and include opportunities for youngsters to be involved in community activities without direct adult supervision.

Prior to entering the program or placement in the MTFC home, we review a prototype of the daily point and level system with the youth, typically while the youth is in detention. The program supervisor also holds a preplacement meeting with the youth's parents to explain how the program works and to get their approval and consent to participate.

On the day of placement, the program supervisor arranges for the youth to be discharged from detention and drives him or her to a meeting with the MTFC parents at the program office. This is typically the first contact between the youth and the MTFC parents. At this initial meeting, attended by the MTFC parents and the youth, we review the Level 1 point program. The youth then goes home with the MTFC parents and the program begins.

ONGOING CONSULTATION AND SUPERVISION OF THE MULTIDIMENSIONAL TREATMENT FOSTER CARE PARENTS

Consultation with the MTFC parents is a cornerstone of the model. Without ongoing consultation, our experience has been that difficult-to-manage adolescent problem behaviors (particularly extreme negative behaviors) quickly shape adults to behave in reactive and potentially nontherapeutic ways. For example, given adolescent sulking or noncompliance, the "natural" adult reaction includes anger and irritability. Research on family interactional processes with antisocial youths has demonstrated that such angry adult reactions can function to set off a chain of events and processes in which the probability of continued misbehavior on the part of the adolescent actually increases over time. This is because it is the relative rate, rather than the overall rate of reinforcement for behavior, that appears to have the most influence on shaping behaviors over time (the matching law; McDowell, 1988).

Adults who respond in-kind to adolescent negativity may lose the chance to teach or have other positive socializing interactions with the teenager. Ultimately, these types of sequences put the relationship and ultimately the placement in jeopardy. Preservice training alone cannot maintain MTFC parents' motivation or competence to perform the skills taught, nor is it sufficient to address the range of intervention strategies necessary to effectively treat the complex behavioral problems of these youngsters. A central feature of the Oregon Social Learning Center (OSLC) MTFC model is frequent contact with, and support and supervision of, the foster parents.

The program supervisor is the primary consultant to the MTFC parents, providing consultation each week in a group meeting and during daily telephone contact. Group meetings focus on development and review of the youths' daily programs, feedback to MTFC parents on their strengths and on areas needing improvement, feedback from MTFC parents on how the program can increase the effectiveness of the support it provides, and coordination of special services such as tutoring or psychiatric consultation. Goals of the group meetings are to support and motivate MTFC parents and to develop a professional team approach to youths' care. The program supervisor provides consultation and on-call crisis intervention to MTFC parents on a 24-hour basis.

We structure daily telephone contact with the foster parents through the use of the Parent Daily Report Checklist (PDR), a brief (5-minute) interview designed to measure the occurrence of problems during the past 24 hours shown in Exhibit 5.1. In addition to obtaining data on the occurrence of problems, PDR is used to track the number of points the youth has gained and lost during the past 24 hours and to get information about school problems or incidents that might affect the youth's treatment (e.g., a negative telephone contact with biological parents). PDR data is always collected for the past 24 hours so that MTFC parents are not asked to recall over long periods of time. Studies have shown that this short-term recall is related to the accuracy of the information being obtained. We use PDR data from the previous week during weekly group meetings as a starting point to talk about case problems and progress and to help the program supervisor systematically track case progress over time.

INDIVIDUAL TREATMENT FOR THE YOUTH

The program assigns an individual therapist or skills trainer to each youth, depending on whether the youth has mental health needs or social skills deficits. Extremely challenging cases call for both a therapist and a skills trainer. A more detailed description of the skills trainer and therapist roles appears in the next section on stratification of staff roles. Unlike many treatment models in which individual therapy is the central focus of treatment, in MTFC the therapist or skills trainer's role (from here on called worker) is to support the youngster's adjustment in the MTFC home where the main treatment effect is expected to occur. The worker's job is to support the youth and help him or her acquire and practice the skills needed to relate successfully to adults and peers.

The youth and worker have at least weekly face-to-face meetings, along with more frequent telephone contacts. During the first three or four meet-

EXHIBIT 5.1
Parent Daily Report Checklist

Parent Daily Report Checklist

Monitor Program   Week of: _____(F-Th)
YOUTH _____PDR CALLER _____
FOSTER PARENT _____PHONE _____

BEHAVIORS	SU	M	TU	W	TH	
Arguing						SUN/Rec time:
Back-talking						Unsupervised time:
Bedwetting						
Competitiveness						
Complaining						
Defiance						
Destructive, vandalism						MON/Rec time:
Encopresis						Unsupervised time:
Fighting						
Irritability						
Lying						
Negativism						
Boisterous/rowdy						TUE/Rec time:
Not minding						Unsupervised time:
Staying out late						
Skipping meals						
Running away						
Swearing/obscene lang.						
Tease/provoke						WED/Rec time:
Depression/sadness						Unsupervised time:
Sluggish						
Jealous						
Truant						
Stealing						
Nervous/jittery						THU/Rec time:
Short attention span						Unsupervised time:
Daydreaming						
Irresponsibility						
Marijuana/drugs						
Alcohol						
School problem						

TOTAL POINTS: _____ _____ _____ _____ _____ (Behaviors are on day
TOTAL POINTS LOST: _____ _____ _____ _____ _____ they occur.)

Friday: Total Points _____ Points Lost _____ Recreation Time _____
Saturday: Total Points _____ Points Lost _____ Recreation Time _____

ings, the goal is to form a relationship and identify the youth's interests. Some youths resist participating in therapy-oriented sessions, having had bad experiences in the past or anxiety about being pressured to talk about problems. The tone of the initial sessions is kept light, and if the youth seems closed or anxious, we encourage the worker to engage in activities with the youth rather than continue sitting in the office talking.

The worker explains his or her role as being that of an ally and "someone to help you navigate your way through the program." The worker tells the youth that if he or she wants to change something about the point program, or earn a particular privilege, the worker will help negotiate that with the program supervisor. It is important to convey to the youth that the worker can help him or her work within the system but also that the basic rules of the program are firm (e.g., requirements for supervision will not be relaxed until the youth proves himself or herself by advancing to Level 3).

During weekly clinical meetings, the program supervisor and the individual and family therapists identify areas to work on with the youths. For example, if a youngster is engaging in a lot of arguing in the MTFC home, the worker might be given the task of talking to him or her about that ("I noticed that you lost a lot of points last week for arguing. What is that all about?"). Often the youth will claim not to know the reason that a problem is occurring or say that the MTFC parents are being unfair ("They are just picking on me"). The worker then frames the problem in a neutral way and offers to help the youth ("Let's you and I work to figure out a way that you can avoid losing points"). In doing so the worker is on the youth's side and opens the door for the youngster to develop and practice more adaptive skills. Possibly, on further examination, the arguing will be framed as the youth having a hard time dealing with hearing "no" or being disappointed. In that case, in their sessions the worker will role-play saying and hearing "no" with the youth. This is done with humor and a light touch. The purpose is to pre-teach the youngster so that he or she can practice reacting differently in the coming week. The worker might also offer a reward for improvement in a problem behavior during the coming week.

In the first month of the program, the youth's relationship with the individual worker is sometimes used in a strategic way to stabilize the youth. For example, if the youth is at high risk to run away, the worker might have frequent telephone contact with the youth and ask him to call her if he feels stressed or upset.

Running away is a behavior many youths who have been placed repeatedly in out-of-home care engage in when they are frustrated or upset. Leaving a place where they feel helped and cared about is an impulsive response to stress and uncertainty. The worker can help counteract the youth's urge to run by providing small rewards early on and by planning and engaging him in fun activities. An external reason not to run (however small) appears to provide the necessary motivation to stay put. Most often, if youths can experience accomplishment and success in the program initially, they will not run from future challenges.

The individual worker's role is that of an ally and a coach. They are a sympathetic ear but are careful not to reinforce the youth's problem behavior (e.g., making excuses or complaining) during sessions. They keep the program supervisor informed about what transpired during the sessions and are careful not to make promises to the youngster that have not been cleared with the program supervisor. Before offering a reward for decreasing a problem behavior, workers first clear the idea with the program supervisor who, in turn, clears it with the MTFC parents. This communication between team members is necessary to avoid making the MTFC parents feel as though the program is bypassing them and possibly undermining their family schedule (e.g., when the worker treats the youth to a snack before dinner).

FAMILY TREATMENT

The goal of family treatment is to help parents prepare for their youth's return home and specifically to become more effective at supervising, encouraging, supporting, and following through with consequences with their youngster. One way to accomplish this is to teach parents the point and level system that is part of the youth's daily program in the MTFC home. As in sessions with the youth, the first family therapy sessions are devoted to the family therapist forming a relationship with the parents (or relatives or other aftercare adults) with an emphasis on recognizing strengths in the family. The family therapist's task is to try to identify and understand, from the parents' point of view, the barriers that have interfered with the parent–child relationship in the past. The therapist asks the parents about the evolution of the problem and supports them in their view.

By the time their son or daughter enters MTFC, most parents feel highly discouraged and defeated. Further, they may feel blamed for their child's problems and act in a highly defensive and guarded way. During the initial sessions, it is important for the family therapist to engage the parents, to be supportive of the parents, and to be sympathetic to their situation.

During the youth's stay in the program, both the therapist and the program supervisor encourage the parents to have frequent contact with staff to get updates on their child's progress. As the adults who know the child the best, parents are asked for continual input into treatment. The program supervisor gives parents her 24-hour telephone number as well as a number for the family therapist.

Home visits are an integral part of the reunification process designed to transfer treatment gains to the home setting. Home visits provide an opportunity for parents to practice new skills at supervising, setting limits, and providing encouragement to their youngster with full backup from MTFC staff. Visits begin as soon as the youth reaches Level 2 (usually 3 weeks after placement) and are scheduled on the average of twice monthly throughout the placement. The first visit is typically short (2–4 hours), followed by a day-long visit, and eventually weekend-long visits. In the rare instances in which parents are unable or unwilling to closely supervise their youth, visits take place in the program offices or another supervised setting. The program supervisor is responsible for approving and scheduling all home visits. Prior to their first visit, the family therapist reviews with the parents the program supervision expectations shown in Exhibit 5.2.

A major aim of the visits is to give parents an opportunity to demonstrate to their child that they are part of the treatment team and that when he or she returns home, there will be changes. To illustrate this clearly to the youth and to help parents develop or refine specific parenting skills that will be crucial for their youngster's continued success, the family therapist teaches

EXHIBIT 5.2
Supervision Expectations for Home Visits

During home visits, youths need to be supervised at all times by a parent or other adult living in the home. It is most helpful if you, as a parent, can stick to the schedule that your son or daughter is following in the treatment foster home. Your program supervisor is available to brief you on the details of that schedule.

Telephone Use

Home visits are not a time for youngsters to contact friends. Therefore, the youth's use of the telephone to talk to friends is not allowed unless approved by the program supervisor. Approved telephone contact with friends is to be supervised during home visits.

Going Places

Families are encouraged to do things together during home visits. You are free to take your youngster anywhere that you are going. The key is that she or he be supervised at all times. Wandering around stores presents a risk for some youths. If your child has had problems with stealing, be sure to carefully supervise him or her in settings where stealing might occur.

Having Friends Over

This is done with the prior permission of the program supervisor only. If the program supervisor has approved contact with friends, your child and his or her friends need to be supervised by an adult during home visits.

Bringing Things Back to the Foster Care Home After the Home Visit

Your child may want to bring some of his or her possessions back to the foster care home. This can be done only with prior approval of the program supervisor.

What to Do If Things Aren't Going Well

Many youngsters will try to test the limits and rules during home visits. Parents are key players in their child's treatment. It is important for your child to see you as cooperating with the program rules. If your child acts up during a home visit, call the program supervisor to talk about the situation. It is much better if you can call early in the process, when your child is just starting to misbehave, rather than waiting until there is a full-blown conflict. The most important thing to remember is to call if there is a conflict or any type of rule breaking on your child's part. It is not a failure or a bad reflection on you as a parent if you call. By calling you are playing an active and positive role in your child's treatment.

Will This Level of Supervision Last Forever?

No. As your child becomes better at making responsible choices and decisions, she or he will get increased privileges. Your program supervisor will talk to you about when and how this will happen. By the time your child comes home to live with you, he or she will not need the constant level of supervision that you are being asked to provide now.

---

parents to use a simplified version of the point and level system that parallels the one used in the MTFC home. The family therapist works with the parents to develop the modified version of this system to implement during visits. Initial home point programs typically include one or two behaviors for which the youth can earn points. Parents are encouraged to take away points for noncompliance, arguing, or other problem behaviors. Initially, parents only give and take points; the consequences occur in the MTFC home. Eventually, the home point program becomes more articulated and includes the parents giving and taking away privileges. Ideally, when the youth returns home, the daily point system used in the MTFC home and in the family home should be identical. Using the same or a highly similar point program in the MTFC and family home helps the youth to generalize treatment gains across settings. Program staff are on-call to parents during home visits and parents are encouraged to call if their son or daughter breaks basic supervision rules or refuses to comply. In those instances, the visit is ended.

Other components of family therapy typically include a focus on problem-solving and communication skills, methods for deescalating family conflict, and instruction on how to advocate for school services for the youngster. The family therapist and the parents work together to anticipate and address potential areas of family conflict or other threats to the youngster's stability on returning home. The family therapist participates in weekly clinical meetings and receives supervision from the program supervisor.

LIAISON WITH SCHOOLS

Youths in MTFC attend public schools. Although school has been an area of major difficulty for virtually all of the youths enrolled in MTFC, we find that with close supervision and follow-through, most youths can do surprisingly well in public school settings. Prior to enrolling the youth in school, we set up an initial meeting with the appropriate school staff (usually the counselor or vice-principal) to acquaint them with the basic features of the program and to reassure them that program staff will be on-call to help deal with any problems that occur.

To monitor in-school performance, attendance, and behavior, youths carry a school card that lists each class. For each class period, there is a place for teachers to rate the youth's behavior as acceptable or unacceptable, to note whether homework has been completed, and to sign their names (see Exhibit 5.3). MTFC parents collect school cards daily, and teacher ratings are converted into points earned or lost on the daily program. To check for possible forgeries, MTFC parents also call the school at least weekly to check on attendance. MTFC program staff are on-call to schools to remove youngsters should they become disruptive. In addition to these standard program features, we conduct school-based interventions, as needed.

Cutting class and aggression during unstructured school activities (e.g., lunch and time between classes) are the most common problems. We have designed specific interventions for these and other school-related problems. Depending on the size of the program, it is helpful to have a staff position

EXHIBIT 5.3
School Card

SCHOOL CARD

Class	Today's Assignment	Assignment	*Overdue Homework	Tardy	Behavior	Initial
		Yes/No	Yes/No	Yes/No	Good/Poor	
		Yes/No	Yes/No	Yes/No	Good/Poor	
		Yes/No	Yes/No	Yes/No	Good/Poor	
		Yes/No	Yes/No	Yes/No	Good/Poor	
		Yes/No	Yes/No	Yes/No	Good/Poor	
		Yes/No	Yes/No	Yes/No	Good/Poor	
		Yes/No	Yes/No	Yes/No	Good/Poor	

*Please identify overdue homework assignments on the back of this form.

dedicated to conducting interventions in the school and acting as a school liaison.

AFTERCARE SUPPORT

Once the youngster has returned home, parents are invited to participate in an aftercare group with other parents. The group meets weekly. Together with input from participating parents, we have developed an aftercare curriculum and manual entitled *Success Begins at Home* (Antoine & Chamberlain, 1995). The table of contents is shown in Exhibit 5.4. The manual includes two parts: a leader guide and a parent guide. A program supervisor or therapist and an MTFC parent or biological parent coleads the group. The format of the aftercare sessions includes focusing on a specific skill (e.g., setting up effective consequences), discussing current problems and progress, and describing a home practice assignment. To engage parents in the group, we have used several methods to motivate attendance and completion of the home practice assignments, such as serving a meal at the session and having a weekly drawing for movie tickets. During aftercare, program supervisors remain on-call to families, as needed. PDR calls continue with parents, beginning with daily calls and graduating to weekly calls by 6 months postplacement.

STRATIFICATION OF STAFF ROLES

Typically, youth treatment programs assign staff members to a "generalist" role; that is, staff work across multiple domains that may include youth

EXHIBIT 5.4
Table of Contents for the *Success Begins at Home* Curriculum Guide

Encouragement
    Building Encouragement
    Encouraging Good Behavior
    Overcoming Blocks
    Tracking Your Own Behavior
    Cooperation
    Effective Listening
    Encouragement Vignette

Teaching New Behaviors
    Use Encouragements
    Attainable Goals
    Setting Up For Success
    Introducing Incentive Charts
    Tracking Progress
    Rewards, Not Bribes
    Attainable Goals Vignette

Setting Limits
    Identifying Problems
    Committing to Consistency
    Time Out
    Privilege Removal
    Work Chores
    Keeping It Small
    House Rules Vignette
    Setting Limits Vignette

School Success
    School Involvement
    Discouraging Negative Emotions
    Encouraging Progress
    School Attendance and Behavior
    Teacher Contacts
    School Success Vignette

Problem Solving
    Step by Step
    Identifying Problems
    Generating Ideas
    Evaluating Progress
    Problem-Solving Vignette
    Related Materials

---

therapy, family therapy, and linking with other agencies providing services. It has been our experience that, when working with severely delinquent youngsters, this model is often insufficient. Various factors, including the complexity of the families receiving services, the high level of conflict among family members, the severity of the youth's behavioral problems, and the likelihood that they will be involved with multiple service providers, have a tendency to place generalist staff members in positions in which they must continuously balance the opposing needs of different constituencies. Within this context, it is challenging to develop and maintain a trusting relationship with any of the parties involved in treatment: conflict is common between the youth and foster parents, between the biological parents and family therapist, or between other involved parties.

A distinguishing characteristic of the OSLC MTFC model is its use of a treatment team in which roles are clearly defined to carry out the treatment plan for each youth. There is little overlap in the responsibilities of team members. Staff members advocate the needs of those individuals with whom they work (i.e., parents and youths). This ensures that the youth, biological parents, foster parents, and other service providers all have a clear role in the treatment process.

In addition to a separation of staff roles, there is also stratification; that is, there are multiple layers of staff involvement with the teenager, the family, and the foster family. For example, it is common for conflict to arise between a youth and his or her foster parents. If there is only one staff member working with the MTFC family and the youth, that individual must mediate the conflict and try to balance the needs of the youth and the foster parents. It is often difficult for staff to emerge from such a situation without angering or offending someone. With stratified staffing, in the MTFC model, when a conflict arises, the next layer of involvement might be for the youth to phone his or her individual worker. The worker's support provides critical cooling-off time and diffuses the conflict. If this strategy is not sufficient, it is then possible to involve the program supervisor (another layer of involvement). The program supervisor can support the foster parents in their efforts to resolve the conflict and can work with the youth worker to better understand the youth's point of view. If it is necessary to meet to discuss the problem, foster parents and the youth each have an advocate. By slowing down the process and providing support to all involved, conflicts rarely escalate to a point that threatens the foster placement. Moreover, conflicts appear to decrease in frequency over time. The case example provided at the conclusion of this chapter shows how a program supervisor, an individual therapist, and a skills trainer worked together to deal with a girl's unwillingness to address her long-standing issues relating to self-destructive interpersonal skills.

Stratification of staff roles also helps in responding strategically to treatment resistance. Such resistance may come from the youth, the biological parents, or the foster parents. For instance, it is typical for parents to be given homework assignments in family therapy that involve various behavior management strategies. Some parents struggle to complete these assignments. However, it can be counterproductive for the family therapist to confront parents about their noncompliance. In these situations, the program supervisor will play an authoritative role, contacting the parents and pushing for them to complete assignments. Throughout this process, the family therapist will continue to support the parents, joining with them to figure out how to comply with the demands of the program. Thus, not only does stratification reduce conflict between the youth and others, it also helps to reduce conflict between biological and foster parents and program staff. In the section that follows, we provide descriptions of staff roles.

Role of the Program Supervisor

The program supervisor organizes all aspects of the MTFC treatment. This person is the leader of the treatment team and is the primary advocate for the MTFC parents. The key role of the program supervisor is to oversee and integrate the activities of the other team members. The program supervisor works to ensure that all team members are following the same treatment protocol, that team members are informed about the activities of all others, and that the needs and concerns of all parties—youths, foster parents, and biological families—are heard. Although the treatment team may not maintain a strict hierarchy and ideally is a collaborative effort, the program supervisor is the team leader. Therefore, this individual ultimately articulates the treatment plan, resolves disputes among team members, and sets the tone for the treatment process. Within the MTFC model, this individual is typically someone who has experience in several of the other roles on the team and who can provide insight into the particular tensions involved in providing effective treatment.

Given the multidisciplinary nature of the team, effective communication is essential for treatment to proceed smoothly. This communication occurs through weekly team meetings, electronic mail (e-mail), and informal conversations among team members. The program supervisor strongly emphasizes a high level of information sharing so as to promote consistent treatment of youths by all team members. Although this approach may appear to be labor and personnel intensive, the long-term benefits of effective intervention justify using resources in this way (see chapter 4 for cost analysis of the MTFC intervention). Figure 5.2 depicts the program supervisor's role relative to the role of the other team members.

Role of the Family Therapist

A key component to the success of the MTFC program is the degree to which the youth can generalize from (i.e., transfer) the gains made during treatment to posttreatment environments. Parents (or other adult guardians) are the primary social agents who determine the quality and consistency of this generalization in aftercare. In a series of analyses described in detail in chapter 6, we found that the extent to which four factors occurred, youths had positive outcomes in follow-up. These factors were that the youth (a) was well supervised, (b) was not allowed to have unsupervised time with delinquent peers, (c) was reinforced for appropriate or positive behaviors, and (d) that parents or guardians used consistent and fair discipline for rule violations and misbehavior. Transferring these conditions into follow-up obviously involves both com-

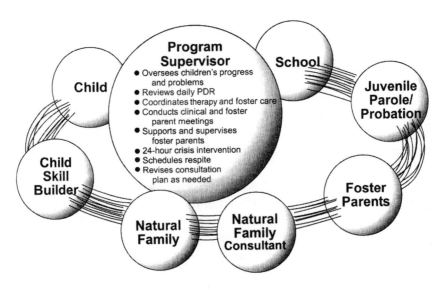

Figure 5.2. The Multidimensional Treatment Foster Care Model. From "Family Connections: A Treatment Foster Care Model for Adolescents With Delinquency," by P. Chamberlain, 1994. Copyright 1998 by Northwest Media, Inc. Adapted with permission.

mitment and skill on the part of adult caretakers. Although it is tempting to think that participation in the program fundamentally changes delinquent youths, the fact is that without continued parental (or adult) support and socialization in follow-up, gains do not remain. Therefore, teaching parents how to effectively supervise, discipline, and encourage their child is a major task undertaken during the placement in MTFC. The family therapist's role is to prepare and support the adults to develop these skills.

The family therapist in MTFC relies primarily on components of the parent management training model (PMT). These components have been adapted from those developed and tested with families of antisocial children and adolescents (Taylor, Eddy, & Biglan, 1999). In the MTFC program, a consulting role is established with the youth's parents. Many participating families have had multiple experiences with service providers and often these have involved blame, confrontation, avoidance, and other negative events. Thus, it is important that the therapist develops an alliance with the family and establishes a relationship that is supportive and constructive prior to introducing parent-training techniques.

As with most PMT models, we emphasize the in-home practice of skills talked about in treatment sessions. As the parent learns particular skills, supervised visits with the youth provide opportunities for this practice. Parents implement specific practice assignments during the youth's home visits. Not only do parents and the youth have a chance to try new ways of relating through these assignments, but also, the balance of power gradually shifts. Additionally, the youth is more accepting of the guidance and support the parents provide. Ultimately, home visits extend to overnights and then weekends and are gradually lengthened until the youth returns home.

Roles of the Skills Trainer and Individual Therapist

Youths are at the center of the MTFC treatment process. As the previous discussion may suggest, these youths are likely to have problems not only with antisocial behavior but also in other domains of functioning. As a result, two types of staff support may be assigned to the youth: the skills trainer and the youth therapist.

The *skills trainer* teaches youths positive behavior and problem-solving skills through intensive one-on-one interaction and skills practice in the community. For example, some youths attract negative attention and hostility when interacting with others because of their lack of eye contact; sulking affect; and rude, curt manner of speaking. A skills trainer would break down basic conversational skills into steps and role-play these with the youth. The skills trainer and youth would then go out into the community and practice the skills, and the trainer would provide reinforcement and feedback. A skills trainer is especially useful in the school setting. He or she can help youths learn appropriate classroom behavior and conflict resolution skills as needed.

We train skills trainers in applied behavior analysis, which they use to examine potential antecedents to and reinforcers for problem behavior in the youth's environment. We also instruct them in the use of shaping procedures to teach new behaviors. Skills trainer interventions often center on behavioral contracting with the youth, such as a reward for passing a certain number of days without a particular problem (as reported by the foster parents).

Initially, the primary role of the *youth therapist* is to serve as an advocate and support person as the youth adjusts to life in the foster home. Many youths, despite their tough demeanor, are highly anxious when they are first placed in the program. In addition, many youths have poor social skills and are unable to advocate for themselves effectively. The youth therapist may also participate with the youth, the parents, and the family therapist in family therapy sessions, again serving primarily as an advocate for the youth. This is especially helpful in families in which there is a great deal of conflict and in which treatment sessions can be very chaotic and emotional. Finally, in some circumstances, youths may address issues of past maltreatment or family of origin with their therapists. However, this typically does not occur until the youth has spent some time in the foster home and his or her behavior has stabilized.

Role of the Consulting Psychiatrist

Many youths enter the program with multiple diagnoses that include disruptive behavior disorders such as conduct disorder and attention deficit disorder, as well as posttraumatic stress disorder, depression, dysthymia, bipolar disorder, and obsessive–compulsive disorder. Often, along with these diagnoses come complex medication regimens that have developed as the youth has moved from one setting to another. Although it is possible to refer these youths for medication evaluations to providers in the community, the ability to consult directly with a psychiatrist who is familiar with the program elements is extremely useful. It allows for careful examination of the accuracy of diagnoses as well as a clarification of the specific medications judged most effective for addressing particular symptoms. Working together, the psychiatrist and program staff are able to evaluate the impact of medication changes on the child's functioning. Consequently, once the child or youth has stabilized in the foster home, it is often possible to greatly reduce the number and dosage of medications.

Role of the Parent Daily Report Caller

Because a high level of contact with foster parents is so critical to the success of treatment, the MTFC model employs a staff member whose role is to contact foster families each day via telephone. In smaller programs, the program supervisor can perform this role. During the phone conversation, the caller reviews a behavior checklist called the parent daily report (PDR; Chamberlain & Reid, 1987). The PDR consists of a list of 40 items that reflect problem behaviors exhibited by disruptive children. The PDR caller asks foster parents to indicate which of the behaviors occurred in the past 24 hours. The checklist takes approximately 5 minutes for the foster parent and PDR caller to complete. The PDR caller then sends the gathered information to the program supervisor along with notes about any additional information that the foster parent provided during the phone call. PDR information provides a thumbnail sketch of the youth's functioning and can be used to track progress or to identify problematic patterns of behavior. PDR has also been found to be a useful instrument for program evaluation research. We hire experienced MTFC parents to work as PDR callers. Frequently they have retired from foster parenting before beginning to work for the program in this new capacity. There are advantages to having a foster parent in this role. It provides a career track for former foster parents who want to remain affiliated with the program but are ready for a new role, and MTFC parents enjoy having daily contact with someone who has "been there."

Role of the Program Director

The director oversees all clinical and management aspects of the program, obtains funding, designs and monitors evaluation activities, and serves as a backup for program supervisors. The director reviews the PDR data each week (the program supervisor reviews it daily) and sets the direction for development of and changes in program policies and practices. The director also often attends the weekly clinical meetings and advocates for the program at the local and state level.

CASE EXAMPLE: MISTY

Misty first came to the attention of the juvenile justice authorities when she was 10 years old. She and her male cousin, who was 12 at the time, were caught breaking into cars that were parked in the center of their small Oregon coastal town. Her second arrest involved a minor assault on a classmate who had apparently been saying derogatory things about Misty's grandmother. By the time Misty was 14, she had 10 police offenses and had been held in detention on three separate occasions. Misty was known for her explosive temper. Her use of loud, extremely foul language had gotten her in trouble several times. She had been expelled from school because of this, and several police reports noted negative verbal behavior on Misty's part.

Misty's family members were no strangers to the criminal justice system. Her father, who had long since left the family, had done time in the state prison for drug-related offenses. Misty's cousin and her uncle both had several run-ins with local police involving drug use, assaults, and burglary. Misty's mother had been hospitalized several times because of mental health problems, and she was unable to provide a home for her children. At the time of referral, Misty was 16 and living in a small trailer with her grandmother. Her uncle and his new wife and their three children (including Misty's co-offending cousin) were also living on the property. What prompted Misty's referral for placement in out-of-home care was her involvement in an incident during which she stabbed her cousin in the hand with a kitchen knife. Misty's grandmother reported this to the police and said that she could no longer care for Misty.

About this time, in response to an ad she saw on the television, Misty's mother called the Sally Jessy Raphael television talk show to tell them her story. The mother and Misty were selected to participate in the show and headed off to New York for the filming. It was the first time either of them had left Oregon. During the show, Misty's mother complained about her daughter's problems, saying that Misty was violent, having unprotected sex, swearing at home, and being defiant. Misty responded by saying several foul things to her mother. This was aired on national television.

Sally Jessy Raphael asked Misty: "Why do you attack family members?"
    Misty: "Because they piss me off."
    Sally Jessy Raphael: "Your mother said you punched her in the face, your uncle says you punched him. You threatened to hit John the producer of the show, and you have threatened to hit me."

Sally Jessy Raphael walked back and forth in front of Misty in a threatening way. Then suddenly a large man in fatigues appeared on stage and addressed Misty: "Punk you got a problem? Answer me."

Misty: "Yes sir."

After a few more interchanges between Misty and the "sergeant," Misty was off to boot camp. Footage was then shown of Misty during her first day at boot camp doing push-ups and responding to the sergeant's commands with "yes sir." What was not shown was the fact that Misty was sent home from boot camp on the second day for medical reasons after she had an anxiety attack and was transported to the local emergency room. Misty was returned home to Oregon to live with relatives. Within one week she was back in detention following an altercation with a neighbor.

After a 2-month stay in detention, Misty was placed in the MTFC program with Marla and Dave, who were experienced foster parents. They lived in a small community located about 30 minutes from Eugene with their 8-year-old son TJ. Marla and Janet, the MTFC program supervisor, set up a point and level system for Misty that emphasized rewarding Misty for coping positively with stressful situations. For example, Misty got extra points for dealing with disappointment in a calm manner and for complaining or otherwise expressing dissatisfaction without using a "potty mouth" (Marla's words). Misty's adjustment in the foster home was positive. Marla and Dave saw her as being a scared young girl with lots of skills deficits who wanted to please them and be accepted by peers. Misty was caring and supportive with TJ and, as a result, Marla asked her if she would be interested in volunteering at the daycare center Marla ran with a group of other women. Misty readily accepted and the volunteering soon turned into a paying job.

Things did not go so well at school. From the beginning, Misty was concerned about rumors that she said were being spread about her. After her second week of enrollment, she got into a physical fight with another girl. Both girls were suspended. Barb, Misty's MTFC individual therapist, attempted to talk about the incident with Misty, but Misty would have none of it. She saw the incident as being completely the other girl's fault and said that she saw absolutely no options for her to have behaved differently. Barb, being skilled in working with resistant teenagers, suggested that they consider a long-term strategy.

> You and this girl are going to have to figure out how to coexist in the same school. It's my job to help you work it out so you don't have to suffer anymore. You think it over and I will, too, and we'll put our heads together to come up with a plan.

Predictably, Misty did not come up with any ideas and thought that all of the suggestions that Barb had would not work. The situation was discussed in the weekly clinical staffing and, with guidance from that meeting and cooperation from Marla and Dave, Barb suggested the following to Misty:

It is good that you are taking this situation seriously and trying to figure out what will and will not work for you, because this is important—not so much because of this girl, but because as you mature you will have to deal with unreasonable people a lot. They are everywhere. We can't jump to a simple solution. This is a complicated problem. If it worked to have a simple solution, you would already have figured it out because you are a smart kid and a sensitive one, too. Look how great the little ones at Sunshine (the daycare) relate to you. I don't see that everyday. Maybe that's playing into the problem. You may be more sensitive than most people. Maybe we need to work on getting you to have a thicker skin in some situations. Being sensitive is such a good thing, but it can set you up to be really hurt when you think people are being unfair. So, in the meantime, before we figure this out, let's see if Janet (the program supervisor) will go for giving you an extra incentive to practice being thick-skinned at school given what you have to deal with there.

We framed the problem as Misty being highly sensitive, something no one had ever called her before, and importantly, we set it up so that her buy-in to change was not required for the intervention to proceed. An incentive of $1 a day was set up for her to earn every day she had a thick skin, defined as each day she did not blow up or get in a fight at school. This allowed for providing her with concrete reinforcement for not engaging aggressively with peers. The aim was to increase her skills for and practice of ignoring peer provocations. In the meantime, Barb took on the task of working with Misty to develop alternative responses to situations when she felt attacked or put down by others, but Misty remained unwilling to consider that she should behave any differently. She felt that it was the other people who had the problem, not her.

However, the incentive for having a thick skin seemed to work well for 2 months with no further incidences at school. Then Misty was expelled for sexual harassment. She called an overweight male peer "boob boy." Barb was becoming quite frustrated at Misty's resistance to talking about problems that she was having at school with peers. Barb had tried several different approaches, and none of them had gone anywhere. Misty was clear that she did not have any problems and did not want Barb to be bugging her just like everyone else. Barb felt that continuing to try to focus this way with Misty was beginning to threaten their relationship, which she thought was otherwise very positive. Misty never missed an appointment and was obviously responsive to Barb's approval. During the clinical staffing it was decided to use the expulsion incident as an opportunity for reorienting the individual therapy. An intervention was planned that used the program supervisor's position of authority but focused this authority not on the youth but on the individual therapist.

During an individual therapy session, Janet knocked and entered the room where Barb and Misty were meeting.

Janet: "I have a few things I need to talk to you about."

Misty (defiantly): "What now?"

Janet: "Not to you, to Barb."

[Silence]

Janet: "Barb, I am really concerned that you are not doing your job with Misty. Here she is in the same type of situation that she was when she first entered the program. Nothing has changed. She has not been taught the things we are supposed to be teaching her, like how to keep her mouth under control and how to stay out of fights. The judge is not going to be happy with us. If you can't do the job, then maybe we need to get someone else in here that can be more effective. Think it over."

Janet then left the room.

Misty's reaction was unbelieving. "I thought she was going to yell at me, and she yelled at you."

Barb was silent and looked stressed. Misty immediately became more cooperative, saying that she was the one who was messing things up, not Barb. She even suggested that they do some role-plays, a strategy that Barb had previously tried to use for practicing responses to provocations, but previously Misty had refused to cooperate.

During the next session, Barb and Misty made a videotape of several role-plays to demonstrate to Janet that they were working hard on the problem. During the role-plays it became obvious that Misty tended to be at a loss for words in stressful situations if she was restricted from swearing and using foul language. The problem of practicing how to express oneself in a socially acceptable way when under stress became a new target behavior for Misty. This was framed to her as a skill that, if practiced, would increase over time. To provide Misty with opportunities to practice we enlisted the help of Latisha, an MTFC skills trainer.

Latisha is a young woman in her 20s who just graduated from college with a bachelor's degree in psychology. Latisha had received training as a skills trainer that emphasized methods for reinforcing youth positive behavior and staying out of discipline confrontations. Latisha and the other MTFC skills trainers participated in a weekly supervision meeting with an experienced MTFC program supervisor. Latisha was assigned to work with Misty with the goal of increasing Misty's exposure to community activities and hobbies that were appropriate for a girl her age. They had done a range of things, including going shopping for Misty's prom dress, exercising, and participating in an art class. They had what might be described as an older-sister/younger-sister relationship, with Latisha providing encouragement, guidance, problem-solving advice, and occasionally a sympathetic ear.

At the clinical staff meeting, it was decided to program regular opportunities for Misty to practice talking about difficult and potentially stressful situations in a socially acceptable manner. Barb continued to meet weekly with Misty, and in addition, Latisha set up a nightly telephone call with her.

During the nightly call, the idea was to spend about 10–15 minutes each weeknight talking about how Misty's day had gone. Misty could talk about the fun and good things but also about the disappointments and stress. If she swore or used rough or crude language, Barb told Latisha to say "I've got to go" and hang up immediately. Latisha was to keep track of the calls, and for every one with no inappropriate language, Latisha and Misty would be given $1 to spend on fun activities of their choice. This intervention was implemented for 30 days without one incident that necessitated a hang-up. Misty improved markedly in her ability to express negative feelings without resorting to problem verbal behavior. She was readmitted to school, and her adjustment with peers improved.

Misty responded well to the structure provided by the MTFC program. It became clear that she was happy and productive when she was busy. The MTFC family therapist worked throughout Misty's placement with the grandmother to help her find ways to provide Misty with closer supervision and regular reinforcement for going to school and being home on time and other activities that showed that she was staying on track. It was a problem that the uncle's family lived on the grandmother's property because the co-offending cousin was not subject to restrictions or rules. He did not attend school or work, and he regularly stayed out all night with drug-using friends. The MTFC team was very concerned about Misty falling in with her old negative crowd when she returned home.

In planning for the transition home, the program supervisor helped arrange for an after-school job for Misty, and Marla hired her to help clean the daycare on weekends. The grandmother and Misty attended weekly family therapy sessions, and Misty met once a week with Latisha and monthly with Barb.

One month after her return home, Misty and her mother went back to New York to do a follow-up Sally Jessy Raphael program, "Boot Camp: Where Are They Now?" The opening scenes at the boot camp showed Misty on the ground with a guard yelling at her to apologize to her mother.

> Sally Jessy Raphael opens the show: "We've seen lots of terrible teens throughout the years crossing this stage—swearing, kicking, yelling, screaming—I guess we sent the worst of them to the one place where we hoped they might shape up: boot camp. We are looking at some of these graduates and asking ourselves where are they now? How is Misty doing?"
>
> *Misty's mother:* "After the show, her and her cousin got in a fight; she stabbed him with a knife, then she went into juvenile detention for 4 months, then she went into foster care. But she got her GED. She's not as violent after that. She's improved a little bit."
>
> *Sally Jessy Raphael:* "She stopped with the drugs?"
>
> *Mother:* "Yea."
>
> *Sally Jessy Raphael:* "With the alcohol?"

Mother: "Yes."

Sally Jessy Raphael: "But she's still having sex?"

Mother: "Yea."

Sally Jessy Raphael: "Let's have Misty come out, let's find out." Misty walks on stage.

Sally Jessy Raphael: "Mother says you are not doing drugs anymore. You want to be a veterinarian?"

Misty: "A vet technician."

Sally Jessy Raphael: "Well, tell me, do you think that your attitude has improved?"

Misty: "Yea, I'm not violent, I don't have mood swings or anything."

Mother: "You need to get a job—you're gonna be 18 soon—who's gonna take care of you?"

Misty: "Me."

Sally Jessy Raphael: "It's good that she knows that."

Mother: "What about the sex thing all the time?"

Misty: "I don't have sex all the time, Mother."

Mother: "It still concerns me what are you gonna do if you end up getting pregnant?"

Misty: "We use protection."

Mother: "Protection doesn't always work, hon."

Sally Jessy Raphael: "If I had to bet on something—if you were a horse— I'd bet you were gonna be OK. If you find out what it is to have money, you're gonna do OK. I believe in you."

[Audience claps. Commercial break.]

Announcer: "And now from our Reaction Room."

Mother: "I can't talk to her about anything—I have no right to talk to her. I am not doing this to make things hard for her, I am doing this to help her."

Misty: "Boot camp never changed me—I burglarized after that. I went to detention for 4 months. I attempted assault. And then I went to foster care, and the foster care and the therapy that I was going through, that's what changed me."

Misty is now 19 years old. She lives in a large Pacific Northwest city working as a veterinary assistant. She shares an apartment with two other girls and has a boyfriend who works for an airline company. She has had no further contact with the legal system.

CONCLUSION

The OSLC MTFC program is a family-based alternative to residential, institutional, and group care for adolescents with significant histories of chronic and serious delinquency. Most of these youths also have serious behavioral, emotional, and mental health problems. In their review of service system components, Rivera and Kutash (1994) noted that the use of treatment foster care programs was first seen in the United States in the mid-1970s as an alternative to institutional placements and has grown steadily within the child welfare, juvenile justice, and mental health systems. A conservative estimate of the number of TFC programs in the United States (estimated on the basis of Foster Family-Based Treatment Association membership) shows that at least 350 programs are providing care. These range from small, locally based programs to large multisite agencies. Judging by these conservative estimates, foster care is providing services for at least 1,200 youths in the United States on any given day, and provides more than 6 million "client-days" per year, at a cost of at least a half billion dollars per year.

The research on the OSLC MTFC reviewed in chapter 4 shows that, compared with group-oriented treatments, participation in MTFC leads to more positive, long-term outcomes. The program components, staffing roles, and principles of practice described in this chapter are the core features of the model that can be put into place to produce those outcomes. In addition to focusing on producing positive outcomes, we are interested in understanding key mechanisms or mediators of change within the MTFC model. This understanding would help in determining what factors are important in the replication of the model and has implications for designing interventions in the context of other types of delinquency treatment programs. This topic is addressed in chapter 6.

6

MEDIATORS OF
TREATMENT OUTCOME

The importance of finding positive effects resulting from application of a treatment model for a serious and costly problem like delinquency is obvious. However, what is perhaps more important to society at large is to understand what it was about the effective model that facilitated positive treatment so that those principles can be applied more broadly to a variety of interventions. In this way, identification of the specific mechanisms that explain how the intervention worked has broader implications for creating change in social policy and improving existing treatment resources. One way to accomplish this broader task is to design treatment studies that are not only theory-based but that also measure the occurrence and influence of key mechanisms that predict successful long-term outcomes.

As the information base on the development of child antisocial behavior has increased, and as theories of prevention and intervention have been developed and tested, commentators (Mrazek & Haggerty, 1994) have noted that researchers have not capitalized on the unique opportunities for investigating and manipulating key mechanisms thought to predict outcomes. In addition to examining whether a particular intervention works, explanatory clinical trials would investigate *how* the intervention works (i.e., what are the specific components or mechanisms).

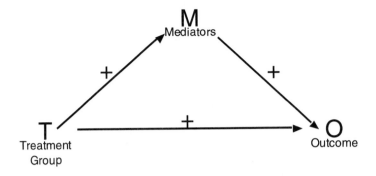

Figure 6.1. Association between treatment group (T), mediators (M), and outcomes (O). Positive association between T and O disappears in the presence of the T to M to O path.

Researchers have labeled variables that explain "how" as *mediators* (Holmbeck, 1997). A mediating variable generates the effect that an independent variable has on a dependent variable. As is shown in Figure 6.1, in the context of a randomized clinical trial, the independent variable T (i.e., treatment group or condition) is hypothesized to cause changes in the levels of the mediators (M), which in turn are hypothesized to cause changes in the outcome of interest (O). Baron and Kenny (1986) have defined the mediation effect as occurring when four conditions are met: (a) T is significantly associated with M, (b) T is significantly associated with O, (c) M is significantly associated with O, and (d) the impact of T on O is significantly less after controlling for M.

In our research on the effects of Multidimensional Treatment Foster Care (MTFC), we have developed and implemented a strategy to measure and test the effects of four specific mechanisms that we hypothesized mediated treatment effects. We selected these mediators on the basis of two criteria: They have each been identified in numerous longitudinal studies as predicting the development and escalation of delinquency, and they are potentially malleable factors. The four key mediators that we attempted to manipulate in the MTFC condition during the study comparing MTFC with group care (GC; described in chapter 4) were supervision, discipline, positive reinforcement from caretaking adults, and decreasing association with deviant peers. In the GC condition, the four mediators were left free to vary. In addition to hypothesizing that boys in MTFC would have fewer arrests in follow-up than those in GC, we predicted that to the extent that the adults in charge in both treatment conditions supervised, disciplined, positively reinforced, and prevented the boy from association with deviant peers, the greater the decrease would be in the boys concurrent and subsequent antisocial behaviors.

Researchers in the area of the effects of residential care were also interested in identification of mediating mechanisms. For example, Wells (1991) called for residential treatment providers to establish a common set of definitions for specific treatment modalities or components. Colton (1990) argued that research on residential care had overemphasized the focus on child characteristics and had not looked enough at the specific characteristics of the treatment setting as being potentially predictive of outcomes. It was our aim to partially remedy this gap. We wanted to measure what went on in MTFC and GC settings, specifically with regard to the four identified variables that we thought would mediate treatment outcomes.

The study design presented in chapter 4 (Figure 4.2) shows that first boys were randomly assigned to participation in MTFC or GC and assessed at baseline (before placement). Then, they were placed in either MTFC or GC settings, and after they had been placed for 3 months, another assessment in the placement setting occurred. The goal of the 3-month assessment was to measure the presence or absence of the four variables that we thought would mediate subsequent antisocial outcomes. The idea was that, regardless of placement setting (in MTFC or GC), boys who were receiving good supervision, consistent and fair discipline, positive reinforcement from adults, and who were not permitted to associate with delinquent peers (especially when not supervised) would have positive outcomes. The first step was to figure out how to measure the four key variables of interest. This was more complex than one might expect because in essence we were asking adults if they were competent at their jobs (i.e., "How well do you supervise him?"). We quickly learned that virtually all adult caretakers reported that they provided complete or nearly complete supervision, consistent discipline, and lots of daily reinforcement. From a measurement standpoint, there was very little variance in the scores that the adults provided. A critical issue identified by numerous investigators is the need to integrate measures from multiple perspectives and from multiple sources to produce generalizable descriptions of key constructs.

THE NEED FOR MULTIPLE PERSPECTIVES[1]

To better define the four variables that we hypothesized would predict later criminality, we used a multiagent, multimethod strategy of data collection. The idea was that any one individual has a unique bias that characterizes his or her perspective. Various types of measurement methods (e.g., questionnaires and in-person interviews) also contribute to systematic bias, and that bias, in turn, contributes to unreliability (reviewed in Patterson, 1982).

---

[1]The remainder of this chapter focuses on results from a series of analyses that examined the key components of treatment that mediated long-term outcomes. Parts of the information we review contain reports on fairly technical statistical information. Unless clinicians and policymakers reading this chapter are looking for potential remedies for problems with insomnia, they may want to focus only on the sections entitled "Summary of Study Results" and "Conclusion."

In addition, there is a consensus among researchers that collecting data over multiple data points (during repeated assessments) gives a better estimate of the phenomena of interest than single-point assessments (Collins & Horn, 1991; Willet, Ayoub, & Robinson, 1991).

We used a two-step approach to measure supervision, discipline, adult relationship, and deviant peer contact. First, before boys were placed in the various settings, we interviewed the adults in charge (senior line staff in GC and foster parents in MTFC). We developed an ecological interview that focused on examining the key assumptions that the adult caretakers had about what factors influenced whether a boy was successful in their programs. Second, once boys were placed for 3 months, we conducted an assessment with boys and caretakers during an in-person interview and during two brief telephone contacts. The purpose of this second assessment was to examine the daily practices and daily experiences that boys were having in the various GC and MTFC placements.

STAFF ASSUMPTIONS: THE ECOLOGICAL INTERVIEW

We designed the ecological interview to examine caretakers' assumptions around four questions: (a) Who do adults think most influences the boy's success in the program? (b) Who does the boy spend his time with while he is in the program? (c) How much supervision do adults perceive that they provide? (d) What are the adult perceptions of who most influences or controls disciplinary practices?

Who Influences Success?

Adults in MTFC and GC differed on how much influence they thought they had on boys' success. A score that measured the difference between the relative influence of adult caretakers and peers showed that in MTFC the adults believed that overall, adults were much more influential than peers (p = .01). On a scale of 1 to 10, GC staff saw less than a 1-point difference between the relative influence of caretakers and peers. MTFC adults saw more than a 3-point difference. Although caretakers in both program models ranked themselves as having the most influence on a boy's success, in MTFC they were seen as significantly more powerful than in GC.

Who Do Boys Spend Time With?

The caretaking adults reported that, on average, boys in GC were thought to be more likely to spend time with peers than those in MTFC (p = .003). Boys in MTFC were reported to be more likely to spend time one-on-one with an adult (p = .01) than were boys in GC. We developed a summary score to measure how much individual adult contact, relative to peer contact, was thought to occur (i.e., the proportion of time a boy spent with adults plus peers, with peers only, and alone was subtracted from the proportion of time spent with adults only). We found a significant difference on this score between the two approaches ($p = .0002$).

How Much Supervision Do Staff Caretakers Provide?

The supervision score measured adult tracking of boys' lateness coming home, school performance, and school tardiness. We found no differences between the groups, indicating that adults in both types of programs reported that they monitored these activities equally well. We also measured supervision by asking adult caretakers to estimate the number of hours per day that boys spent without direct supervision by an adult and the number of hours per week of unsupervised free time. Boys in MTFC settings were thought to spend less time per day without direct adult supervision ($p = .05$) and less unsupervised free time per week, although the latter difference was not statistically significant.

Adult Perception of Discipline Practices

As could be expected by the differing program philosophies, in MTFC settings adults reported that they had the main control over discipline. We examined three aspects of discipline: (a) who decides if discipline is needed, (b) who decides what the discipline will be, and (c) who administers the discipline. In GC programs, although adults reported that they retained a good measure of control, they reported scores significantly lower than those in MTFC on a composite score that summarized these three aspects of discipline.

PROGRAM PRACTICES

Next we assessed actual program practices after boys in the study had been in their placements for 3 months. At that time we conducted a series of five telephone interviews with caretakers and then with boys, each time using the Parent Daily Report (PDF) Checklist (Chamberlain & Reid, 1987, described in chapter 5). Three scores were developed to reflect three perspectives on daily program practices: the adult caretakers' reports, the boys' reports, and discrepancy scores, which are the difference between the caretakers' and boys' reports. We arbitrarily defined the discrepancy score as being the adult report minus the boy report, so that a positive discrepancy score indicates that the caretaker is reporting more incidents than the boy, and a negative score indicates that the boy is reporting more events. All scores on

TABLE 6.1
Average Youth Problem Behavior Occurrences Within the Past 24 Hours

Report	GC		MTFC	
	M	*SD*	*M*	*SD*
Adult caretaker report	3.7	2.3	3.6	1.7
Boy report	6.6$_a$	3.9	2.9$_a$	2.3
Discrepancy score	−2.9$_b$	4.4	0.7$_b$	0.7

Note. Means with the same subscripts are significantly different at $p < .05$. GC = group care; MTFC = Multidimensional Treatment Foster Care.

daily practices reflect an average rate per day of the behavior of interest and are based on five days of data from each agent.

RATES OF BOY PROBLEM BEHAVIOR OCCURRENCE

Caretakers in the GC and MTFC programs reported that boys engaged in approximately the same average level of problem behaviors per day (3.7 and 3.6, respectively; see Table 6.1). However, boys in the two programs differed considerably in their own reports of how many problem behaviors they engaged in per day: GC boys reported engaging in an average of 6.6 problem behaviors, while MTFC boys reported an average of 3 ($p = .008$). The discrepancy score showed a significant difference in both magnitude and direction across the two program models. In GC, there was more disagreement on boys' rates of daily problem behaviors than in MTFC: $F(1, 24) = 6.87, p = .02$. In MTFC, the positive score indicated higher adult than boy report score, whereas in GC the negative sign indicated higher boy than adult report scores.

DISCIPLINE PRACTICE

After reporting on the occurrence of problem behaviors, we independently asked both the boys and the caretakers if boys were given consequences for their misbehaviors. As would be expected, in the adult-mediated MTFC model, consequences occurred more frequently, according to both boys ($F[1, 22] = 6.17, p = .02$) and caretakers ($F[1, 24] = 9.86, p = .004$) than in GC. In both settings, the discrepancy score (caretaker report – boy report) revealed that, regardless of program setting, caretakers reported delivering more consequences than boys said they received (see Table 6.2).

SUPERVISION PRACTICES

We collected data from both boys and caretakers on the amount of time spent with adult caretakers and the amount of time spent without adult

TABLE 6.2
Proportion of Youth Problems Consequated

Report	GC		MTFC	
	M	SD	M	SD
Adult report	0.34$_a$	0.28	0.62$_a$	0.18
Boy report	0.15$_b$	0.15	0.37$_b$	0.26
Discrepancy score	0.16	0.25	0.24	0.27

Note. Means with the same subscripts are significantly different at $p < .05$. GC = group care; MTFC = Multidimensional Treatment Foster Care.

supervision. In GC, caretakers reported that they spent an average of just over 3 hours per day with a particular boy, whereas in MTFC, caretakers reported spending over 5 hours a day with a particular boy. This difference was significant: $F(1, 24) = 5.11, p = .03$. In both settings, there was no significant difference in the amount of agreement between adults and boys on this measure. When asked about unsupervised time, caretakers in both models underestimated the amount of unsupervised time boys had compared with boys' reports. In GC, boys reported an average of over 1 hour per day without adult supervision, and in MTFC boys reported an average of 12 minutes per day. The discrepancy between reports was significantly different between the two models: $F(1, 24) = 4.99, p = .04$ (see Table 6.3).

PEER CONTACT AND INFLUENCE

Because of the fundamental difference between program structures, boys in GC have more opportunity for peer associations. This is reflected in boy and caretaker reports of the time spent recreating with peers: GC boys spent from 1.75 (caretaker report) hours to 3 (boy report) hours daily, and MTFC boys spent from 1 hour (boy report) to 1.3 hours (caretaker report). We found greater discrepancy between boy and adult reports in GC than in MTFC programs.

We then asked boys and caretakers to report how much time boys spent with peers from outside of their programs who had histories of delinquency. There were substantial discrepancies between boy and caretaker reports in both GC and MTFC, but in opposite directions. In GC, boys reported spending more time with delinquent peers than adults reported, whereas in MTFC, adults reported boys spending more time with delinquent peers than boys said they had. The discrepancy score was marginally different between the two groups: $F(1, 24) = 3.8, p = .06$ (see Table 6.4).

Finally, we examined how adults and boys rated the degree to which peers influenced boys. On a 10-point scale (i.e., 1 = no influence), MTFC boys reported less negative influence from peers than did GC boys: $F(1, 24)$

TABLE 6.3
Adult Contact and Supervision With Youths

Report	GC		MTFC	
	M	SD	M	SD
Average minutes with caretaker				
Adult caretaker report	189.0[a]	139.0	311.0[a]	134.0
Boy report	188.0	134.0	266.0	174.0
Discrepancy score	1.6	98.6	45.0	174.0
Average minutes without adult supervision				
Adult caretaker report	7.8[a]	12.3	3.2[a]	25.0
Boy report	78.8	90.0	35.1	46.0
Discrepancy score	−71.0[b]	93.0	−11.0[b]	31.0

Note. Means with the same subscripts are significantly different at $p < .05$. GC = group care; MTFC = Multidimensional Treatment Foster Care.

$= 6.52, p = .02$. There was no significant discrepancy between boy and adult reports (see Table 6.4).

This study was an initial step toward beginning to define and measure assumptions and practices of residential care models for delinquent youths. We examined the areas that were thought to influence or mediate the effects of outcomes. In general, there was a great deal of consistency between program assumptions and practices for the two models of care. In the GC programs that were more peer-focused, peers were thought to have more influence, and more time with peers was endorsed. Peers were also reported to have a negative influence on boys' daily life. This finding is in line with research conducted by Elliott, Huizinga, and Ageton (1985) and others reviewed in chapter 2 that negative peer influence potentiates delinquency.

SUMMARY OF STUDY RESULTS

Differences were found in the two program models in terms of the amount and type of discipline and supervision strategies used. In MTFC, adults provided consequences more often, provided tighter supervision, and restricted contacts with peers more often than in GC. This is consistent with the theoretical orientation of the MTFC approach, which views adults as the key change agents and minimizes unsupervised contact with peers.

In both program models, caretakers reported approximately the same level of daily problem behaviors in boys, but boys differed in their reported levels with those in GC reporting over twice the rate as those in MTFC. In MTFC, caretakers reported more problems than did boys, whereas in GC, caretakers reported fewer problems than did boys. This led us to speculate that either MTFC caretakers were hypervigilant or GC caretakers were lax in their tracking of problem behaviors.

TABLE 6.4
Peer Contact and Influence on Youths

Report or rating	GC		MTFC	
	M	SD	M	SD
Average minutes recreating with peers				
Caretaker report	106.0ₐ	85.0	77.0	97.0
Boy report	185.0ₐ	174.0	71.0ₐ	79.0
Discrepancy score	−78.9	158.0	6.1	58.0
Average minutes with nonprogram delinquent peers				
Caretaker report	1.0	3.4	33.0	71.0
Boy report	18.0	33.0	4.5	9.8
Discrepancy score	−17.0	34.0	28.0	73.0
Ratings of influence by negative peers				
Caretaker rating	2.9	1.2	2.2	0.98
Boy self-rating	2.3ₐ	1.1	1.4ₐ	0.61
Discrepancy score	0.65	1.8	0.79	0.99

Note. Means with the same subscripts are significantly different at $p < .05$. GC = group care; MTFC = Multidimensional Treatment Foster Care.

The discrepancy scores for the two groups focused on the concurrence of boy and caretaker reports. Patterns of discrepancies for the two program models were distinct. In GC, caretakers and boys disagreed more (relative to those in MTFC) on amount of contact with adults, supervision practices, occurrence of problem behaviors, amount of peer contact, and magnitude of the negative influence of peers. In MTFC, there was greater disagreement (relative to GC) on the amount of time spent with nonprogram delinquent peers.

MEDIATED EFFECTS

The next step was to determine if the differences that we observed in the two models related to differences in outcomes. More specifically, do boys who are well supervised, more consistently disciplined, and well mentored during treatment have lower subsequent levels of arrests in follow-up compared with those who have less supervision and so forth? Does the amount of unsupervised time with delinquent peers while a boy is in treatment relate to his level of arrests in follow-up?

DEPENDENT VARIABLES

To test these questions, we examined the scores on the daily practices mentioned above relative to official records of criminal activity and self-reports of criminal activity in follow-up. We measured arrests from official electronic records. The cumulative number of days a youth had at least one arrest between placement and 1 year following exit from treatment were computed and converted to an average arrest per year score. We collected arrest data from the county juvenile courts from each of the counties a youth resided in during the placement and the 1-year follow-up periods. In addition to official arrest data, at 6-month intervals following enrollment in the study, all youths completed the Elliott Behavior Checklist (EBC; Elliott, Ageton, Huizinga, Knowles, & Canter, 1983), a confidential self-report of delinquency with both content and construct validity (Elliott et al., 1985). We used the average of scores at the 12-month, 18-month, and 24-month post-enrollment assessments on the General Delinquency subscale of the EBC.

MEDIATIONAL ANALYSIS

An overview of the mediational analysis is presented next; for a full description, please see Eddy and Chamberlain (2000). The purpose of the analysis was to determine if the four variables of interest mediated the outcomes in a way that could help explain what factors during treatment contributed to positive change for boys who were successful in follow-up. As discussed above, a mediator is a variable that generates the effect of an independent variable on a dependent variable. Changes in a true mediator are both *caused by* an independent variable and are *the cause of* changes in a dependent variable. In this study, the independent variable, treatment group (MTFC vs. GC), is hypothesized to have caused levels of the four variables of interest (i.e., supervision, discipline, positive relationship with a mentoring adult, and social distance from deviant peers) to increase, which in turn is hypothesized to have caused decreases in the outcome, youth antisocial behavior. We used the latent modeling analysis strategy to incorporate multiple indicators of each of the hypothesized mediators into the model to help deal with the bias that measurement error can introduce in the estimation of mediated effects (e.g., Judd & Kenny, 1981).

Fifty-three (23 in GC, 30 in MTFC) of the 79 participants in the randomized trial were included in these analyses. The 26 other participants were excluded because they were not placed in GC or MTFC at the time of the 3-month assessment when we assessed the mediating variables. These participants were not present at the 3-month assessment due to a variety of reasons, including running away and expulsion from the program (i.e., this was the case for 17 of 40 GC boys and 9 of 39 MTFC boys).

The final sample of 53 youths had fewer days with criminal referrals prior to baseline than the 26 excluded youths (average of 7 days with at least one criminal referral [SD = 5] vs. 13 days [SD = 6]; $t[77] = 4.81$, $p < .01$). Similarly, the sample of 53 had spent fewer days in detention in the year prior to baseline (average of 50 days [SD = 53] vs. 119 days [SD = 92]; $t[76] =$

4.23, $p < .01$). However, averages for the number of self-reported crimes in the year prior to baseline, the number of prebaseline felony referrals, the age of first criminal referral, and the age at entry into the study were not significantly different between the included and excluded groups. Within the sample of 53, there were no differences between GC and MTFC youths in terms of the number of days with at least one criminal referral prior to baseline, the number of self-reported crimes, the number of felony referrals, the age of first criminal referral, and age at baseline.

Each of the variables central to the mediational analysis (i.e., treatment condition, family management variables, deviant peer variables, and follow-up antisocial behavior measures) were correlated at least $r = .20$ or greater with each of the other variables (see Table 6.5). At the baseline assessment, the MTFC and GC means for antisocial behavior in the 6 months prior did not differ. At the midpoint and follow-up assessments, the MTFC and GC group means differed significantly for each of the variables in the analysis, with MTFC means in all cases in the more favorable direction (i.e., lower antisocial behavior scores, more positive family management scores, lower deviant peer association scores).

All four of Baron and Kenny's (1986) conditions for mediation were successfully met in our analyses: (a) group assignment (MTFC or GC) was significantly associated with the mediators during the midst of placement (ß $= .89, p < .01$), (b) group assignment was significantly associated with subsequent youth antisocial behavior (ß $= -.51, p < .05$), (c) family management skills were significantly associated with youth antisocial behavior (ß $= -.71, p < .01$), and (d) the impact of group on youth antisocial behavior was not significant in the presence of the mediators after controlling for prebaseline levels of antisocial behavior (ß $= .31, ns$). The mediated model tested in the fourth condition (i.e., d) fit the data (χ^2 [21] $= 21.6, p = .43$, GFI $= .92$).

We then tested whether it was plausible to consider the path from group to youth antisocial behavior as equal to zero. The chi-square for this model (χ^2 [22] $= 21.8, p = .47$, GFI $= .92$) did not differ significantly from our preliminary mediated model. Thus, this simpler model was retained and is illustrated in Figure 6.2. The indicators of each of the constructs loaded moderately to highly, and prebaseline levels of antisocial behavior were not significantly related to group. The paths from group to mediators, from mediators to follow-up antisocial behavior, and from pretreatment behavior to follow-up antisocial behavior were all significant. The indirect effect of group through the mediators construct was significant ($t = -2.72, p < .05$) and accounted for 32% of the variation in the follow-up antisocial behavior construct.

CONCLUSION

As we had hypothesized, the family management skills (i.e., supervision, discipline, and positive adult relationship) and deviant peer association

TABLE 6.5
Descriptive Statistics for the Variables in the Mediational Model

Variable	6 months prebaseline			Placement midpoint				Placement to 1 yr post Rx exit	
	1	2	3	4	5	6	7	8	9
Mediator									
1. Group									
2. Official criminal referral (prebaseline)	−.09								
3. Self-reported delinquency (prebaseline)	.07	.44****							
4. Positive adult–youth relationship	.34***	−.07	.05						
5. Discipline	.69****	−.12	.01	.41****					
6. Supervision	.51****	−.03	−.06	.35***	.53****				
7. Deviant peers	−.78****	.16	.15	−.36***	−.65****	−.51****			
8. Official criminal referrals	−.29**	.22*	.37***	−.33***	−.44***	−.25**	.35***		
9. Self-reported delinquency	−.31**	.20*	.23*	−.22*	−.32***	−.21*	.25**	.35***	
GC									
M		3.00	20.30	−.26	−.52	−.26	.75	3.70	10.60
SD		1.76	17.17	0.70	0.76	0.61	0.62	2.74	11.00
MTFC									
M		2.63	23.43	.23	.48	.29	−.64	2.10	4.58
SD		2.16	25.76	0.67	0.25	0.32	0.51	2.55	7.77

Note. For each midpoint and follow-up variable, group means were significantly different at $p < .05$. Group means were not significantly different for prebaseline variables. GC = group care; MTFC = Multidimensional Treatment Foster Care. GC, *N* = 23; MTFC, *N* = 30.
*$p < .10$. **$p < .05$. ***$p < .01$. ****$p < .001$.

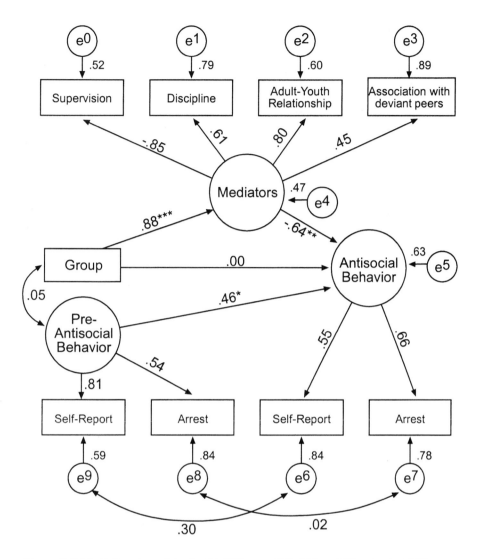

Figure 6.2. Mediational model. $\chi^2 = 21.802$, $p = .472$, GFI = .920, adjusted GFI = .837, $N = 53$. *$p < .05$. **$p < .01$. ***$p < .001$.

all functioned as mediators of the effect of treatment condition on subsequent youth antisocial behavior. Thus, not only was MTFC a more effective treatment for severe antisocial behavior than were traditional group home services in this sample, but a significant part of the influence of MTFC on youth behavior was due to the levels of these mediators during treatment.

This analysis underlines the importance of both parenting and deviant peers in modifying the frequency of youth antisocial behaviors, even for severely and chronically delinquent boys. Parenting characterized by firm limit setting, consistent consequences for misbehavior, close supervision of youth activities and whereabouts, limitation of contact with deviant peers, and positive interactions between the youth and his caretakers does make a difference. Further, the analysis affirms that it is not too late to modify antisocial "careers," even during adolescence. This analysis also points to the potential dangers of bringing high-risk youths together for group treatment (see Dishion, McCord, & Poulin, 1999).

In the next chapter, we review research on the prevalence and form of severe antisocial behavior in girls and discuss implications for treatment. We describe an ongoing clinical trial aimed at developing a treatment for severely antisocial girls referred from the juvenile justice system, along with preliminary data on differences in initial characteristics and treatment process for boys and girls.

7

ANTISOCIAL BEHAVIOR AND DELINQUENCY IN GIRLS

The idea that treatment for girls should be gender specific and that male treatments do not adequately address the unique needs of girls is well accepted in clinical circles. However, the pathways to adolescent antisocial behavior are not nearly as well understood for girls as they are for boys. It is not surprising then that we lack a theoretically grounded treatment model for antisocial behavior and related problems that consider gender.

Several authors have noted that female adolescents who are involved in the juvenile justice system are not treated comparably to their male counterparts (Bloom, 1998; Chesney-Lind, 1998). The juvenile justice system tends to either ignore girls or deal with them more harshly for less serious crimes than boys (Chesney-Lind, 1999). There may be numerous reasons for this, including the perception that girls are criminal "lightweights" (Giordano & Cernkovich, 1997), the attitudes of social control agents in male-dominated juvenile justice systems (Schlossman & Cairns, 1991), or the characterization of girls as being difficult to work with because they are emotionally demanding (Zanarini & Gunderson, 1997). As a result, even though experts recognize that juvenile justice, educational, and child welfare systems should be sensitive to gender-related issues, there is far less empirical information on the development of the antisocial process in girls than in boys. This gap contributes to the underdevelopment of cohesive and appropriate services geared to the needs of girls.

Understanding girls' pathways to antisocial behavior is complicated by contradictory findings from studies on age of onset. Some research indicates that, whereas the majority of boys who have severe and chronic problems with delinquency in adolescence have childhood histories of antisocial and aggressive behavior, for most seriously delinquent girls, antisocial behavior emerges for the first time during adolescence (Cohen, Cohen, Kasen, Velez, & Johnson, 1993). Other studies examining age at onset of conduct problems for boys and girls have found that first symptoms and less serious presentations of problems appear at similar ages (reviewed in Keenan, Loeber, & Green, 1999). If the emergence of serious forms of antisocial behavior in early adolescence is more precipitous for girls than for boys, this sudden onset could contribute to the lack of theoretically and developmentally based treatment models for girls. We simply know less about factors that predict or protect against the development of severe conduct problems and delinquency in girls. Therefore, juvenile justice interventionists hold a weakened position when it comes to knowing what should be included in the design of developmentally grounded, gender-relevant intervention models.

Apparently the juvenile justice system is not alone in this regard. There is evidence that other community service systems short-change girls. They tend not to be referred to or make use of mental health, social services, or educational delivery service systems as often as do boys. In fact, there is evidence that utilization rates for such services are lower for adolescent girls than for any other cohort (i.e., younger girls, younger and adolescent boys; Offord, Boyle, & Racine, 1991). Caseau and colleagues (Caseau, Luckasson, & Kroth, 1994) examined whether girls with mental health problems were underidentified in public schools as being seriously emotionally disturbed (according to the Individuals with Disabilities Education Act; P.L.101-476). They found that girls were underrepresented in special education services, yet private psychiatric hospitals treated them more often. These authors suggested that the relatively high rate of psychiatric hospitalization for girls in their sample could be attributed to an overall denial of educational services to girls, especially services at an early stage of intervention. Although female adolescents use fewer services, in the juvenile justice system they are more likely than boys to be incarcerated for minor offenses (Chesney-Lind, 1988), even though they commit fewer and less serious offenses than do boys (Ageton & Elliott, 1978). Chesney-Lind's review showed that, despite the relatively minor nature of their offenses, more female adolescents than male end up in adult jails nationwide.

In this chapter, we review research on the prevalence and form of severe antisocial behavior in girls and discuss implications for their long-term adjustment into adulthood and motherhood. We describe an ongoing clinical trial aimed at developing a treatment for severely antisocial girls referred from the juvenile justice system. We review the study design and measurement strategy, and then present the risk factor profiles of participating girls and compare them with those of boys with similar juvenile justice backgrounds. We focus on similarities and differences in the histories of trauma, mental health symptoms, and family risk factors that girls and boys in our studies have experienced.

OVERVIEW OF RESEARCH ON THE PREVALENCE AND FORM OF SEVERE ANTISOCIAL BEHAVIOR IN GIRLS

Over the past two decades, epidemiological studies have shown mixed results on the relative prevalence of severe conduct problems during adolescence for boys and girls (reviewed in Zoccolillo, 1993). A consistent finding (except in the Isle of Wight sample; Graham & Rutter, 1973) is that the high male-to-female ratio diminishes from preadolescence to adolescence. For example, findings from the Dunedin studies (Anderson, Williams, McGee, & Silva, 1987; McGee, Feehan, Williams, & Anderson, 1992) showed significant differences by gender in the prevalence of conduct problems at age 11 years (i.e., 1.9% girls; 6.3% boys) but no differences at age 15. However, 15-year-old boys and girls differed in the rate of aggressive conduct problems (i.e., 0% of girls; 3.1% of boys). Zoccolillo (1993) raised the question of whether this finding, which is replicated elsewhere (e.g., Esser, Schmidt, & Woerner, 1990), is due to a later onset of conduct problems or due to a lack of sensitivity of methods for detection of early symptoms in girls.

Some studies have shown that the magnitude of sex differences in aggression depends on how aggression is defined. For example, when researchers administered measures of conflict and aggression to fourth graders, boys and girls reported equal rates of conflicts with peers. However, physical aggression was more common for boys, whereas snubbing and ignoring were more common for girls (Cairns & Cairns, 1994). In assessing developmental changes from fourth through ninth grades, Cairns, Cairns, Neckerman, Ferguson, and Gariepy (1989) found that rates of physical aggression declined for conflicts between boys, whereas social alienation and ostracism dramatically increased in conflicts between girls. Other studies have found no overall gender differences in aggressive behavior, but boys tend to show more physical aggression and girls more verbal aggression (Hartup, 1974).

Indirect aggression, which is not overt but rather delivered circuitously, appears to be more characteristic of girls than boys (Cairns, Cairns, Neckerman, Ferguson, et al., 1989). Crick examined gender differences in the form of male and female aggression in two recent studies (Crick, 1995; Crick & Grotpeter, 1995). She assessed overt and "relational" forms of aggression in elementary school children. Overt aggression included physical and verbal aggression of the type typically studied. Relational aggression included exclusion, gossip, and collusion directed at relational bonds between friends. Using peer nominations, similar proportions of boys and girls were classified by their peers as nonaggressive (73% of boys, 78% of girls). However, boys and girls differed dramatically in how they expressed aggression; 15.6% of boys and only 0.4% of girls were classified exclusively as overtly aggressive, whereas 17.4% of girls and 2.0% of boys were classified exclusively as relationally aggressive. An additional 9.0% of boys and 4.0% of girls displayed both overt and relational aggression.

Underwood (1995) examined whether nonverbal behaviors such as disdainful facial expressions, ignoring, and eye rolling would be perceived by children as hurtful. She compared the effects of these "socially aggressive" behaviors with those of physical aggression for 9-, 12-, and 15-year-olds. For all three groups, mean ratings of hurtfulness for social aggression were greater for girls than for boys. The findings support the notion that forms of aggression other than physical fighting and threats are salient for girls.

Gender differences have been found both in the type of aggression expressed and in the interactional contexts in which they occur. Beginning in early childhood, boys are more likely to engage in rough-and-tumble play, whereas girls typically play less physically and in dyads. Sex role prohibitions against physical aggression are stronger for girls, and physically aggressive girls are more disliked by peers than their male counterparts (Pepler, 1995). Yet, by adolescence physical aggression is not as rare among girls as one might expect. According to self-report data from the Ontario Child Health Study, 7% of girls (compared with 12% of boys) said they had physically attacked someone (Offord et al., 1991). Similarly, Cairns and his colleagues (Cairns, Cairns, Neckerman, Ferguson, et al., 1989) found that 25% of 7th-grade girls and 12% of 11th-grade girls admitted to engaging in physical fights with a female friend. These data on physical aggression are consistent with the notion that for girls, aggression tends to be expressed in close relationships rather than in the community at large (Pepler & Craig, 1999).

Although, in general, girls may be at lower risk for conduct problems than boys, those who are aggressive as adolescents are more likely than male adolescents to exhibit comorbid depression (Loeber & Keenan, 1994). Crick and her colleagues (Crick & Grotpeter, 1995) found that, regardless of gender, relationally aggressive children were significantly more rejected by peers and reported more loneliness and depression. Relationally aggressive children demonstrated more hostile attributions to ambiguous social scenarios than did nonaggressive children and reported feeling more upset in these situations.

AGGRESSION AND EARLY MOTHERHOOD

Several researchers have found a relationship between aggressive behavior during childhood and adolescent childbearing. Cairns, Cairns, and

Neckerman (1989), for example, found that membership in an aggressive peer group in the seventh grade related to dropping out of school, which in turn related to adolescent childbearing. Further, two-thirds of the adolescent mothers in that study were the girls considered to be "high risk" because of aggression, poor academic performance, and low socioeconomic status.

Underwood, Kupersmidt, and Coie (1996) examined the frequency and timing of adolescent childbearing as a function of aggression and peer sociometric status. Peer nominations were made for status (i.e., popular, average, rejected, neglected, and controversial) and aggression when girls were in the fourth grade. Eleven years later, county birth certificates were examined for the 79% of the original sample who still resided in the area. Half of the aggressive girls became mothers compared with 25% of the nonaggressive girls ($p < .05$). *Controversial* girls—those who in the fourth grade were well liked by some peers and disliked by others—also had a 50% childbearing rate, which was significantly higher than for any other peer sociometric status group. The researchers considered aggression and controversial status separately in these analyses. There was only a 19% overlap between controversial and aggressive girls. Besides an elevated frequency of births, these investigators also found that both aggressive and controversial girls gave birth earlier and had more births than those in other groups.

The Underwood et al. (1996) study identified two vulnerable subgroups of female adolescents: those who are aggressive and those who have controversial peer status. Controversial children have certain shared characteristics with aggressive children. Most importantly, both groups engage in antisocial and risk-taking behaviors and break rules (Coie & Dodge, 1988; Coie, Dodge, & Coppotelli, 1982). Capaldi (1991) found that similar factors contributed to boys' engaging in early sexual intercourse. In Capaldi's longitudinal study, levels of antisocial behavior and association with deviant peers during the fourth grade contributed to boys' engaging in sexual intercourse by the ninth grade. Peer status and aggression may relate to adolescent motherhood because they both shape the social world in which the girls operate (Cairns, Cairns, & Neckerman, 1989), especially in terms of future friendship selection.

Once an adolescent becomes a mother, she is at risk for multiple and cascading negative effects. At the very least, being a mother constrains her social, academic, and work opportunities. In numerous studies, adolescent motherhood has been associated with serious educational, financial, and relationship problems for teenage girls (Furstenberg, Brooks-Gunn, & Chase-Lansdale, 1989) and, in turn, with negative effects on psychological functioning (Kellam, Adams, Brown, & Ensiminger, 1992). The earlier adolescent mothers have their first child, the more negative the effects appear to be on the mother. For example, if mothers are 15 years or younger at the time that they give birth, they complete one-and-a-half fewer years of schooling than those who have children born in later adolescence (Hofferth & Moore, 1979).

PROBLEMS FOR THE NEXT GENERATION:
TRANSMISSION OF TRAUMA

Children of adolescent mothers are at risk for negative outcomes. In particular, mothers with a history of severe antisocial behavior as adolescents put the next generation at risk in a multitude of ways. As adults, girls who have been antisocial as adolescents are more likely than non-antisocial girls to (a) affiliate with antisocial men (Quinton & Rutter, 1988); (b) be in violent, abusive relationships (Rosenbaum & O'Leary, 1981); (c) get divorced (Rosenbaum, 1989); (d) exhibit poor parenting skills (Capaldi & Patterson, 1991); and (e) have lower incomes and receive welfare. These and related outcomes result in a greatly increased risk for a child to behave in an aggressive and antisocial manner. For example, the Oregon Youth Study (Capaldi, 1991) has followed a sample of at-risk boys for 10 years, since they were in the fourth grade. In that sample, mothers who gave birth to their first child by age 20 were twice as likely (35% vs. 18%) to have study sons with arrest records before boys were age 14.

In their follow-up of institution-reared girls ($n = 81$) and boys ($n = 90$), Rutter and Quinton (1984) found that women who had experienced severe breakdowns in their upbringing were more likely to have significant difficulties raising their own children, and more of these girls gave up care of their children to other people. In contrast, as adults, men who were institution-reared rarely had their children taken into care. The institution-reared girls were significantly more likely than control girls to become teenage parents (41% vs. 5%), whereas for boys the difference was much smaller (8.9% institution-reared vs. 2.45% control).

More broadly, there is evidence in the psychiatric literature that women with chronic or recurring problems tend to transmit problems to their offspring. Other than through genetic means, there are two primary psychosocial mechanisms through which this transmission is hypothesized to occur. The first, documented in numerous studies, is that disturbed or deviant mothers are more likely to provide their children with poor parenting (Hare & Shaw, 1965; Keller et al., 1986; Lyons-Ruth, Zoll, Connell, & Grunebaum, 1989). The second is that such mothers tend to marry men who also have severe psychiatric, personality, or substance abuse problems (Merikangas & Spiker, 1982; Westen, Ludolph, Misle, Ruffins, & Block, 1990; Zoccolillo, Pickles, Quinton, & Rutter, 1992), or who are violent (Lewis, Yeager, Cobham-Portorreal, Showalter, & Anthony, 1991). Andrews, Brown, and Creasey (1990) found that daughters of mothers with chronic problems reported three times more early trauma experiences than those whose mothers had no disorder or only one episode. They were also subjected to physical or sexual abuse by their mothers' partners significantly more often. On the other hand, selection of a nondeviant male partner has been shown to have a protective effect (Rutter & Quinton, 1984). In summary, the presence of psychiatric problems, including severe conduct problems in female adolescents, is increasingly recognized as a significant problem that is likely to have negative ramifications both for their own adult adjustment (Robins & Price, 1991; Zoccolillo et al., 1992) and for the future adjustment of their offspring.

RESEARCH ON INTERVENTION EFFECTIVENESS

The numbers of girls being referred to services by the juvenile justice system has increased nationally during the past decade, as it has in our community. In 1984, after our Multidimensional Treatment Foster Care (MTFC) program for male juvenile offenders had been established for only one year, it became apparent that there was an increasing community demand to serve girls. We went to the literature to search for promising intervention strategies for this population.

Several studies document that severe antisocial behavior in adolescence leads to extremely poor adult adjustment for women (e.g., Robins & Price, 1991; Zoccolillo & Rogers, 1991). Robins and her colleagues have shown in several studies that, whereas men who were antisocial adolescents are more likely to engage in criminal activities as adults, women are more at risk for diverse types of poor outcomes. For example, Robins and Price (1991) found that, regardless of other types of psychiatric problems, conduct problems in girls predicted poor long-term outcomes such as internalizing disorders, early pregnancy, and high use of social services.

The few studies that have evaluated the effects of confinement or therapeutic interventions aimed at girls portray a grim picture. For example, Lewis and colleagues (1991) found that for a sample of incarcerated boys and girls, significantly fewer girls had been rearrested in adulthood (71% vs. 95% of the boys). However, long-term outcomes for girls were poor. Of 21 participants in the original sample, only 6 had completed high school, 4 had participated in prostitution, 19 had attempted suicide (with 1 success), 15 had serious drug problems, 13 were or had been involved in seriously violent relationships with men, and 1 had died of AIDS. These authors also followed 159 women who had been committed to the California Youth Authority from 1961 to 1969, and who had been randomly assigned to incarceration or community treatment. Before the random assignment, girls had an average of 4.6 arrests, and two thirds of the sample were primarily status offenders (i.e., nonserious offenses for which an adult would not be charged, such as running away or minor in possession). Following treatment, persistent offending continued; the treatment had no effect. The mean number of arrests was 7.2, and the seriousness of the girl's offenses increased. As adults, only 4% had no further arrests, 27% had at least two arrests, 40% had been arrested for crimes against persons, and 60% were incarcerated at least once during the period of the adult follow-up.

TABLE 7.1
Youth Demographics

Variable	Boys (n = 51)		Girls (n = 37)	
	M	SD	M	SD
Age at intake	14.54	1.50	14.8	1.45
Age of first offense	11.91	2.22	12.89	1.32*
Number of prior placements	2.52	7.64	4.26	4.79*
Total arrests	10.84	5.87	8.43	4.12*
Mean total risk factors (of 18 measured)	6.96	2.30	7.34	2.40

*$p < .05$.

Zoccolillo and Rogers (1991) examined long-term outcomes for 55 White, middle-class, female adolescents who had been hospitalized and who had severe conduct problems (i.e., they met the criteria for conduct disorder). At 2 to 4 years postdischarge, they found a 6% mortality rate (twice the national rate), a 35% pregnancy rate (compared with an 8% state rate), and high school dropout rates that were significantly higher than the national average. Although many of these girls had comorbid emotional disorders, the authors concluded that it was the presence of severe conduct problems that determined their poor long-term prognosis.

A MULTIDIMENSIONAL TREATMENT FOSTER CARE APPROACH FOR GIRLS WITH SEVERE ANTISOCIAL BEHAVIOR

In 1988 we published a study where we examined gender differences in initial risk factors and responsiveness to MTFC for 88 consecutive boys and girls referred by juvenile justice (Chamberlain & Reid, 1994). Table 7.1 shows data on age, arrest, and placement history for the 51 male and 37 female participants of that study, and Table 7.2 identifies pretreatment family and child risk factors.

As can be seen in Table 7.1, the boys tended to be younger at the time of their first arrest by almost 10 months, and boys had more total offenses and felonies at the time of referral to MTFC. Girls, on the other hand, showed more evidence of family disruption and chaos. Girls had been placed out of their family homes significantly more often and had been sexually abused at four times the rate of the boys. Girls were also more likely than their male counterparts to have attempted suicide and to have run away two or more times.

Outcomes examined included posttreatment rates of criminal offenses and program completion rates. In addition to measuring outcomes, we looked at the daily rate of problem behaviors for boys and girls during the first and

TABLE 7.2
Youth Risk Factors

Risk factors	Boys		Girls	
	N	%	N	%
Family risk factors				
One-parent family at intake	30	57	17	52
Income less than $10,000	28	53	17	52
Parents ever divorced	41	77	31	87
Three or more siblings	15	28	10	29
Siblings institutionalized	11	21	9	26
Adopted	5	9	7	20
Mother hospitalized	5	9	3	9
Father convicted	8	15	6	18
Family violence	35	66	26	74
Abuse				
Victim of physical abuse	27	51	12	34
Victim of sexual abuse	6	11	17	49
Perpetrated sexual abuse	8	15	0	0*
Child risk factors				
Attempted suicide	3	6	10	29*
Two or more runaways	29	56	30	86*
Charged with felony	47	89	18	51*
Firesetting	8	15	1	3
Serious drug or alcohol	23	43	18	51
Chronic truancy	41	77	29	83
Less than 1 year below grade level	24	45	22	63

*p < .05.

last months of their participation in MTFC, as reported by the MTFC parents. We were interested in examining how behavior problems unfolded over time, as the MTFC parents had told us they preferred to provide placements for boys because it was less stressful. We were curious about this because boys appeared to be a higher risk for causing problems in the foster homes as they had committed more property and person-to-person crimes than had girls before treatment.

Prior to intake, the 51 male participants had an average of 10.8 offenses (SD = 5.87) and the 37 female participants had an average of 8.43 offenses (SD = 4.12, p < .05). We found significant gender differences on age of first offense (boys were younger) and on number of prior out-of-home placements (girls had more). Girls also had attempted suicide and had run away more frequently, whereas boys had more felonies.

The MTFC treatment was equally effective in reducing criminal offenses for boys and girls. On rates of status offenses, both girls and boys decreased their rates of offending over time, as they did on person-to-person crimes. On property crimes, both sexes dropped significantly, with boys showing a greater decrease in the rate of property crimes than girls. Program completion rates also showed no difference for boys and girls (i.e., 71% of boys and 73% of girls completed). This was a post hoc analysis, complete with all of the limitations associated with this type of retrospective approach. However, on major outcomes (criminal offenses and program completion) relating to program goals, girls did as well as their male counterparts in MTFC. Although this was a service program with no funded research component, clinically we were aware of differences that we wanted to explore using the limited types of data we had been able to collect.

We examined the patterns of problem behavior demonstrated by girls and boys in their MTFC homes. The Parent Daily Report (PDR) checklist that was administered during treatment to MTFC parents daily (Monday–Friday) by telephone generated data on problem behavior patterns. To compare initial levels of conduct problems, as well as the patterns over time, we examined the rate of foster-parent-reported problems for the first month (20 calls) and the sixth month (20 calls), which was typically the last month of placement. Researchers have used PDR in treatment outcome (Dadds & McHugh, 1992) and longitudinal research (Patterson, Reid, & Dishion, 1992) to assess the presence of and changes in rates of conduct and emotional problems.

We found a gender-by-time interaction ($p = .005$), indicating that boys began the program with higher daily rates of problem behaviors and these decreased over time, whereas girls had the opposite pattern: Their foster parents reported fewer problem behaviors at first and over time these increased. Whether girls "wore" more on the foster homes in which they were placed or became more aggressive and noncompliant over time in the home could not be determined from these data. We hypothesize that in not targeting relational or social forms of aggression in these girls, we missed a key set of problem behaviors that compromised their relationship with their MTFC parents. The subtle nature of these behaviors coupled with our lack of an intervention strategy to help foster parents deal with them precluded inclusion of relational or social aggressive behaviors as treatment targets. Likewise, we did not target teaching girls alternative ways of expressing their concerns and anger that could help them maintain positive relationships with the adults who were attempting to help them. At any rate, these data were consistent with the perception by MTFC parents and program staff that girls were more difficult to treat than boys.

Although girls might have benefited from MTFC as much as boys in terms of reductions in criminal offense rates, we realized that we needed to reconceptualize and adapt aspects of our MTFC model to be more responsive to the clinical needs of girls. Also, solid treatment effectiveness conclusions could not be drawn from the pilot study described above because there was no control group, and the one-year follow-up period limited the look at long-term recidivism. In 1996, we began a study to examine the histories and risk factors of girls in the juvenile justice system and the effectiveness of an MTFC model modified to address the clinical needs of girls referred from juvenile justice.

THE OREGON STUDY OF FEMALE
DELINQUENCY: PROCESSES AND OUTCOMES

We are currently funded by the National Institute of Mental Health (MH54257) to study female adolescents (ages 12–18) referred from the juvenile justice system. Participants are randomly assigned to one of two treatment conditions: MTFC or group care (GC). All participating girls have been screened by their local juvenile justice department staff and recommended for placement in out-of-home care due to severe and chronic delinquency. After girls are referred to the study, we obtain consent to participate from the girls and their guardians. Next, girls are assessed using a multimethod, multiagent (i.e., different types of measures gathered from a variety of reporters) assessment strategy. We focus on several domains that are thought to influence girls' long-term adjustment. These include criminal behavior, mental health, history of trauma and abuse, parenting practices girls have experienced, educational history, substance use, sexual history, and relational aggression. After the baseline assessment, girls are placed in either MTFC or GC (determined by random assignment).

In MTFC one girl is placed in a family home where the foster parents have been recruited and trained, and are supervised to provide a set of treatment components that are hypothesized to be related to specific short- and long-term outcomes. In GC, girls are placed with from 6 to 15 peers who are experiencing similar problems with delinquency. The primary purpose of the study is twofold: to evaluate systematically the short- and long-term outcomes for girls participating in the experimental intervention (MTFC) relative to those in the control condition, and to evaluate the contribution of the treatment components to immediate and long-term outcomes. Short-term outcomes include association with antisocial peers, negative departures from treatment, contact with prosocial peers, school adjustment and performance, and high-risk sexual contacts. Long-term outcomes of interest include delinquency; drug use; relationships with non-antisocial romantic partners; and rates of school completions, occupational functioning, early pregnancies, and sexually transmitted diseases. In addition to examining the effects of the treatment condition on short- and long-term outcomes, we look at the relationships between the girl's history and her subsequent adjustment.

In this study we have hypothesized that, regardless of placement setting (MTFC or GC), girls' better short- and long-term outcomes will be determined by the extent to which they receive a set of key treatment components. These components include close supervision, consistent discipline, positive caring by a mentoring adult, relationship-building skills, monitoring of and help with school work, and education on avoiding high-risk sexual contacts. Further, we expect that to the extent that the posttreatment living situation supports these components, girls will do well in follow-up.

At this point, 36 girls have been enrolled in the study. Their characteristics and risk factors are discussed next.

CHARACTERISTICS AND RISK FACTORS OF STUDY PARTICIPANTS

Trauma and Abuse

To examine the history of trauma and abuse, we asked girls to complete the Assessing Environments III (AEIII) and the Lifetime Childhood Sexual Experiences questionnaires. The AEIII questionnaire was developed for use in studies investigating punitive childhood experiences of adolescents and adults (Berger, Knutson, Mehm, & Perkins, 1988). Zaidi and colleagues (1991) developed the childhood sexual history questionnaire for the National Center for Post-Traumatic Stress Disorder, and we have adapted it to a computer-based administration format. Psychometric properties for both of these measures have been found to be good.

On the AEIII, we calculated the percentage of girls in the study who met the criteria for having been physically abused, as defined by Berger and colleagues (1988). Compared with a sample of over 4,500 college men and women, 64% of study girls met the Berger and colleagues criteria for physical abuse compared with 9% in the college sample.

History of Childhood Sexual Experiences

Girls' histories of sexual abuse were equally severe. We analyzed the percentage of girls who reported experiencing a series of 14 sexual acts, the average age at the first time they experienced the act, and the percentage of those who experienced each act who were younger than age 12 when it first occurred. As can be seen in Table 7.3, the majority of these girls have experienced severe forms of sexual abuse at young ages. The average age at which at least one of these sexual experiences occurred for study girls was 7.1 years.

Family Factors

We examined girls' histories of stability and transition in parent figures. We asked them who they have lived with (i.e., parent figures), from their birth through the present, and then we asked them to report any changes throughout their lives. We counted each change in the parent figures living with them as one parental transition. So, for example, if they were residing with their mother and father when they were born and then their father left (1) and mother's new boyfriend moved in (2), that would be two parental transitions. If they were then placed in foster care (3), were returned to live

TABLE 7.3
Lifetime Childhood Sexual Experiences (Reported at Referral)

In your lifetime, did someone ever . . .	Affirmative responses[a]		Age (years)		Age at 1st time (years)		Experienced it 1st under age 12	
	%	n	M	SD	Min.	Max.	%[b]	n
Make inappropriate comments about sex or about sexual parts of your body	75.9	22	7.18	3.97	2	14	77.3	17
Flash or expose their sexual parts to you	75.9	22	7.00	4.41	2	15	72.7	16
Spy on or watch you while you were bathing, dressing, or using the bathroom	55.2	22	8.67	4.41	3	15	60.0	9
Ask you to watch sexual acts including masturbation or intercourse	32.1	9	7.89	4.86	3	15	66.7	6
Touch an intimate or private part of your body in a way that surprised you or made you uncomfortable	70.0	21	7.14	4.34	2	14	66.7	14
Rub their genitals against you	72.4	21	8.90	4.46	3	15	52.1	11
Ask you to touch them in an intimate or private part of their body	79.3	23	7.96	4.46	3	16	65.2	15
Force you to kiss them in a sexual rather than an affectionate way	53.3	16	8.56	4.37	3	14	56.3	9
Ask you to have genital intercourse	72.4	21	11.71	3.07	5	17	33.0	7
Ask you to perform oral intercourse on them	69.0	20	10.60	4.60	3	17	35.0	7
Perform oral intercourse on you against your will	37.9	11	8.18	5.07	3	15	54.5	6
Ask you to have anal intercourse	27.6	8	13.25	2.76	8	15	25.0	2
Try to have any type of intercourse with you against your will but not actually do so	46.4	13	9.38	4.52	3	15	61.5	8
Make you pose for sexy or suggestive pictures	20.0	6	11.17	4.07	3	14	16.7	1

Note. Min. = minimum; Max. = maximum.
[a]*N* = 30. One or two girls did not answer 11 items. Thus, % represents valid percentages (omitting missing data from the denominator).
[b]The denominator for this percentage is the number of girls who had the specific experience.

with an aunt and uncle (4), and then the uncle left (5), a total of five transitions would be counted. We counted as a transition any time a parent figure came in or out of the girls' home or when they were placed in the custody of another adult or in residential care. At baseline, girls have had an average of 16 parental transitions, a little over one for each year of their lives.

We examined rates of parent criminality for the girls studied and compared the rates with those for parents of a group of boys who had also been referred by juvenile justice and who had participated in a parallel study conducted from 1990 to 1996 (Chamberlain & Reid, 1998). The two samples (girls and boys) were similar in age at referral (means: girls, 14.6 years; boys, 14.4 years) and on the percentage that had been adopted (girls, 8%; boys, 9%). Differences were found for rates of parents who had been convicted of a crime. Forty-three percent of girls' mothers had been convicted of a crime, compared with 9.5% of boys' mothers. Seventy percent of girls' fathers had been convicted of a crime versus 22% of boys' fathers. Both of these differences were significant ($p = .05$). Seventy-two percent of the girls had at least one parent convicted as compared with 22% of the boys. We examined the rates of out-of-home placements for girls and boys and again found a significant difference ($p < .01$), with girls averaging 3.9 previous out-of-home placements and boys averaging 1.33.

Although, unfortunately, we did not measure history of trauma or sexual experiences in our male offender sample, our data on parent criminality and rates of out-of-home placements suggest that girls who were referred from juvenile justice come from families that are extremely chaotic and distressed, even compared with the highly distressed families of juvenile justice–referred boys. The high rate of early sexual abuse and large number of parental transitions contributes to the picture of extreme instability, neglect, and abuse this group of girls has experienced. These data suggest that studies examining precursors to the development of antisocial behavior would be remiss if they failed to look at the possible impact of multiple and sustained traumas and lack of parental guidance and care on girls' developmental trajectory.

Mental Health Problems

We assessed mental health problems through examination of the self-report of symptoms on the Brief Symptom Inventory (BSI; Derogatis & Spencer, 1982), where we compared scores on five scales for girls and boys. We also administered the DISC-2 Interview (Shaffer, Fisher, Piacentini, Schwab-Stone, & Wicks, 1989), which tracks girls' mental health diagnoses using the *DSM–IV* criteria. In addition, we have coded files to determine what percentage of girls and boys have made a documented suicide attempt. On this variable, we found a significant difference between girls and boys with 64% of girls and 3% of boys having attempted suicide. Girls' and boys' scores on the five BSI scales reflect the same trend. In Table 7.4, we show the percentage of girls and boys in the two juvenile justice–referred samples who met clinical cutoff criteria on five of the BSI scales. On every scale, more

TABLE 7.4

Percentage of Boys and Girls From the Juvenile Justice System Meeting
Clinical Cutoffs on *Brief Symptom Inventory*

Diagnosis	Boys ($n = 52$)	Girls ($n = 36$)
Depression	8	40
Anxiety	11	80
Paranoid	10	67
Somatic	5	87
Hostility	4	47

girls than boys report levels of symptoms that put them in the clinical range. DISC-2 data confirm a high rate of endorsement of psychiatric symptoms for girls; of the 36 girls interviewed so far, 53% of them have met criteria for three or more Axis I disorders on the *DSM–IV*. This is clearly a highly distressed group of youngsters who have substantial mental health problems.

Criminal and Antisocial Behavior

It is well documented in the literature that girls tend to commit fewer and less serious crimes than boys. In our samples, boys referred to a parallel study had 14 offenses prior to entering the study. The first 25 girls who entered the study have an average of 9.9 prior offenses ($p < .05$). Interestingly, before entering the study, boys had spent an average of 73 days in detention during the past year, whereas girls (with fewer offenses) spent an average of 81 days in detention during the past year.

In addition to collecting data on official reports of criminal activity, we collect youth self-reports of criminal activities at regular intervals. Official reports are known to provide a biased underestimate of the volume and seriousness of criminal acts (Elliott & Voss, 1974) because only a small fraction of such acts are detected by the police, and different precincts and communities vary in which offenses are written up and processed. Several investigators have agreed that compared with official reports, self-reports better capture the actual nature, incidence, and frequency of juvenile offending (Capaldi & Patterson, 1996; Erickson & Empey, 1963). All girls in the ongoing study and boys from the previous study completed the Elliott Behavior Checklist (EBC; Elliott, Ageton, Huizinga, Knowles, & Canter, 1983), a confidential self-report of delinquency. The report asks youths how many times they engaged in any of the criminal behaviors during a specific time frame. Scores on three subscales are reported: General Delinquency, Index Offenses, and Felony Assaults. The EBC has demonstrated good psychometric properties.

Table 7.5 lists scores for girls and boys on three EBC scales. As can be seen, boys report committing more serious offenses (index offenses and felony assaults). Surprisingly, girls report committing more delinquent acts in the general delinquency category than do boys. We also examined boys' and girls'

TABLE 7.5
Youth Incidents in the Past Year From the *Self-Reports Elliott Scale*

Incident	Boys	Girls
Index offenses	63	31
Felony assault	13	10
General delinquency	385	502
Loud or rowdy	12	83
Drunk or public	7	26
Obscene phone calls	5	50

reports of how many of their friends engaged in delinquent behaviors. Youths were asked to report if from none (1) to all (5) of their friends had committed a series of delinquent acts in the past 6 months. Table 7.6 shows that girls consistently rate their friends as being significantly more delinquent than do boys.

GENDER-RELATED ADAPTATIONS TO THE OREGON MULTIDIMENSIONAL TREATMENT FOSTER CARE MODEL

As has been discussed in this chapter and elsewhere (Keenan et al., 1999), most theories of criminality are largely founded on characteristics and observations of males and the social conditions that affect them. Historically, theories of female criminality have tended to center on individual and pathological factors, whereas male crime has been explained by social and cultural factors (Bloom, 1998). During the past two decades, increasing attention has been paid to the possible role of contextual (family, peer, and system) factors in female delinquency. It is now recognized that girls in the juvenile justice system have multiple and complex needs in addition to controlling their criminal, antisocial, and often self-destructive behavior. Interventions need to be tailored to the specific problems and barriers to productive adjustment that these girls face.

The Oregon MTFC model attempts to provide girls with several basic program components plus individualized services and supports that address their specific needs. Basic program components are organized around the notion of providing a safe and supportive family living environment. Because the girls we are working with have such severe histories of chaos and disruption in their living situations, a primary goal is to stabilize them and to stop the pattern of moving from one placement to the next, especially when placement changes are unplanned and are a reaction to a negative set of circumstances. Like their male counterparts referred from juvenile justice, girls enrolled in our MTFC program have histories of chronic and severe delinquency and need to be well supervised by adults and separated from delinquent peers, particularly in situations in which they are unsupervised. They also seem to benefit from being given clear and teaching-oriented di-

TABLE 7.6
Boys' and Girls' Ratings of Their Friends' Delinquency

Friend incident	Boys	Girls
Hit or threatened	2.9	4.1
Damaged property	2.8	3.8
Drove without permission	2.2	3.4
Stole more than $50	2.6	3.3
Sold drugs	2.6	3.5
Drank	3.5	4.2

rection and mentorship by a positive female adult (i.e., the female MTFC parent). The role of the female MTFC parent is well defined in this regard.

To help accomplish these goals, program staff closely supervise MTFC parents during daily telephone calls and weekly meetings. Staff give special attention to interactional dynamics between the foster mother and girl in an attempt to head off escalating negative confrontations and the buildup of angry feelings that can potentially lead to a replication of the girl's history of disrupted relationships with significant adults.

Another important consideration is the orientation of girls toward planning for their futures. Findings from the work of Rutter (1989) and others (Walsh, 1999) suggest that, for female adolescents, a planning orientation protects against future antisocial behavior. In the MTFC model, each girl works weekly with an individual therapist who is available to address issues of the girl's choosing. The therapist introduces the notion of future planning and assists the girl to identify short- and long-term goals and to take steps toward their actualization. In addition, the girl's therapist helps her problem solve around difficulties she may be encountering in the MTFC home, in school, with peer relations, or in other situations. The individual therapist follows the girl's agenda with regard to working on issues related to sexual and physical abuse. Clinically, we think it is unwise to push girls to deal with these issues given that doing so typically increases their levels of anxiety and stress. Therapists encourage girls to identify themes and topics to work on in the context of the individual therapy.

The program provides family treatment to girls' biological (or adoptive) families to prepare for reunification. The goal of family treatment is to help parents prepare for their girl's return home and specifically to become more effective at supervising, encouraging, supporting, and following through with consequences with their youngster. One mechanism for accomplishing this is to teach parents to use the point and level system that is part of the daily program in the MTFC home. The family therapist devotes the first sessions to assessing family strengths and areas that need to be improved. The family therapist tries to understand the barriers to effective parenting that have interfered with the parent–child relationship in the past. Parents are asked about and supported in their view of the evolution of the problem.

Both the therapist and program supervisor encourage parents to have frequent contact with staff for updates on their daughter's progress in the program. As the adults who know the child best, parents are asked for continual input into their child's treatment. Parents are given both the therapist's and program supervisor's 24-hour telephone numbers.

Program staff schedule home visits throughout the placement. The first visit is typically short (2–4 hours), followed by a daylong visit, and eventually weekend visits. If the parent is unable or unwilling to closely supervise the youth during the visit, visits take place in the program offices or in another supervised setting.

In MTFC, girls attend public schools. Although school has been an area of major difficulty for many of them, we find that with close supervision and follow-through, most girls can do surprisingly well in public school settings. To monitor in-school performance, attendance, and behavior, girls carry a school card that lists each class. For each class period, there is a place for teachers to rate the girl's behavior as acceptable or unacceptable, to note whether homework has been completed, and to sign their names. The MTFC parents collect the school cards daily, and teacher ratings are converted into points earned or lost on the daily program. Program staff are on-call to remove youngsters from school should they become disruptive. In addition to these standard program features, we conduct school-based interventions, as needed.

CONCLUSION

The data presented in this chapter suggest that the developmental histories of the girls in this juvenile justice sample are filled with extreme and complex trauma. This history appears to put girls at risk for a pattern of daily behavior that is filled with intra- and interpersonal chaos and relational or social aggression. When this chaotic and stressful daily life is coupled with a complex trauma history and includes delinquency and conduct problems, the clinical treatment task is quite complex.

The Oregon Girls Study attempts to organize a treatment approach within a developmental model of female conduct problems. A better understanding of the developmental histories and gender differences in female conduct problems may lead to better defined and targeted treatments. For example, in our sample most girls have already participated in numerous programs that have attempted to treat them for the symptoms of trauma and chaotic histories (e.g., sexual abuse, depression, posttraumatic stress disorder, school problems, family problems, conduct problems), but few, if any, provided a comprehensive approach that focused on their behavioral problems and on increasing positive functioning in their daily lives. It is our experience that, when daily functioning is ignored or undertreated, there tends to be a misuse or overuse of control procedures (i.e., medications and, in our sample, longer periods of incarceration) and an increasing perception that "nothing works."

Initial data from our ongoing girls study is also commensurate with recent developmental work on girls' aggression by others (e.g., work cited throughout this chapter by Rutter, Pepler, Cairns, Crick, and Underwood) in that adolescent female aggression is expressed differently than male aggression. Moreover, female aggression tends to be expressed in interpersonal contexts (i.e., close personal relationships rather than the community at large). In our opinion, until these recent developmental findings on the demographic and topographical differences between boys' and girls' aggression and conduct problems are better disseminated, many treatment agents and agents of social control will fail to identify these gender differences and will continue to label adolescent female aggression in negative and global ways (e.g., diagnosis of "attitude" problems, mental health syndromes, and being labeled "bad girls"). This lack of theoretical and developmental specificity could contribute to intervention models that fail to focus on the present and that are unsuccessful in improving girls' long-term adjustment. This lack of specificity may also lead to the aforementioned perception of hopelessness and thus, to the selection of more restrictive and less contextualized interventions (e.g., incarceration, hospitalization) over that of less-restrictive, community-based psychosocial interventions such as MTFC.

As noted earlier, the social–interactional treatment strategies we use in MTFC have been shown to reduce both male and female adolescent delinquency rates. However, our previous studies and the initial demographic data from our current study suggest that if the relational and social aggressive behaviors associated with the conduct disorders in girls are not directly treated, the girls will remain at risk for negative long-term interpersonal and developmental outcomes (e.g., adult mental health problems, early pregnancy, and poverty). These negative outcomes also include the transmission of trauma, aggression, mental health, and conduct problems intergenerationally. Thus, we are anxious to determine if our attempts to clinically alter a previously successful MTFC model for boys to better understand and treat gender differences such as relational aggression and other behavioral manifestations of traumatic childhoods (e.g., lack of future planning) will ultimately improve the life course trajectories of girls with conduct disorder.

I explore another application of the MTFC model in the next chapter, involving adapting the model for use with young children. Just as the high number of female adolescent delinquents led my colleagues and I to examine tailoring MTFC to the special needs of girls, so the rise in young children in foster care who have complex behavioral and emotional problems led us to create a version of MFTC for this special population.

8

AN APPLICATION OF MULTIDIMENSIONAL TREATMENT FOSTER CARE FOR EARLY INTERVENTION

Despite federal efforts in the early 1980s to direct state agencies to develop programs that prevented placement of children in substitute care and to reunify those who were already in care with their families (Adoption Assistance and Child Welfare Act, 1980), between 1985 and 1995 the number of children in care had increased by 65%. This enormous growth of the foster care population produced a national crisis in the child welfare system, including a shortage of qualified foster parents and caseworkers (Klee, Kronstadt, & Zlotnick, 1997). During the same period, there was an increasing recognition that the children being placed into care had high rates of behavioral, emotional, developmental, and medical problems that were comparable to rates observed in clinical populations (Glisson, 1994; Landsverk, Litrownik, Newton, Ganger, & Remmer, 1996). Not only were more children coming into care, but many of these were children who were challenging to manage.

This chapter is based on the work of Philip A. Fisher, PhD, Oregon Social Learning Center (Fisher & Chamberlain, 2000; Fisher, Ellis, & Chamberlain, 1999; Fisher, Gunnar, Chamberlain, & Reid, 2000) and was coauthored with him.

A shift also occurred in the age of children who were placed in that the proportion of younger children increased. The proportion of foster children younger than age 6 years had increased at about double the rate of the total population of children in care (U.S. General Accounting Office, 1994). Ruff, Blank, and Barnett (1990) suggested that this increase was due to multiple factors, including the birth of more drug-affected babies, increases in efforts for early identification, and the spread of HIV. Taken together, the increase in numbers of children needing placement, the increased severity of their problems, and the trend toward younger age at placement are all factors that have placed increased stress on the foster care system in the United States during the past two decades.

These national trends were mirrored in our local community such that by the early 1990s there were increasing numbers of younger emotionally and behaviorally disturbed children presenting their foster parents with severe and complex problems. Our Multidimensional Treatment Foster Care (MTFC) program began getting referrals to develop placements for preschoolers who had failed in regular foster home placements. It was not unusual for us to be asked to find a home for a 4-year-old who had disrupted more than five previous foster home placements during the previous 6 months. At first we took only cases for which child welfare caseworkers were unable to find suitable homes. Many of these children had extreme or high-profile behavior problems. For example, caseworkers had grave concerns about the appropriateness and safety of foster home placement for a 5-year-old girl who had burned down her family home and was diagnosed with severe attachment disorder and posttraumatic stress disorder.

The increased level of attention to individual problems and focus on close supervision in MTFC provided local caseworkers with an alternative to residential or regular foster home placement for these types of youngsters. However, our MTFC model had been developed to serve older youngsters who had conduct problems and were aggressive, and it quickly became clear to us that we needed to adapt our policies and procedures to meet the developmental needs of this preschool population.

THE EARLY INTERVENTION FOSTER CARE MODEL

Reviews of the literature on risk factors among preschool foster children highlighted three interrelated types of problems that commonly occurred in this population. These included behavioral problems, difficulties with regulation of emotions, and developmental delays. It seemed that a modified MTFC model was an appropriate mechanism for intervention for these youngsters because of the extensive evidence that parenting practices within families mediate the course of these risk factors (see review in Patterson, Reid, & Dishion, 1992). Specific parenting practices that have shown to be effective include engagement with and monitoring of the child, consistent discipline, and positive reinforcement. A further rationale for the focus on parenting strategies is that, prior to entry into school, parental figures are the child's primary agents of socialization. Researchers have found that at this developmental stage, interventions that strengthen the parenting of foster and biological families exert a powerful preventative effect on long-term outcomes (see review in Reid & Eddy, 1997). By affecting change in each of these areas, we hoped to alter the life course trajectory of these children away from subsequent school failure, antisocial behavior, and other conduct problems and toward more positive psychosocial adjustment.

Beginning in 1993, Phil Fisher, a research scientist at Oregon Social Learning Center (OSLC) who up to that point had focused his research on early childhood development, began to lead the effort to adapt the OSLC MTFC model for use with preschoolers. To fund this effort, OSLC received Medicaid authorization from the State of Oregon to treat children who had been placed in foster homes by the state child protective services agency. Referrals included preschool children who had been removed from their family homes because of maltreatment. Typically, these younger children were referred to OSLC because of the extremely challenging aggressive and oppositional behavior that led to their placement disruptions from multiple foster homes. The protective services agency hoped that by placing them in the OSLC program there would be improvements to their behavior and a decrease in the disruption rate. After treating several youngsters who had had disruptions in previous placements, we found that after stabilizing them to the point at which they had a sustained decrease in conduct-related problems, emotional regulation problems and developmental delays could be subsequent targets of the Early Intervention Foster Care (EIFC) intervention.

THE THREE TARGETS OF THE EARLY INTERVENTION FOSTER CARE INTERVENTION

Behavioral Problems

Reducing behavioral problems is typically the most immediate need for most high-risk, preschool-age children in foster care, and therefore is usually the first target of the EIFC intervention. Unlike adolescents, after they are placed, preschoolers tend not to have a "honeymoon period" with an initial low rate of problems. For many, behavior problems have resulted in disruptions from multiple previous foster placements. They are clearly anxious and tend to relate to adults and peers in a negative, aggressive way. This is not surprising given that many have histories of witnessing violence and being victims of abuse. In addition, most have experienced repeated trauma. Although their specific symptoms and circumstances vary, these children have all experienced either neglect or extremely poor parenting.

Treatment provides them with a consistent, safe home environment with clear parental expectations and a great deal of nurturing. We specifically train EIFC foster parents to provide a high rate of positive reinforcement for prosocial behaviors and deliver mild and consistent consequences for problem behaviors. We provide EIFC foster parents with daily telephone support, on-call (7 days, 24 hours) access to program supervisors and therapists, and weekly training and support group meetings. Additionally, home visits are regularly scheduled to provide in-home modeling and support.

EIFC maintains the basic elements of the OSLC MTFC model but adapts the behavioral techniques to be age appropriate. For instance, with older adolescents, behavioral contracting to teach positive behavior involves the use of "level systems" in which children work toward increasing responsibility and self-maintenance over a period of days or even weeks. With latency-age youths, contracts typically involve star charts in which youths receive daily rewards for achieving a certain criterion level of stars. With preschoolers, we use more immediate contingencies. Foster parents are trained in the effective use of more concrete token systems, in which immediately following a positive behavior children receive as reinforcement items such as poker chips, stickers, ink stamps on their hand or on a sheet of paper. Depending on the particular child, these tokens may be of sufficient reinforcement value to be used independently, or they may be exchanged for larger rewards once the child has accumulated a certain number of tokens.

There is also a greater emphasis on redirection and distraction techniques with the preschool population. For instance, if a child is starting to play with a toy belonging to another child in the home, or perhaps is refusing to comply with a request, it is often possible to distract the child's attention to an alternative, more appropriate focus. If this is not effective, or if the behavior is more problematic, we teach foster parents to use a brief "time out" procedure. A key issue is helping foster parents find a balance between encouragement of positive behaviors and limit-setting for problem behaviors. As with the adolescents, young children with severe behavior problems tend to elicit negative reactions from others, so the environment of the foster home has potential to become overly punitive. An overall aim of the training and support of foster parents is to help maintain a high ratio of encouragement to limit-setting interactions. The daily contact and consultation with foster parents helps to monitor and encourage this balance.

Developmental Delays

It is not surprising that children with the maltreatment histories of those referred to this program should manifest developmental delays. Indeed, in many ways, more surprising is the extent to which these youths prove resilient in the face of overwhelming challenges to their development. However, if delays in particular areas do exist they can pose a threat to successful outcomes over time. The developmental model of antisocial behavior that has been specified through several longitudinal research programs (Patterson et al., 1992; Reid & Eddy, 1997) documents that as children make the transition into primary school, those who have difficulties conforming to the expectations of the classroom are more likely to experience peer rejection, and labeling by teachers, and consequently experience more problems in the school environment over time. Thus, even if a treatment program is effective at improving behavior in preschool-age foster children, failure to remedy developmental delays may lead to the reemergence of these problems in kindergarten or first grade.

We derived our approach to assessing and treating developmental delays in the EIFC foster care program from the procedures developed by Bricker and colleagues (Bricker, Bailey, & Bruder, 1984; Bricker & Cripe, 1992). Linked systems and activity-based intervention (ABI) are two noteworthy aspects of this approach. Within the linked-systems approach, the screening, assessment, and treatment processes are all part of an integrated effort. Screening identifies children in need of further assessment for developmental delays; assessment specifies the areas in which the delays exist; and treatment targets those areas. ABI is a specific type of treatment for developmental delays within which the environment of the child is structured so as to maximize the opportunities for practicing particular skills. This somewhat naturalistic approach is thought to generalize more readily than direct instruction methods.

Within the EIFC program, an early interventionist screens all children at the time of placement. Those with evidence of delays receive a more in-depth assessment using the Assessment, Evaluation, and Programming System (Bricker, Ayers, Slentz, & Kaminski, 1997). The linked-systems tool also has a curriculum associated with it; once particular delays are determined to exist, the child's treatment team may draw on the linked-systems curriculum to include activities that will facilitate remediation of those delays. This allows a highly individualized approach to remedying developmental delays that can be tailored to each child. Staff in the EIFC program work with both foster parents and preschools and day care centers to address developmental delays using the activity-based intervention approach. This work often includes the development of an individual family service plan and an individualized education plan once the child reaches school age. Focusing on the developmental needs of the child serves to address areas that could cause difficulties during the transition to primary school.

Emotion Regulation

Positive emotional development is a critical component of psychosocial adjustment. However, for many children in the EIFC program, there have been multiple challenges to emotional development. Parental psychopathology and substance use, chaos, and trauma all have the potential to affect emotional development significantly. The specific mechanisms of disruption to emotional regulation have been studied as early as infancy. Tronick and Gianino (1986; Gianino & Tronick, 1985), for instance, have proposed a Mutual Regulation Model (MRM) in which they describe emotion regulation in the infant as part of a larger dyadic process. The MRM articulates the intra-individual and social–interactional processes involved in the development of emotion regulation. The MRM describes the infant and mother as sharing the goal of obtaining a state of emotional reciprocity. The MRM describes the infant as having the dual tasks of regulating both his or her internal emotional state and his or her engagement with the external environment (Tronick & Gianino, 1986). More recently, work by Field (1994) described similar processes, but used the term *attunement*. Field (1987) noted that the mother serves the role of modulating the infant's optimal level of stimulation and arousal. Ideally, infant–mother interactions become synchronous over time. If this is not the case, "the infant experiences behavioral and physiological disorganization, and the mother's and the infant's behavioral and physiological rhythms become asynchronous. This is manifested in affective disturbance and changes in the infant's motor, physiological, or biochemical activity levels" (Field, 1994, p. 214).

If mutual regulation does not occur, in particular if the mother does not respond to the infant's other-directed regulatory behavior, the infant will increasingly favor self-directed regulatory behavior (Gianino & Tronick, 1985). Because self-directed regulatory behavior is by nature less effective in infants, those for whom this is the primary means of regulation are likely to manifest less adequate emotion regulation capabilities, and to exhibit stress coping styles that are less interpersonally engaging (both in the infant–mother relationship and in subsequent relationships). Research on infants of depressed mothers (e.g., Tronick, Als, Adamson, Wise, & Brazelton, 1978) has documented the emergence of these aberrant coping styles. Similarly, Field (1994) summarized her own and her colleagues' research documenting that infant emotion regulation is affected by maternal absence and separation, by emotional unavailability, and by maternal depression. Specifically, these factors all involve depriving the child of his or her primary regulator of stimulation. Therefore, in cases of maltreatment including neglect and abuse, in which maternal absence, unavailability, and depression are common, deviations from typical emotion regulation processes may be expected (Thompson & Calkins, 1996).

The lack of emotion regulation among maltreated preschoolers in foster care is often quite marked. Frequent and prolonged tantrums, destruction of property, and even suicidal ideation are not uncommon phenomena. In addition, many foster parents working with this population report great emotional changeability: A child will move from happy to greatly distressed with little warning and at times without an apparent precipitating incident. Such occurrences are potentially threatening to the development of positive relationships and place the child at great risk for disrupted placements. Interestingly, these problems typically respond to the same system of clear limits and contingencies as is used for dealing with problem behavior. Over time, as the child stabilizes in the foster home and begins to process a broader array of information in the daily environment, greater stability of emotions and better emotional regulatory capabilities become evident.

RESULTS OF A PILOT STUDY EVALUATING THE EFFECTIVENESS OF THE EARLY INTERVENTION FOSTER CARE PROGRAM

The National Institute of Mental Health Prevention branch funded a pilot study of the EIFC program that ran from January 1997 through January 1998. The objectives of the study included examining the psychosocial functioning of maltreated preschoolers in foster care and gathering preliminary evidence of the potential for a foster care-based preventive intervention to reduce risk among maltreated preschoolers for entry into the antisocial developmental trajectory. To accomplish these objectives, we collected data from three groups of 10 children: children referred for services to the EIFC program by the state child welfare system after one or more placement disruptions or because of highly disruptive and aggressive behavior; nonreferred children receiving regular foster care services through the state system (RFC group); and a community comparison group (CC) of same-age children living with their natural families. The pilot study did not include random assignment to the EIFC and RFC conditions. As a result of nonrandom assignment in the pilot study, children in the EIFC condition were generally more troubled and had more severe maltreatment histories than those in the RFC group.

We conducted analyses of variance (ANOVAs) on three parenting scales (see Figure 8.1 for graphs of results). For monitoring, there was a statistically significant effect for group, $F(2, 18) = 18.01, p < .001$. Post hoc analyses revealed that at both time points the RFC group was significantly different from both the EIFC and CC groups, which were not different from each other. For discipline, there was an effect for time, $F(1, 18) = 5.06, p < .05$, with the mean number of discipline items dropping from initial to final assessment. There was also a significant effect for group, $F(2, 18) = 21.69, p < .001$, again with the RFC group significantly different from both the EIFC and CC groups, which were not different from each other at both time points. We observed a similar statistically significant pattern for the group factor on the positive reinforcement scale, $F(2, 15) = 4.96, p < .05$, with the RFC foster parents scoring significantly lower than either EIFC or CC caregivers at both time points.

A. Monitoring

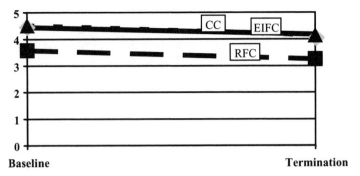

B. Consistent discipline

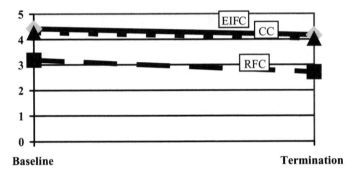

C. Positive reinforcement

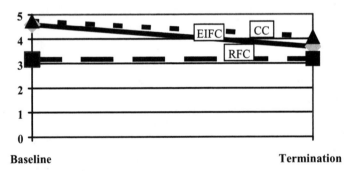

Figure 8.1. Before-and-after measures of monitoring (A), consistent discipline (B), and positive reinforcement (C). CC = community comparison group; EIFC = Early Intervention Foster Care group; RFC = regular foster care group.

There was a marginally significant Time × Treatment Group interaction, $F(2, 12) = 3.24$, $p = .08$, in the amount of stress reported by foster parents as a result of child problem behaviors. Post hoc analysis indicated that EIFC decreased stress, whereas the RFC group showed an increase in reported stress. Effects are illustrated in Figure 8.2.

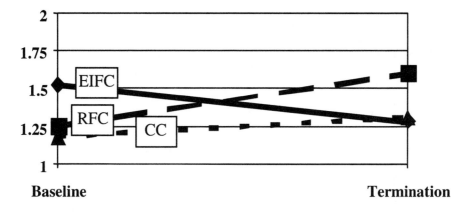

Figure 8.2. Before-and-after measure of stress reported on the Parent Daily Report Telephone Checklist (Chamberlain & Reid, 1987). EIFC = Early Intervention Foster Care group; RFC = regular foster care group; CC = community comparison group.

A mixed-model ANOVA examining number of child symptoms reported by caregivers showed a significant effect for group, $F(2, 26) = 21.27$, $p < .001$, and a significant Group × Time interaction, $F(2, 26) = 4.33$, $p < .05$. Post hoc analyses indicated that the EIFC group, whose reported symptoms decreased, and the RFC group, whose reported symptoms increased, drove this interaction. Figure 8.3 illustrates these effects.

Figure 8.4 shows the plot for each group's weekly cortisol values. As is evident, in the EIFC group, following an initial elevation in cortisol over the first 5 weeks, levels decreased for the next 5 weeks. They again began to increase slightly in Weeks 11 and 12, but the overall trend is a negative quadratic. In contrast, the regular foster care group showed a positive qua-

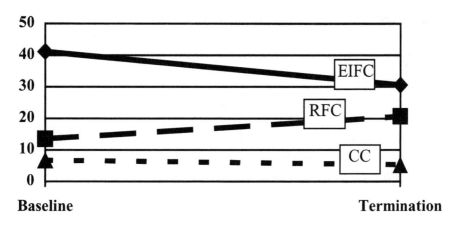

Figure 8.3. Before-and-after measure of psychological symptoms reported on the Early Childhood Inventory (Gadow & Sprafkin, 1994). EIFC = Early Intervention Foster Care group; RFC = regular foster care group; CC = community comparison group.

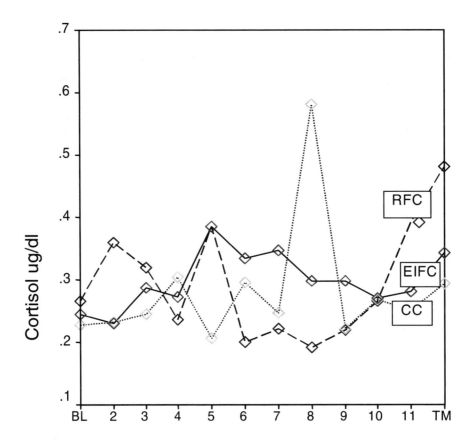

Figure 8.4. Weekly basal cortisol (mid-morning collection). RFC = regular foster care group; EIFC = Early Intervention Foster Care group; CC = community comparison group; BL = baseline; TM = termination.

dratic trend of general decrease in cortisol over the first 6 weeks of the study, but then an increase, rising sharply over the last 4 weeks. A group by time multiple analysis of variance (MANOVA) revealed trends in the effect for time, $F(2, 11) = 4.01$, $p = .10$, and for the Group × Time interaction, $F(10, 22) = 2.18$, $p = .10$. As expected, a test of the within-subject Group × Time quadratic interaction effect was also close to significant ($p = .06$). This reflects the reverse quadratic effects for the EIFC and regular foster care groups.

To further examine group differences in the weekly cortisol levels, we analyzed within-subject variability in weekly cortisol for each of the groups. We computed a within-subjects mean for each child across the 12 weeks of data collection and then computed the absolute value of the difference between the mean and each weekly cortisol level. We then aggregated data for the first and last month of data collection and thereby created a mean variability score for these two time periods. Figure 8.5 shows the values for the three groups. A repeated measures MANOVA revealed significant effects for group, $F(2, 25) = 4.27$, $p < .05$; time, $F(1, 25) = 5.49$, $p < .05$; and for the

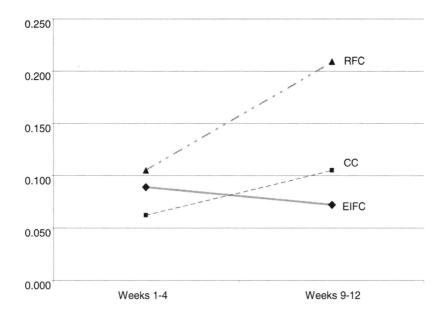

Figure 8.5. Mean absolute value differences from within-subject salivary cortisol means, by group, Weeks 1–4 versus Weeks 9–12. RFC = regular foster care group; EIFC = Early Intervention Foster Care group; CC = community comparison group.

Group × Time interaction, $F(1, 25) = 5.49, p < .05$. Within-subject variability increased for RFC over time and decreased for EIFC over time. Needless to say, the results reported here are very preliminary in nature. They do, however, suggest that children in the EIFC group over time became more similar to the community control group in both basal cortisol and in circadian release patterns, whereas children in the regular foster care group diverge increasingly from the community control group.

Given the multitude and magnitude of risks faced by maltreated preschoolers in the foster care system and the growing numbers of children in these circumstances, there is evidently need for empirically tested early intervention programs specifically designed for this population. The research described here may be considered the first step in the development of such an intervention. What remains are several critical stages of research. First, it will be necessary to conduct a randomized efficacy trial in which the impact of the intervention under ideal circumstances can be evaluated. Such a study is currently under way (Fisher, 1999; Fisher, Ellis, & Chamberlain, 1999). If researchers observe changes similar to those obtained in the present study in the ongoing efficacy trial, the next step will be to conduct a larger scale effectiveness trial in which the emphasis would shift to demonstrating that the impact of the intervention is not lost in the dissemination of the approach to community settings. Only after these steps have been successfully undertaken will it be appropriate to begin to emphasize the incorporation of this approach into public policy discussions. And only after public policy changes have been implemented on the basis of empirically tested intervention methods can we hope to see a reduction in the risks faced by very young children in foster care.

CONCLUSION

The process of moving from conducting exploratory and pilot studies to a larger scale efficacy trial provided the theoretical and empirical underpinnings for the first steps in developing the EIFC approach. This stepwise process has been a productive model for development of programmatic intervention research. Moving empirically tested interventions into larger and more diverse communities and social services agencies is a far more complex and less prescribed undertaking. In the next chapter, I discuss issues relating to dissemination and implementation of MTFC.

9

SOME CHALLENGES
OF IMPLEMENTING
SCIENCE-BASED INTERVENTIONS
IN THE "REAL WORLD"

We began our dissemination efforts in the late 1980s and early 1990s in response to requests from agencies and state and county departments asking us to present workshops on the Multidimensional Treatment Foster Care (MTFC) model. As demand grew for more in-depth information on the model, we augmented 1- or 2-day workshops with periodic weeklong seminars in Oregon. Today MTFC is being used in over a dozen sites throughout the U.S. and in Sweden and Norway. When we began the process of bringing the MTFC intervention to communities several years ago, we anticipated few of the challenges we have since encountered. Our dissemination efforts have taught us that transferring an intervention model from a research-based environment to settings within existing community agencies is not as simple as training agency staff. In this chapter, I describe common barriers and how we have attempted to understand and resolve the problems we have encoun-

This chapter was written in collaboration with Philip A. Fisher, PhD.

tered so far in our efforts to disseminate MTFC. The steps and strategies that we use to help communities implement MTFC will also be described.

Once we moved beyond the "show and tell" stage where we gave 1-day talks about the MTFC model, we began to learn how to get involved in the details of helping agencies implement MTFC effectively. It soon became clear that doing high-quality dissemination would be extremely challenging on many levels and that it was not realistic to try to accomplish this set of complex tasks out of our left pocket. Therefore, in 2001 we established a separate organization, TFC Consultants Inc., whose sole responsibility is planning, implementing, and monitoring the effectiveness of implementations of the MTFC model.

BEGINNINGS AND EXAMPLES

Publication of results from studies on MTFC led to inquiries from various agencies wanting to implement the model. Then, in 1996, MTFC was selected as 1 of 10 national Blueprint Programs by the Colorado Center for the Study and Prevention of Violence, the Centers for Disease Control, and the Office of Juvenile Justice and Delinquency Prevention (Elliott, 1998). More recently, the Oregon MTFC model was highlighted in two Surgeon General reports on children's mental health services and youth violence (U.S. Department of Health and Human Services, 2000a, 2000b). The Safe, Disciplined, and Drug Free Schools Committee from the U.S. Department of Education also named Oregon MTFC an exemplary program. With increased national recognition, more and more communities have begun to ask the question, "What would it take for us to start an MTFC program?"

The first agency to seriously attempt to implement MTFC on a large scale was Youth Villages in Tennessee. In the early 1990s, we began training their staff. Initially, a group of Youth Villages administrators and direct line staff came to our center to observe the program. In addition, we have sent trainers to their site on numerous occasions. Throughout the years we have kept in contact, and some of their staff members continue to have weekly telephone consultation sessions with MTFC program supervisors about individual cases. Youth Villages implements MTFC at several sites in Tennessee. In some of these sites they closely adhere to the MTFC model; in others their practices do not resemble those of MTFC. Currently, Youth Villages serves over 400 children and adolescents per day in Treatment Foster Care (Mendel, 2001), making it the largest site that we know of to implement the model. Youth Villages has not conducted a formal outcome study; however, they report that they are able to serve many more youths in less restrictive placements than they did before being trained in MTFC. They also report that youths are more successful at remaining at home postplacement than they had been before implementation of the model. Youth Villages also reports that MTFC costs substantially less than residential care (Mendel, 2001).

Another more recent implementation of the model has been with the Laurel Hill Youth Services program in Williamsport, Pennsylvania. The program director, David Hall, and three staff members from Laurel Hill were trained in January 2001 and began implementation at their site soon afterward. By six months after the initial training, they had served nine youths, and an additional two had completed the program and had been successfully returned home. The Laurel Hill program serves youths referred from juvenile justice who are in need of out-of-home placement. The program appears to be working well at their site, particularly in dealing with youths who would have been placed in more restrictive residential programs before MTFC was implemented. We continue to do telephone consultations with Laurel Hill staff, view videotapes of their family therapy sessions, and review Parent Daily Report (PDR) data they collect on program youths. They are slated to expand to a second site in the spring of 2003.

Two international applications of MTFC are currently being conducted in Sweden and Norway. Both are being run by private agencies that serve youths referred from child welfare who have severe emotional and behavioral problems. Training for those sites has involved several intensive workshops and visits by their staff to the Oregon site. Preliminary data on outcomes for children served in the Swedish program appear promising (K. Hannson, personal communication, August 2001). The Norway site has just begun.

OVERVIEW OF STEPS FOR IMPLEMENTATION

Implementation of MTFC in other sites involves a series of well-planned steps.[1] We begin by conducting an Organizational Readiness interview with interested agencies. The aim of this interview is to assess such areas as organizational structure, history of service provision, experience implementing other evidence-based models, current resources and staffing patterns, relationships with key community stakeholders (e.g., juvenile justice, mental health), and potential barriers to implementation.

The readiness interview provides information that is then used to map out agency strengths with regard to their potential to conduct MTFC, as well as information about potential barriers to implementation that need to be addressed before implementation can begin. Examples of strengths include a previous history of good collaboration with the local juvenile department or a positive record of recruiting foster parents. Common barriers are having staff housed in a number of different locations or union rules against staff being on call.

After working through the issues identified in the readiness interview, the site identifies a core team of staff members to be trained. The core team

---

[1]The steps described here have so far been used in 12 agencies located throughout the United States. We will continue to revise these methods to improve the effectiveness and relevancy of the training.

should minimally include an administrator, a program supervisor, family and individual therapists, and a foster parent trainer/recruiter (who also conducts PDR calls). The team attends a 4-day training in Oregon during which they participate in training sessions, MTFC parent meetings, and clinical staff meetings. Prior to their Oregon training, we identify the program consultant from the Oregon site. Following the 4-day training and after the agency has recruited foster parents, we send a foster parent trainer to train the first cohort of MTFC parents and prepare them to use the PDR checklist. We have developed a web-based application of the PDR so that sites enter individual child data each day, which are then monitored by the Oregon program consultant. Sites are ready to place youth following the foster parent training and the PDR hook-up.

Once youths are placed, the Oregon program consultant conducts weekly telephone consultation with the program supervisor(s) and therapists and reviews the daily PDR data for all cases placed in the site's program. The PDR checklist was originally developed as an outcome measure in the context of research studies on parent–child interaction patterns. The PDR checklist provides data on the parent's perception of the occurrence of specific child behaviors during the past 24 hours. In MTFC, PDR also includes data on the daily number of points youths have earned and lost and why, and on the number of minutes that they have been unsupervised during the past 24 hours. Each day, MTFC parents are telephoned and asked about the occurrence or nonoccurrence of a list of problem behaviors that are tailored to the developmental level of the child and about the points earned and lost. Having daily data allows the consultant to focus on the specifics of youth and foster parent adjustment during weekly consultations, and key components of the treatment (e.g., reinforcement level, discipline, supervision) can be tracked through this mechanism.

PDR was originally developed as a research tool to augment home observations conducted by trained observers in family homes. PDR data are a compromise between the types of microsocial data that can be obtained during in-home observations and more global parent reports of child functioning. We use PDR both as an outcome measure and as a tool to continuously track case progress and the level of program implementation and fidelity. During the first year of implementation, PDR is reviewed daily and discussed during weekly telephone consultations. In addition, the program consultant views videotapes of the foster parent and clinical meetings. The program consultant also makes three on-site training visits, usually one each quarter for 2 days each, during the first year.

POTENTIAL BARRIERS TO IMPLEMENTATION

From the site's perspective, being on the receiving end of this intensive consultation package can be challenging, especially when complex conditions exist at the site, such as managing high caseloads while simultaneously trying to learn about and convert to a new way of working. Many agencies also have high staff turnover that complicates staff morale and willingness to implement a new program model. Some agencies find it challenging to manage staff with diverse theoretical orientations that may be incompatible with each other or with the MTFC approach.

Another challenge includes overcoming community perceptions that youths with such severe and persistent problems can be dealt with effectively and safely in the context of a family setting. In looking at the types of programs now in place in the United States for such youth, many, if not most, current practices appear to have more to do with setting up things to be convenient for the programs and adults who run them than with getting positive outcomes for youths and families. Notable exceptions are the family-oriented Multisystemic and Functional Family Therapy models that I described earlier. The notion that youth with multiple and severe conduct problems can be dealt with in group settings using the rationale that the group interaction will somehow have a therapeutic effect is both counterintuitive and not supported by any empirically based studies. If community referral agents are negative about the new MTFC program's ability to handle youth, initially it will be difficult to get the flow of referrals started. Until the program has a few "successes," referrals may be slow in coming.

Other aspects of the initial implementation of the MTFC model can be complex because they require that several program functions be brought online in a planned and timely way. Without a clear plan for program development that includes a well thought out timeline for implementation of key start-up functions, the program will flounder and may ultimately fail. Start-up requires the commitment of sufficient staff and administrative resources that are coordinated and complementary. After obtaining funding, hiring staff, and receiving initial training in Oregon, the next challenge is recruiting and preparing MTFC parents to provide placements. At this stage, the program is faced with a series of tasks including

- recruiting a pool of qualified foster parents,
- certifying foster parents in a timely way,
- matching referrals to homes, and
- orienting foster parents and staff to a way of working that promotes cooperative teamwork.

It is common for beginning programs to have difficulty recruiting foster parents during the start-up phase. At times they might have youths referred but no MTFC parents ready to provide placements for them. Then, when foster parent recruitment efforts begin to pay off, sometimes referrals to the program are no longer in place. Experience has shown that MTFC parents without placements do not last long (i.e., if programs have delays in using homes, they lose them). Start-up involves not only being able to recruit and train qualified staff and MTFC parents but doing it in a timely way that is coordinated with availability of referrals.

Certification of MTFC parents can also be a barrier. Requirements vary widely from state to state. Program developers should thoroughly understand the certification requirements and processes in their area. It is helpful to have worked out a clear arrangement with the agencies responsible for certification and to know which personnel from which agency will work with the new MTFC program. Specific roles that the MTFC program and the agency will play in the certification process should also be known. We have found that in many areas it is common for certification agencies to expect that it will take several months for foster parents to meet their requirements. Having foster parents go through a lengthy process can be viewed as a test of their level of commitment. This usually makes for an unworkable situation, and we have found that such a waiting period is not necessary for screening good MTFC parents. It has been our experience that the process can be expedited if the certification agency considers the certification of certain parents a priority (emergency or expedited certification is a common practice). Beginning MTFC programs need to clearly understand their certification process and have it in place prior to recruiting foster parents. This topic is addressed in the readiness interview.

Some sites have had experience with recruiting foster parents and have existing foster homes that they want to convert to MTFC placements. This can be a big advantage if the foster parents are willing to play a more active treatment-oriented role and if the implementing agency is prepared to shift their way of working and compensation level. What does not work is the agency deciding to convert to MTFC and then "telling" the foster parents that things are changing without giving them a choice about their participation in the new scheme. Often foster homes that have functioned well more independently are not willing to accept the close staff involvement and teamwork that MTFC requires.

Staff turnover can be a major barrier, especially at the program supervisor level. In our experience, if the MTFC program can keep stable program supervisors in place, foster parent turnover is usually quite low.

CREATING THE MULTIDIMENSIONAL TREATMENT FOSTER CARE CULTURE

In training new sites we attempt to first talk about several basic "big picture" assumptions underlying the model. The idea is to set up a culture within which their MTFC program can survive and hopefully thrive. One aspect of the big picture has to do with the relationship between the program staff (especially the program supervisor) and the MTFC parents. The importance of establishing a supportive and collaborative relationship between the program supervisor and the foster parents cannot be overemphasized. Usually, all parties agree that a high degree of collaboration makes sense, and even the idea that foster parents can help shape the intervention agenda is largely noncontroversial. However, as new programs have been implemented, it has become clear to us how difficult achieving this collaboration can be. For example, it is often hard for new program staff to break with the idea that the therapist's agenda should drive treatment. In MTFC what happens in the foster home is primary, but we have found that it is often difficult to operationalize this idea and to implement it in daily practice.

Therefore, much of the training and supervision in the MTFC model includes a focus on creating a program culture in which all staff members are trained to operate in ways that reinforce the idea that the relationship between the MTFC parent and the youth is key to achieving positive case outcomes. Program staff members need to work to empower foster parents and give them the skills and supervision to make smart decisions about the use of daily contingencies in their interactions with youths. Program supervisors work to prevent things from happening that undermine the foster parent's reinforcing role or relationship with the youth. This includes occasionally protecting foster parents from unpopular decisions such as saying "no" to a youth request. This is done by having the program supervisor be the one to deliver the bad news. This stratification of authority helps the foster parent stay in a supportive role and puts the program supervisor in the line of fire. Program supervisors are trained to develop a good understanding of how and when to step in so they can structure daily operations and supervise other program staff and MTFC parents to reinforce the overall goals of the program. In terms of training to this issue, we have found that it is most effective for new program staff to see examples of how these dynamics work in our foster parent meetings and talk with existing MTFC parents and their program consultants. This first occurs during the initial 4-day training in Oregon.

In MTFC, we place a strong emphasis on interventions that attend to specific aspects of daily behavior. This is another aspect of program culture that is sometimes very different from the way new sites are accustomed to operating. They may be more accustomed to responding to case needs when there are crises. In MTFC, we take a different approach, which is to pay attention when things are going well.

Rather than staffing and organizing to react to antisocial behavior, we attempt to carefully attend, at a daily level, to what the youth is doing correctly. This requires that a consistent level of staff and MTFC parent time and attention be spent on noncrisis topics. The MTFC program culture is to intervene sooner rather than later and to try to direct the bulk of the attention to normative or positive behavior. We have put structures in place to help accomplish this goal, such as the daily point and level system described in chapter 5 that MTFC parents conduct each day. This attention-to-positive-behaviors strategy requires ongoing supervision of staff to maintain the focus.

Typically, much of our weekly consultation surrounds the concept of shaping behavior. This approach essentially involves a focus on promoting behavior change through a series of approximations toward an ultimate goal, although the initial change that is reinforced is typically much more modest in nature. For instance, a child who has extreme tantrums and runs away when confronted might actually be rewarded for an episode in which he or she threw a tantrum but did not run away. Changing the expectations of staff concerning what effects behavioral interventions may ultimately achieve in the short run and focusing them on goals that are more easily attained is a critical part of the consultation process. As staff from agencies that are receiving consultation begin to grasp these concepts, their use and acceptance of the MTFC approach is greatly facilitated.

Because the MTFC model is fairly complex, several key functions and staff roles must be well coordinated for things to run smoothly. However, an MTFC team that accumulates experience working effectively together can deal with increasingly challenging youths over time.[2] Once established, MTFC programs can be expanded relatively easily, and future program development can be tailored to serve a wide range of youths and families.

FROM EFFICACY TO EFFECTIVENESS: HOW HAS MULTIDIMENSIONAL TREATMENT FOSTER CARE PROGRESSED?

Research in the field of dissemination typically has been conceptualized as a series of steps whereby one first develops and validates interventions under ideal conditions and then tests them in community settings under "real-world" conditions with more diverse populations. In developing and testing the MTFC model, we have used a different process, which reflects a blending of these steps from the outset. The original funding for the MTFC programs was from local contracts. Cases were referred from local juvenile departments and mental health and child welfare systems. Participants in the various applications of the MTFC program described in this volume have reflected real-world conditions. For example, in the development phases of MTFC, we made no attempts to screen out cases in which youths had multiple problems

---

[2]The MTFC programs in Oregon have benefited tremendously from having highly skilled and dedicated staff, especially at the program supervisor level. J. P. Davis has supervised our juvenile justice programs for the past 15 years, and more recently, Dana Smith joined that team as a supervisor. Kevin Moore supervises the MTFC program for youths with developmental delays as well as our Medicaid-funded program. Phil Fisher directs the Early Intervention Foster Care program and research. Peter Sprengelmeyer supervises our intensive home-based program.

(e.g., mental health problems or low cognitive functioning in addition to delinquency).

Once we had developed a strong set of program procedures and a solid referral base, we moved into efficacy tests and conducted controlled studies of key program outcomes in the context of randomized trials. We have used a back and forth process of moving from community development of programs centering on local need to collecting pilot data on program outcomes to conducting full-scale controlled trials. Throughout this process of developing and testing the efficacy of applications of MTFC we have attempted to increase our chances of succeeding with the high-risk populations that we serve by bringing together the greatest number of resources and the highest degree of control over the treatment that we can muster. For example, to promote a high level of coherence of the treatment approach, we insist that MTFC program staff conduct all elements of the treatment (individual, family, and drug and alcohol) that youths receive. Although this approach of maintaining control of key aspects of the case has been effective at producing good outcomes in several MTFC applications, it has contributed to the program's complexity when the focus turns to disseminating the intervention in communities. This was especially the case when those entities trying to replicate MTFC had no previous experience conducting multicomponent interventions (i.e., they were accustomed to working in outpatient, office-based settings).

In this chapter, our preliminary experiences with dissemination of MTFC have been discussed. We have learned that dissemination involves more than just training in MTFC intervention techniques. It must contain equal parts of knowing the intervention techniques and the manner in which these techniques are ultimately implemented. Consequently, we have now begun to devote attention to a much broader set of issues in our work. For instance, we spend considerably more time laying the groundwork for implementation, including doing a thorough pre-implementation site assessment through the readiness interview, problem solving up front around potential barriers, identifying key players in the implementation, and ensuring that those individuals are supportive of the plan. We now routinely have staff from implementing agencies spend time at our center to see MTFC in action. We feel that "seeing" is critical for them to comprehend the culture of our program and the manner in which treatment teams work together. As we continue to implement MTFC in different sites, we continue to learn and to gain a greater appreciation for the demands and constraints that agencies face when trying to operate a multilevel intervention such as MTFC.

AFTERWORD: LOOKING FORWARD

The idea that youths with severe and chronic problems with delinquency can be maintained in community families is counterintuitive in many ways. This reaction is especially understandable within the current context of increasing fear of violence and crime initiated by adolescents. To achieve widespread use of high-quality, community-based treatment programs it is necessary to provide on-the-ground examples of programs that work. We hope that through these examples, communities can overcome perceptions that such youths are beyond reach and that adults are powerless to influence them in meaningful ways. The types of group-oriented programs (e.g., group homes, residential care, group therapy) now used in most communities in the United States have the advantage of being convenient to run. However, there is little to no evidence that they produce positive outcomes for the youths and families they serve. On the other hand, over the past 10 years a number of family-based approaches have produced positive results in carefully controlled clinical trials.

The Multidimensional Treatment Foster Care (MTFC) model highlighted in this book is one such approach. The central aims of MTFC are straightforward. MTFC aims to create supports and opportunities for children and adolescents with a history of severe problems so they can have a successful community living experience. In addition, the MTFC model prepares the parents, relatives, or other aftercare placement resource to use skills and methods that will allow the youngster after returning home to maintain the gains he or she made while in MTFC.

In the early chapters of this book, I reviewed studies and presented theoretical groundwork that supports a series of strategies and practices designed to accomplish these aims. Principles for designing effective community-based programs for youths with chronic delinquency and conduct problems can be drawn from the rich body of previous research on the development of antisocial behavior. Four key elements are indicated:

1. Provide a consistent reinforcing environment where the youth is mentored and encouraged.
2. Provide a clear structure and limits with well-specified consequences that can be delivered in a teaching-oriented way.
3. Provide close supervision of the youth's whereabouts.
4. Prevent associations between the youth and peers with problems (especially conduct-related problems), and help the youth develop skills for having relationships with positive peers.

Intervention models that use these elements can be widely implemented in communities throughout the country if the political "will" and knowledge can be brought together.

In many respects, as straightforward as the ideas and goals of community-based intervention efforts such as MTFC are, the intervention models can be fairly complex to implement. Our ongoing implementation of MTFC programs in the United States and abroad continues to provide us with increased understanding of the challenges involved in the successful operation of a multilevel intervention like MTFC and enables us to develop ever more efficient strategies for meeting and circumventing these challenges. Our work in dissemination of MTFC has been highly rewarding, and it has created opportunities to connect with bright and committed individuals working in different contexts who share similar visions about improving outcomes for children and families at the highest risk. In short, like many important endeavors, dissemination has been at times both challenging and frustrating, but I view it as one of the most highly promising approaches we can take to improving the quality of care in social and mental health services for youths and their families.

REFERENCES

Achenbach, T. M., & Edelbrock, C. S. (1983). *Manual for the Child Behavior Checklist and Revised Child Behavior Profile*. Burlington: University of Vermont.

Adoption Assistance and Child Welfare Act of 1980, Pub. L. No. 96-272 (1980).

Ageton, S. S., & Elliott, D. S. (1978). *The incidence of delinquent behavior in a national probability sample of adolescents* (National Youth Survey, Report No. 3). Boulder, CO: Behavioral Research Institute.

Alexander, J., Barton, C., Gordon, D., Grotpeter, J., Hansson, K., Harrison, R. et al. (1998). *Book three: Functional family therapy*. In D. S. Elliott (Series Ed.), Blueprints for Violence Prevention Series. Boulder, CO: Institute of Behavioral Science, University of Colorado.

Alexander, J. F., & Parsons, B. V. (1973). Short-term behavioral intervention with delinquent families: Impact on family process and recidivism. *Journal of Abnormal Psychology, 81,* 219–225.

Alexander, J. F., & Parsons, B. V. (1982). *Functional family therapy: Principles and procedures*. Monterey, CA: Brooks/Cole.

Alvarado, R., Kendall, K., Beesley, S., & Lee-Cavaness, C. (Eds.). (2000). *Strengthening America's families: Model family programs for substance abuse and delinquency prevention*. Salt Lake City: University of Utah, College of Health.

Anderson, J. C., Williams, S., McGee, R., & Silva, P. A. (1987). DSM-III disorders in preadolescent children. *Archives of General Psychiatry, 44,* 69–76.

Andrews, B., Brown, G. W., & Creasey, L. (1990). Intergenerational links between psychiatric disorder in mothers and daughters: The role of parenting experiences. *Journal of Child Psychology and Psychiatry, 31*, 1115–1129.

Antoine, K., & Chamberlain, P. (1995). *Success begins in the home: A curriculum for family reunification.* (Available from the Oregon Social Learning Center, 160 East 4th Avenue, Eugene, OR 97401)

Asher, S. R., & Dodge, K. A. (1986). Identifying children who are rejected by their peers. *Developmental Psychology, 22*, 444–449.

Bank, L., Marlowe, J. H., Reid, J. B., Patterson, G. R., & Weinrott, M. R. (1991). A comparative evaluation of parent training for families of chronic delinquents. *Journal of Abnormal Child Psychology, 19*, 15–33.

Bank, L., & Noursi, S. D. (2001). The impact of violence on children: Home, community and national levels. *Journal of Community Psychology, 29*(3), 1–5.

Baron, R. M., & Kenny, D. A. (1986). The moderator–mediator variable distinction in social psychological research: Conceptual, strategic, and statistical considerations. *Journal of Personality and Social Psychology, 51*, 1173–1182.

Barrish, H. H., Saunders, M., & Wolfe, M. D. (1969). Good behavior game. Effects of individual contingencies for group consequences and disruptive behavior in a classroom. *Journal of Applied Behavior Analysis, 2*, 119–124.

Bates, J. E., Maslin, C. A., & Frankel, K. A. (1985). Attachment security, mother–child interaction, and temperament as predictors of behavior-problem ratings at age three years. *Monographs of the Society for Research in Child Development, 50*(1–2), 167–193.

Berger, A. M., Knutson, J. D., Mehm, J. G., & Perkins, K. A. (1988). The self-report of punitive childhood experiences of young adults and adolescents. *Child Abuse and Neglect, 12*, 251–262.

Berleman, W. C., & Steinburn, T. W. (1969). The value and validity of delinquency prevention experiments. *Crime and Delinquency, 15*, 471–478.

Bettelheim, B. (1982). The necessity and value of residential treatment for severely disturbed children. *Family and Mental Health Journal, 8*(1–2), 55–61.

Bloom, M. (1998). Primary prevention and foster care. *Children and Youth Services Review, 20*, 667–696.

Blotcky, M. J., Dimperio, T. L., & Gossett, J. T. (1984). Follow-up of children treated in psychiatric hospitals: A review of studies. *American Journal of Psychiatry, 141*, 1499–1507.

Blumstein, A., & Cohen, J. (1979). Estimation of individual crime rates from arrest records. *Journal of Criminal Law and Criminology, 70,* 561–585.

Borduin, C. M., Mann, B. J., Cone, L. T., Henggeler, S. W., Fucci, B. R., Blaske, D. M., et al. (1995). Multisystemic treatment of serious juvenile offenders: Long-term prevention of criminality and violence. *Journal of Consulting and Clinical Psychology, 63,* 569–578.

Bricker, D., Ayers, E. J., Slentz, K., & Kaminski, R. (1997). *Assessment, evaluation, and programming system test for three to six years.* Baltimore: Brookes.

Bricker, D., Bailey, E., & Bruder, M. (1984). The efficacy of early intervention and the handicapped infant: A wise or wasted resource. *Advances in Developmental and Behavioral Pediatrics, 5,* 373–423.

Bricker, D., & Cripe, J. W. (1992). *An activity based approach to early intervention.* Baltimore: Brookes.

Bronfenbrenner, U. (1979). *The ecology of human development: Experiments by nature and design.* Cambridge, MA: Harvard University Press.

Burns, B. J., & Friedman, R. M. (1990). Examining the research base for child mental health services and policy. *Journal of Mental Health Administration, 17,* 87–98.

Burns, B., Hoagwood, K., & Maultsby, L. T. (1997). Improving outcomes for children and adolescents with serious behavioral and emotional disorders: Current and future directions. In M. H. Epstein, K. Kutash, & A. J. Duchnowski (Eds.), *Community based programming for children with serious emotional disturbance and their families* (pp. 685–707). Austin, TX: Pro-Ed.

Cairns, R. B., Cadwallader, R. W., Estell, D., & Neckerman, H. J. (1997). Groups to gangs: Developmental and criminological perspectives and relevance for prevention. In D. M. Stoff, J. Breiling, & J. D. Maser (Eds.), *Handbook of antisocial behavior* (pp. 194–204). New York: Wiley.

Cairns, R. B., & Cairns, B. D. (1994). *Lifelines and risks: Pathways of youth in our time.* Cambridge, England: Cambridge University Press.

Cairns, R. B., Cairns, B. D., & Neckerman, H. J. (1989). Early school dropout: Configurations and determinants. *Child Development, 60,* 1437–1452.

Cairns, R. B., Cairns, B. D., Neckerman, H. J., Ferguson, L. L., & Gariepy, J. L. (1989). Growth and aggression: I. Childhood to early adolescence. *Developmental Psychology, 25,* 320–330.

Capaldi, D. M. (1991). The co-occurrence of conduct problems and depressive symptoms in early adolescent boys: I. Familial factors and general adjustment at Grade 6. *Development and Psychopathology, 3,* 277–300.

Capaldi, D. M., Chamberlain, P., Fetrow, R. A., & Wilson, J. E. (1997). Conducting ecologically valid prevention research: Recruiting and retaining a "whole village" in multimethod, multiagent studies. *American Journal of Community Psychology, 25*, 471–492.

Capaldi, D. M., & Patterson, G. R. (1991). Relation of parental transitions to boys' adjustment problems: I. A linear hypothesis. II. Mothers at risk for transitions and unskilled parenting. *Developmental Psychology, 27*, 489–504.

Capaldi, D. M., & Patterson, G. R. (1994). Interrelated influences of contextual factors on antisocial behavior in childhood and adolescence for males. In D. Fowles, P. Sutker, & S. H. Goodman (Eds.), *Experimental personality and psychopathy research* (pp. 165–198). New York: Springer.

Capaldi, D. M., & Patterson, G. R. (1996). Can violent offenders be distinguished from frequent offenders: Prediction from childhood to adolescence. *Journal of Research in Crime and Delinquency, 33*, 206–231.

Caseau, D. L., Luckasson, R., & Kroth, R. L. (1994). Special education services for girls with serious emotional disturbances: A case of gender bias? *Behavioral Disorders, 20*, 51–60.

Chamberlain, P. (1990). Comparative evaluation of Specialized Foster Care for seriously delinquent youths: A first step. *Community Alternatives: International Journal of Family Care, 2*(2), 21–36.

Chamberlain, P. (1994). *Family connections: Treatment foster care for adolescents with delinquency.* Eugene, OR: Northwest Media.

Chamberlain, P. (1999). Residential care for children and adolescents with conduct disorders. In H. C. Quay & A. E. Hogan (Eds.), *Handbook of disruptive behavior disorders* (pp. 495–505). New York: Kluwer Academic/ Plenum.

Chamberlain, P., & Friman, P. C. (1997). Residential programs for antisocial children and adolescents. In D. M. Stoff, J. Breiling, & J. D. Maser (Eds.), *Handbook of antisocial behavior* (pp. 416–424). New York: Wiley.

Chamberlain, P., & Mihalic, S. F. (1998). *Book eight: Multidimensional treatment foster care.* In D. S. Elliott (Series Ed.), Blueprints for Violence Prevention Series. Boulder, CO: Institute of Behavioral Science, University of Colorado.

Chamberlain, P., Moreland, S., & Reid, K. (1992). Enhanced services and stipends for foster parents: Effects on retention rates and outcomes for children. *Child Welfare, 71*, 387–401.

Chamberlain, P., Patterson, G. R., Reid, J. B., Kavanagh, K., & Forgatch, M. S. (1984). Observation of client resistance. *Behavior Therapy, 15*, 144–155.

Chamberlain, P., & Price, J. (2001). *Testing the effectiveness of a foster parent intervention: A cascading dissemination design.* Manuscript in preparation.

Chamberlain, P., & Ray, J. (1988). Therapy process code: A multidimensional system for observing therapist and client interactions. In R. J. Prinz

(Ed.), *Advances in behavioral assessment of children and families: Vol. 4. A research manual* (pp. 189–217). Greenwich, CT: JAI Press.

Chamberlain, P., Ray, J., & Moore, K. J. (1996). Characteristics of residential care for adolescent offenders: A comparison of assumptions and practices in two models. *Journal of Child and Family Studies, 5,* 259–271.

Chamberlain, P., & Reid, J. B. (1987). Parent observation and report of child symptoms. *Behavioral Assessment, 9,* 97–109.

Chamberlain, P., & Reid, J. B. (1991). Using a specialized foster care treatment model for children and adolescents leaving the state mental hospital. *Journal of Community Psychology, 19,* 266–276.

Chamberlain, P., & Reid, J. B. (1994). Differences in risk factors and adjustment for male and female delinquents in treatment foster care. *Journal of Child and Family Studies, 3*(1), 23–39.

Chamberlain, P., & Reid, J. (1998). Comparison of two community alternatives to incarceration for chronic juvenile offenders. *Journal of Consulting and Clinical Psychology, 6,* 624–633.

Chesney-Lind, M. (1988). Girls in jail. *Crime and Delinquency, 34,* 150–168.

Chesney-Lind, M. (1998). *What to do about girls? Promising perspectives and effective strategies.* Manoa: University of Hawaii.

Chesney-Lind, M. (1999). Challenging girls' invisibility in juvenile court. *Annals, AAPSS, 564,* 185–201.

Cohen, P., Cohen, J., Kasen, S., Velez, C. N., & Johnson, J. (1993). An epidemiological study of disorders in late childhood and adolescence: I. Age and gender specific prevalence. *Journal of Child Psychology and Psychiatry, 34,* 851–867.

Coie, J. D. (1996, August). *Effectiveness trials: An initial evaluation of the FAST Track program.* Paper presented at the Fifth National Institute of Mental Health National Conference on Prevention Research, Washington, DC.

Coie, J. D., & Dodge, K. (1988). Multiple sources of data on social behavior and social status in the school: A cross-age comparison. *Child Development, 59,* 815–829.

Coie, J. D., Dodge, K. A., & Coppotelli, H. (1982). Dimensions and types of social status: A cross-age perspective. *Developmental Psychology, 18,* 557–570.

Collins, L. M., & Horn, J. L. (Eds.). (1991). *Best methods for the analysis of change: Recent advances, unanswered questions, future directions.* Washington, DC: American Psychological Association.

Colton, M. (1990). Specialist foster family and residential child care practices. *Community Alternatives: International Journal of Family Care, 2*(2), 1–20.

Conduct Problems Prevention Research Group. (1992). A developmental and clinical model for the prevention of conduct disorder: The FAST Track Program. *Development and Psychopathology, 4,* 509–527.

Craft, M., Stevenson, G., & Granger, C. (1964). A controlled trial of authoritarian and self-governing regimes with adolescent psychopaths. *American Journal of Orthopsychiatry, 34,* 543–554.

Crick, N. R. (1995). Relational aggression: The role of intent attributions, feelings of distress, and provocation type. *Development and Psychopathology, 7,* 313–322.

Crick, N. R., & Grotpeter, J. K. (1995). Relational aggression, gender, and social-psychological adjustment. *Child Development, 66,* 710–722.

Cummings, E., Iannotti, R. J., & Zahn-Waxler, C. (1989). Aggression between peers in early childhood: Individual continuity and developmental change. *Child Development, 72,* 887–895.

Curry, J. F. (1991). Outcome research on residential treatment implications and suggested directions. *American Journal of Orthopsychiatry, 61,* 348–357.

Dadds, M. R., & McHugh, T. A. (1992). Social support and treatment outcome in behavioral family therapy for child conduct problems. *Journal of Consulting and Clinical Psychology, 60,* 252–259.

Dadds, M. R., Sanders, M. R., Behrens, B. C., & James, J. E. (1987). Marital discord and child behavior problems: A description of family interactions during treatment. *Journal of Clinical Child Psychology, 16,* 192–203.

Dadds, M. R., Schwartz, S., & Sanders, M. R. (1987). Marital discord and treatment outcome in behavioral treatment of child conduct disorders. *Journal of Consulting and Clinical Psychology, 55,* 396–403.

Dalton, R., Muller, B., & Forman, M. (1989). The psychiatric hospitalization of children: An overview. *Child Psychiatry and Human Development, 19,* 231–244.

Day, D. M., Pal, A., & Goldberg, K. (1994). Assessing the post-residential functioning of latency-aged conduct disordered children. *Residential Treatment for Children and Youth, 11*(3), 45–52.

Derogatis, L. R., & Spencer, P. M. (1982). *The brief symptom inventory (BSI) administration, scoring, and procedures manual—I.* Baltimore: Clinical Psychometric Research.

DiJulio, J. J. (1995, May). *Net repairing: Rethinking incarceration and immediate sanctions. A comment on Professor Joan R. Petersilia, "Diverting nonviolent prisoners to intermediate sanctions."* Paper presented at the Conference on the Future of Criminal Justice Policy in California, Berkeley.

Dishion, T. J. (1990). The peer context of troublesome child and adolescent behavior. In I. Leone (Ed.), *Understanding the troubled and troubling youth: Multidisciplinary perspective* (pp. 128–153). Newbury Park, CA: Sage.

Dishion, T. J., & Andrews, D. W. (1995). Preventing escalation in problem behaviors with high risk young adolescents: Immediate and 1-year outcomes. *Journal of Consulting and Clinical Psychology, 63*, 538–548.

Dishion, T. J., Andrews, D. W., & Crosby, L. (1995). Adolescent boys and their friends in early adolescence: I. Relationship characteristics, quality, and interactional processes. *Child Development, 66*, 139–151.

Dishion, T. J., French, D. C., & Patterson, G. R. (1995). The development and ecology of antisocial behavior. In D. Cicchetti & D. J. Cohen (Eds.), *Developmental psychopathology: Vol. 2. Risk, disorder, and adaptation* (pp. 421–471). New York: Wiley.

Dishion, T. J., McCord, J., & Poulin, F. (1999). When interventions harm: Peer groups and problem behavior. *American Psychologist, 54*, 755–764.

Dishion, T. J., & Patterson, G. R. (1997). The timing and severity of antisocial behavior: Three hypotheses within an ecological framework. In D. M. Stoff, J. Breiling, & J. D. Maser (Eds.), *Handbook of antisocial behavior* (pp. 205–217). New York: Wiley.

Dishion, T. J., Patterson, G. R., & Griesler, P. C. (1994). Peer adaptation in the development of antisocial behavior: A confluence model. In L. R. Huesmann (Ed.), *Aggressive behavior: Current perspectives* (pp. 61–95). New York: Plenum Press.

Dishion, T. J., Spracklen, K. M., Andrews, D. W., & Patterson, G. R. (1996). Deviancy training in male adolescent friendships. *Behavior Therapy, 27*, 373–390.

Dodge, K. A. (1980). Social cognition and children's aggressive behavior. *Child Development, 51*, 162–170.

Dumas, J. E. (1989). Treating antisocial behavior in children: Child and family approaches. *Clinical Psychology Review, 9*, 197–222.

Dumas, J. E., Gibson, J. A., & Albin, J. B. (1989). Behavioral correlates of maternal depressive symptomatology in conduct-disorder children. *Journal of Consulting and Clinical Psychology, 57*, 516–521.

Dumas, J. E., & Wahler, R. G. (1983). Predictors of treatment outcome in parent training: Mother insularity and socioeconomic disadvantage. *Behavioral Assessment, 5*, 301–313.

Duncan, G. J., Brooks-Gunn, J., & Klebanov, P. K. (1994). Economic deprivation and early childhood development. *Child Development, 65*, 296–318.

Durkin, R. P., & Durkin, A. B. (1975). Evaluating residential treatment programs for disturbed children. In M. Guttentag & E. L. Streuning (Eds.), *Handbook of evaluation research* (Vol. II, pp. 275–339). Beverly Hills, CA: Sage.

Eddy, J. M., & Chamberlain, P. (2000). Family management and deviant peer association as mediators of the impact of treatment condition on youth antisocial behavior. *Journal of Consulting and Clinical Psychology,* 68, 857–863.

Eddy, J. M., Reid, J. B., & Fetrow, R. A. (2000). An elementary-school based prevention program targeting modifiable antecedents of youth delinquency and violence: Linking the Interests of Families and Teachers (LIFT). *Journal of Emotional and Behavioral Disorders,* 8, 165–176.

Eddy, J. M., Reid, J. B., Stoolmiller, M., & Fetrow, R. A. (2002). *Three year outcomes for a preventive intervention for conduct problems.* Manuscript submitted for publication.

Elliott, D. S. (Ed.). (1998). *Blueprints for violence prevention.* Boulder, CO: Institute of Behavioral Science, University of Colorado.

Elliott, D. S., Ageton, S. S., Huizinga, D., Knowles, B. A., & Canter, R. J. (1983). *The prevalence and incidence of delinquent behavior: 1976–1980. National estimates of delinquent behavior by sex, race, social class, and other selected variables* (National Youth Survey Report, No. 26). Boulder, CO: Behavior Research Institute.

Elliott, D. S., Huizinga, D., & Ageton, S. S. (1985). *Explaining delinquency and drug use.* Beverly Hills, CA: Sage.

Elliott, D. S., & Menard, S. (1992). *Delinquent friends and delinquent behavior: Temporal and developmental patterns.* Unpublished manuscript.

Elliott, D. S., & Voss, H. L. (1974). *Delinquency and dropout.* Lexington, MA: D. C. Heath.

Erickson, M. F., Sroufe, L. A., & Egeland, B. (1985). The relationship between quality of attachment and behavior problems in preschool in a high-risk sample. *Monographs of the Society for Research in Child Development,* 50(1–2), 147–167.

Erickson, M. L., & Empey, L. T. (1963). Court records, undetected delinquency and decision-making. *Journal of Criminal Law, Criminology, and Police Science,* 54, 456–469.

Esser, G., Schmidt, M. H., & Woerner, W. (1990). Epidemiology and course of psychiatric disorders in school-age children: Results of a longitudinal study. *Journal of Child Psychology and Psychiatry,* 31, 243–263.

Farrington, D. P., Loeber, R., & Van Kammen, W. B. (1990). Long term criminal outcomes of hyperactivity—impulsivity—attention deficit and conduct problems in childhood. In L. N. Robin & M. R. Rutter (Eds.), *Straight and devious pathways to adulthood* (pp. 62–81). New York: Cambridge University Press.

Felner, R. D., Brand, S., Adan, A. M., Mulhall, P. F., Flowers, N., Sartan, B., et al. (1993). Restructuring the ecology of the school as an approach to prevention during school transitions: Longitudinal follow-ups and extensions of the school transitional environment project (STEP). In L. A.

Jason, K. E. Danner, & K. S. Kurasaki (Eds.), *Prevention and school transitions* (pp. 103–136). Binghamton, NY: Haworth.

Fergusson, D. M., & Horwood, L. J. (1999). Prospective childhood predictors of deviant peer affiliations in adolescence. *Journal of Child Psychology and Psychiatry and Allied Disciplines, 40*, 581–592.

Field, T. (1987). Interaction and attachment in normal and atypical infants. *Journal of Consulting and Clinical Psychology, 55*, 1–7.

Field, T. (1994). The effects of mother's physical and emotional unavailability on emotion regulation. *Monographs of the Society for Research in Child Development, 59*(2–3, Serial No. 240).

Fisher, P. A. (1999). *Early intervention foster care: A prevention trial* (Grant No. R01 MH 59780). Bethesda, MD: National Institute of Mental Health, Child and Adolescent Treatment and Preventive Intervention Research Branch.

Fisher, P. A., & Chamberlain, P. (2000). Multidimensional Treatment Foster Care: A program for intensive parent training, family support, and skill building. *Journal of Emotional and Behavioral Disorders, 8*(3), 155–164.

Fisher, P. A., Ellis, B. H., & Chamberlain, P. (1999). Early intervention foster care: A model for preventing risk in young children who have been maltreated. *Children Services: Social Policy, Research, and Practice, 2*, 159–182.

Fisher, P. A., Gunnar, M. R., Chamberlain, P., & Reid, J. B. (2000). Preventive intervention for maltreated preschoolers: Impact on children's behavior, neuroendocrine activity, and foster parent functioning. *Journal of the American Academy of Child and Adolescent Psychiatry, 39*, 1356–1364.

Fixsen, D. L., Phillips, E. L., Baron, R. L., Coughlin, D. D., Daly, D. L., & Daly, R. B. (1978, November). The Boys' Town revolution. *Human Nature*, pp. 54–61.

Forehand, R. L., & McMahon, R. J. (1981). *Helping the noncompliant child: A clinician's guide to parent training.* New York: Guilford Press.

Forgatch, M. S. (1994). *Parenting through change: A training manual.* Eugene: Oregon Social Learning Center.

Forgatch, M. S., & DeGarmo, D. S. (1999). Parenting through change: An effective prevention program for single mothers. *Journal of Consulting and Clinical Psychology, 67*, 711–724.

Friman, P. C., Osgood, D. W., Shanahan, D., Thompson, R. W., Larzelere, R., & Daly, D. L. (1996). A longitudinal evaluation of prevalent negative beliefs about residential placement for troubled adolescents. *Journal of Abnormal Child Psychology, 24*, 299–324.

Furstenberg, F. F., Brooks-Gunn, J., & Chase-Lansdale, L. (1989). Teenaged pregnancy and childbearing. *American Psychologist, 44,* 313–320.

Gadow, K.D., & Sprafkin, J. (1994). *Early childhood inventories manual.* Stony Brook, NY: Checkmate Plus.

Gardner, F. E. (1987). Positive interaction between mothers and conduct-problem children: Is there training for harmony as well as fighting? *Journal of Abnormal Child Psychology, 15,* 283–293.

Garrett, C. J. (1985). Effects of residential treatment on adjudicated delinquents: A meta-analysis. *Journal of Research in Crime and Delinquency, 22,* 287–308.

Ge, X., Best, K. M., Conger, R. D., & Simons, R. L. (1996). Parent behaviors and the occurrence and co-occurrence of adolescent depressive symptoms and conduct problems. *Developmental Psychology, 32,* 717–731.

Gianino, A., & Tronick, E. Z. (1985). The mutual regulation model: The infant's self and interactive regulation and coping and defensive capacities. In R. Field, P. McCabe, & N. Schneiderman (Eds.), *Stress and coping* (pp. 47–67). Hillsdale, NJ: Erlbaum.

Giordano, P. C., & Cernkovich, S. A. (1997). Gender and antisocial behavior. In D. M. Stoff, J. Breiling, & J. D. Maser (Eds.), *Handbook of antisocial behavior* (pp. 496–510). New York: Wiley.

Glisson, C. (1994). The effects of services coordination teams on outcomes for children in state custody. *Administration in Social Work, 18,* 1–23.

Gold, M. (1963). *Status forces in delinquent boys.* Ann Arbor: University of Michigan, Institute for Social Research.

Graham, P., & Rutter, M. (1973). Psychiatric disorder in the young adolescent: A follow-up study. *Proceedings of the Royal Society of Medicine, 66,* 1226–1229.

Griest, D. L., Forehand, R., Rogers, T., Breiner, J., Furey, W., & Williams, C. A. (1982). Effects of parent enhancement therapy on the treatment outcome and generalization of a parent training program. *Behavior Research and Therapy, 20,* 429–436.

Guerra, N. G., Huesmann, L. R., Tolan, P. H., Van Acker, R., & Eron, L. D. (1995). Stressful events and individual beliefs as correlates of economic disadvantage and aggression among urban children. *Journal of Consulting and Clinical Psychology, 63,* 518–528.

Haley, J. (1976). *Problem solving therapy.* San Francisco: Jossey-Bass.

Hare, E. H., & Shaw, G. K. (1965). A study in family health. II. A comparison of the health of fathers, mothers, and children. *British Journal of Psychiatry, 111,* 467–471.

Hartup, W. W. (1974). Aggression in childhood: Developmental perspectives. *American Psychologist, 20*, 337–341.

Hawkins, J. D., & Nederhood, B. (1987). *Handbook for evaluating drug and alcohol prevention programs: Staff/team evaluation of prevention programs (STEPP)* (DHHS Publication No. ADM 87–1512). Washington, DC: U.S. Government Printing Office.

Hazelrigg, M. D., Cooper, H. M., & Borduin, C. M. (1987). Evaluating the effectiveness of family therapies: An integrative review and analysis. *Psychological Bulletin, 101*, 428–442.

Henggeler, S. W., Brondino, M. J., Melton, G. B., Scherer, D. G., & Hanley, J. H. (1997). Multisystemic therapy with violent and chronic juvenile offenders and their families: The role of treatment fidelity in successful dissemination. *Journal of Consulting and Clinical Psychology, 65*, 821–833.

Henggeler, S. W., Melton, G. B., Smith, L. A., Schoenwald, S. K., & Hanley, J. (1993). Family preservation using multisysemic therapy: Long-term follow-up to a clinical trial with serious juvenile offenders. *Journal of Child and Family Studies, 2*, 283–293.

Henggeler, S. W., Mihalic, S. F., Rone, L., Thomas, C., & Timmons-Mitchell, J. (1998). *Book six: Multisystemic therapy*. In D. S. Elliott (Series Ed.), Blueprints for Violence Prevention Series. Boulder: Institute of Behavioral Science, University of Colorado.

Henggeler, S. W., Rodick, J. D., Borduin, C. M., Hanson, C. L., Watson, S. M., & Urey, J. R. (1986). Multisysemic treatment of juvenile offenders: Effects on adolescent behavior and family interaction. *Developmental Psychology, 22*, 132–141.

Hoagwood, K., & Cunningham, M. (1992). Outcomes of children with emotional disturbance in residential treatment for educational purposes. *Journal of Child and Family Studies, 1*(2), 129–140.

Hobbs, N. (1982). *The troubled and troubling child*. San Francisco: Jossey-Bass.

Hofferth, S. L., & Moore, K. A. (1979). Early childbearing and later economic well-being. *American Sociological Review, 44*, 784–815.

Holmbeck, G. N. (1997). Toward terminological conceptual and statistical clarity in the study of mediators and moderators; examples from the child-clinical and pediatric psychology literatures. *Journal of Consulting and Clinical Psychology, 65*, 599–610.

Holmes, S. J., & Robins, L. N. (1988). The role of parental disciplinary practices in the development of depression and alcoholism. *Psychiatry, 51*, 24–36.

Jacobson, N. S., & Truax, P. (1991). Clinical significance: A statistical approach to defining meaningful change in psychotherapy research. *Journal of Consulting and Clinical Psychology, 59*, 12–19.

Johnson, R. J., & Kaplan, H. B. (1988). Gender, aggression, and mental health intervention during early adolescence. *Journal of Health and Social Behavior*, 29, 53–64.

Johnson, T. F. (1973). Treating the juvenile offender in his family. *Juvenile Justice*, 24, 34–41.

Johnson, T. F. (1974). Hooking the involuntary family into treatment: Family therapy in a juvenile court. *Family Therapy*, 1, 79–82.

Johnson, T. F. (1975a). Family therapy with families having delinquent offspring. *Journal of Family Counseling*, 3, 32–37.

Johnson, T. F. (1975b). The juvenile offender and his family. *Juvenile Justice*, 26, 23–27.

Johnson, T. F. (1977). The results of family therapy with juvenile offenders. *Juvenile Justice*, 28, 29–34.

Johnson, T. F. (1978). A contextual approach to treatment of juvenile offenders. *Offender Rehabilitation*, 3, 171–179.

Judd, C. M., & Kenny, D. A. (1981). Process analysis: Estimating mediation in treatment evaluations. *Evaluation Review*, 5(5), 60–61.

Katz, L. F., & Gottman, J. M. (1991). Marital discord and child outcomes: A social psychophysiological approach. In J. Garber & K. A. Dodge (Eds.), *The development of emotion regulation and dysregulation: Cambridge Studies in Social and Emotional Development* (pp. 129–155). New York: Cambridge University Press.

Kazdin, A. E. (1987). Treatment of antisocial behavior in children: Current status and future directions. *Psychological Bulletin*, 102, 187–203.

Kazdin, A. E. (1990). Premature termination from treatment among children referred for antisocial behavior. *Journal of Child Psychology and Psychiatry and Allied Disciplines*, 31, 415–425.

Kazdin, A. E. (1993). Treatment of conduct disorder: Progress and directions in psychotherapy research. *Development and Psychopathology*, 5, 277–310.

Kazdin, A. E. (1995). *Conduct disorder in childhood and adolescence* (2nd ed.). Thousand Oaks, CA: Sage.

Kazdin, A., & Weisz, J. R. (1998). Identifying and developing empirically supported child and adolescent treatments. *Journal of Consulting and Clinical Psychology*, 66, 19–36.

Keenan, K., Loeber, R., & Green, S. (1999). Conduct disorder in girls: A review of the literature. *Clinical Child and Family Psychology Review*, 2(1), 3–19.

Kellam, S., Adams, R., Brown, C. H., & Ensiminger, M. E. (1992). The long-term evolution of family structure of teenage and older mothers. *Journal of Marriage and the Family*, 44, 539–554.

Kellam, S. G., Rebok, G. W., Ialongo, N., & Mayer, L. S. (1994). The course and malleability of aggressive behavior from early first grade into middle school: Results of a developmental epidemiologically-based preventive trial. *Journal of Child Psychology and Psychiatry, 35,* 259–281.

Keller, M. B., Beardslee, W. R., Dorer, D. J., Lauori, P. W., Samuelson, H., & Klerman, G. R. (1986). Impact of severity and chronicity of parental affective illness on adaptive functioning and psychopathology in children. *Archives of General Psychiatry, 43,* 930–937.

Kendall, P. C., & Grove, W. (1988). Normative comparisons in therapy outcome. *Behavioral Assessment, 10,* 147–158.

Klee, L., Kronstadt, D., & Zlotnick, C. (1997). Foster care's youngest: A preliminary report. *American Journal of Orthopsychiatry, 67,* 290–299.

Klein, N. C., Alexander, J. F., & Parsons, P. V. (1977). Impact of family systems intervention on recidivism and sibling delinquency: A model of primary prevention and program evaluation. *Journal of Consulting and Clinical Psychology, 45,* 469–474.

Kutash, K., & Rivera, V. R. (1996). *What works in children's mental health services?* Baltimore: Brookes.

Lahey, B. B., & Loeber, R. (1994). Framework for a developmental model of oppositional defiant disorder and conduct disorder. In D. Routh (Ed.), *Disruptive behavior disorders in childhood: Essays in honor of Herbert C. Quay* (pp. 139–180). New York: Plenum.

Lahey, B. B., & Loeber, R. (1997). Attention-deficit/hyperactivity disorder, oppositional defiant disorder, conduct disorder, and adult antisocial behavior: A life span perspective. In D. M. Stoff, J. Breiling, & J. D. Maser (Eds.), *Handbook of antisocial behavior* (pp. 51–59). New York: Wiley.

Landsverk, J., Litrownik, A., Newton, R., Ganger, W., & Remmer, J. (1996). *Psychological impact of child maltreatment* (Final Report to National Center on Child Abuse and Neglect). Washington, DC: National Center on Child Abuse and Neglect.

Laub, J. H., & Sampson, R. J. (1988). Unraveling families and delinquency: A reanalysis of the Gluecks' data. *Criminology, 26,* 355–379.

Lewis, D. O., Yeager, C. A., Cobham-Portorreal, N. K., Showalter, B. A., & Anthony, B. A. (1991). A follow-up of female delinquents: Maternal contribution to the perpetuation of deviance. *Journal of the American Academy of Child and Adolescent Psychiatry, 30,* 197–201.

Lipsey, J. H. (1992). Juvenile delinquency treatment: A meta-analytic inquiry into the variability of effects. In T. D. Cook, H. Cooper, D. S. Cordray, H. Hartmann, L. V. Hedges, R. J. Light, et al. (Eds.), *Meta analysis for explanation: A casebook* (pp. 83–125). New York: Russell Sage Foundation.

Lipsey, M. W., & Wilson, D. B. (1998). Effective intervention for serious juvenile offenders: A synthesis of research. In R. Loeber & D. P. Farrington (Eds.), *Serious and violent juvenile offenders: Risk factors and successful interventions* (pp. 313–345). Thousand Oaks, CA: Sage.

Loeber, R., & Dishion, T. J. (1983). Early predictors of male delinquency: A review. *Psychological Bulletin, 94,* 68–99.

Loeber, R., & Hay, D. H. (1994). Developmental approaches to aggression and conduct problems. In M. Rutter & D. H. Hay (Eds.), *Development through life: A handbook for clinicians* (pp. 488–515). Oxford, England: Blackwell.

Loeber, R., & Keenan, K. (1994). Interaction between conduct disorder and its comorbid conditions: Effects of age and gender. *Clinical Psychology Review, 14,* 497–523.

Long, P., Forehand, R., Wierson, M., & Morgan, A. (1994). Does parent training with young noncompliant children have long-term effects? *Behaviour Research and Therapy, 32,* 101–107.

Lyons-Ruth, K., Zoll, D., Connell, D., & Grunebaum, H. U. (1989). Family deviance and family disruption in childhood: Associations with maternal behavior and infant maltreatment during the first two years of life. *Development and Psychopathology, 1,* 219–236.

Martinson, R. (1974). What works? Questions and answers about prison reform. *Public Interest, 35,* 22–24.

McCord, J. (1997, April). *Some unanticipated consequences of summer camps.* Paper presented at the meeting of the Society for Research on Child Development, Washington, DC.

McDowell, J. J. (1988). Matching theory in natural human environments. *The Behavior Analyst, 11,* 95–109.

McGee, R., Feehan, M., Williams, S., & Anderson, J. (1992). DSM-III Disorders from age 11 to age 15 years. *Journal of the American Academy of Child Adolescent Psychiatry, 31*(1), 50–59.

McMahon, R. J., Forehand, R., Griest, D. L., & Wells, K. C. (1981). Who drops out of treatment during parent behavior training. *Behavioral Counseling Quarterly, 1,* 79–85.

McMahon, R. J., & Wells, K. C. (1989). Conduct disorders. In E. J. Mash & R. A. Barkley (Eds.), *Treatment of childhood disorders* (pp. 73–132). New York: Guilford.

Mendel, R. A. (2001). *Less cost, more safety: Guiding lights for reform in juvenile justice.* Washington, DC: American Youth Policy Forum.

Merikangas, K. R., & Spiker, D. G. (1982). Assortive mating among inpatients with primary affective disorder. *Psychological Medicine, 12,* 753–764.

Miller, G. E., & Prinz, R. J. (1990). Enhancement of social learning family interventions for childhood conduct disorder. *Psychological Review, 100,* 674–701.

Moffitt, T. E. (1990). The neuropsychology of juvenile delinquency: A critical review. In M. Tonry & N. Morris (Eds.), *Crime and justice: A review of research* (Vol. 12, pp. 99–169). Chicago: University of Chicago Press.

Moffitt, T. E. (1993). Adolescence-limited and life-course-persistent antisocial behavior: A developmental taxonomy. *Psychological Review, 100,* 674–701.

Moore, K. J. (2001, August). Generalization of MTFC to youth with borderline cognitive functioning. In P. Chamberlain & P. G. Sprengelmeyer (Chairs), *Applications of the Oregon model to populations of difficult youth.* Symposium conducted at the meeting of the American Psychological Association, San Francisco, CA.

Mrazek, P. G., & Haggerty, R. J. (Eds.). (1994). *Reducing risks for mental disorders: Frontiers for prevention intervention research.* Washington, DC: National Academy Press.

National Institute of Mental Health, Prevention Research Steering Committee. (1993). *The prevention of mental disorders: A national research agenda.* Bethesda, MD: Author.

O'Donnell, J., Hawkins, D. J., & Abbott, R. D. (1995). Predicting serious delinquency and substance use among aggressive boys. *Journal of Consulting and Clinical Psychology, 63,* 529–537.

Office of Juvenile Justice and Delinquency Prevention. (1997). *Boot camps for juvenile offenders.* Washington, DC: U.S. Department of Justice.

Offord, D. R., Boyle, M. C., & Racine, Y. A. (1991). The epidemiology of antisocial behavior in childhood and adolescence. In D. J. Pepler & K. H. Rubin (Eds.), *The development and treatment of childhood aggression* (pp. 31–54). Hillsdale, NJ: Erlbaum.

Olds, D. L., Henderson, C. R., Chamberlin, R., & Tatelbaum, R. (1986). Preventing child abuse and neglect: A randomized trial of nurse home visitation. *Pediatrics, 78*(1), 65–78.

Olweus, D. (1979). Stability of aggressive reaction patterns in males: A review. *Psychological Bulletin, 86,* 852–875.

Parker, J. G., Rubin, K. H., Price, J. M., & DeRosier, M. E. (1995). Peer relationships, child development, and adjustment: A developmental psychopathology perspective. In D. Cicchetti & D. J. Cohen (Eds.), *Developmental psychopathology: Vol. 2. Risk, disorder, and adaptation* (pp. 96–161). New York: Wiley.

Patterson, G. R. (1982). *Coercive family process.* Eugene, OR: Castalia.

Patterson, G. R. (1993). Orderly change in a stable world: The antisocial trait as a chimera. *Journal of Consulting and Clinical Psychology, 61*, 911–919.

Patterson, G. R., Chamberlain, P., & Reid, J. B. (1982). A comparative evaluation of parent training procedures. *Behavior Therapy, 13*, 638–650.

Patterson, G. R., Dishion, T. J., & Chamberlain, P. (1993). Outcomes and methodological issues relating to treatment of antisocial children. In T. R. Giles (Ed.), *Effective psychotherapy: A handbook of comparative research* (pp. 43–88). New York: Plenum.

Patterson, G. R., & Forgatch, M. S. (1985). Therapist behavior as a determinant for client resistance: A paradox for the behavior modifier. *Journal of Consulting and Clinical Psychology, 53*, 846–851.

Patterson, G. R., & Forgatch, M. S. (1995). Predicting future clinical adjustment from treatment outcome and process variables. *Psychological Assessment, 7*, 275–285.

Patterson, G. R., Reid, J. B., & Dishion, T. J. (1992). *Antisocial boys.* Eugene, OR: Castalia.

Pepler, D. J. (1995, June). *Aggression and gender: Self and peer perceptions.* Paper presented at the meeting of the Society for Research on Child Development, Indianapolis, IN.

Pepler, D. J., & Craig, W. (1999). *Aggressive girls: Development of disorder and outcomes.* Toronto, Ontario: York University.

Pfeiffer, S. I., & Strzelecki, S. C. (1990). Inpatient psychiatric treatment of children and adolescents: A review of outcome studies. *Journal of the American Academy of Child and Adolescent Psychiatry, 29*, 847–853.

Quay, H. C. (1979). Residential treatment. In H. C. Quay & J. S. Werry (Eds.), *Psychopathological disorders of childhood* (2nd ed., pp. 387–410). New York: Wiley.

Quay, H. C. (1986). Residential treatment. In H. C. Quay & J. S. Werry (Eds.), *Psychopathological disorders of childhood* (3rd ed., pp. 558–582). New York: Wiley.

Quinton, D., & Rutter, M. (1988). *Parenting breakdown: The making and breaking of inter-generational links.* Aldershot, UK: Avebury.

Reid, J. B. (1995). *Linking interests of families and teachers* (Grant No. MH 54248). Washington, DC: National Institute of Mental Health.

Reid, J. B., & Eddy, J. M. (1997). The prevention of antisocial behavior: Some considerations in the search for effective interventions. In D. M. Stoff, J. Breiling, & J. D. Maser (Eds.), *Handbook of antisocial behavior* (pp. 343–356). New York: Wiley.

Reid, J. B., & Hendriks, A. F. C. J. (1973). A preliminary analysis of the effectiveness of direct home intervention for treatment of predelinquent boys who steal. In L. A. Hamerlynck, L. C. Handy, & E. J. Mash (Eds.), *Behavior therapy: Methodology, concepts, and practices* (pp. 453–478). Champaign, IL: Research Press.

Rivera, V. R., & Kutash, K. (1994). *Components of a system of care: What does the research say?* Tampa: Research and Training Center for Children's Mental Health, University of South Florida, Florida Mental Health Institute.

Robins, R. L. N., & Price, R. K. (1991). Adult disorders predicted by childhood conduct problems: Results from the NIMH Epidemiologic Catchment Area Project. *Psychiatry, 54,* 116–132.

Rosenbaum, A., & O'Leary, K. D. (1981). Marital violence: Characteristics of abusive couples. *Journal of Consulting and Clinical Psychology, 49,* 63–71.

Rosenbaum, J. L. (1989). Family dysfunction and female delinquency. *Crime and Delinquency, 35,* 31–44.

Ruff, H. A., Blank, S., & Barnett, H. L. (1990). Early intervention in the context of foster care. *Developmental and Behavioral Pediatrics, 11,* 265–268.

Rutter, M. (1978). Family, area, and school influences in the genesis of conduct disorders. In L. A. Herson, M. Berger, & D. Schaffer (Eds.), *Childhood and adolescence* (pp. 95–111). London: Blackwell.

Rutter, M. (1989). Pathways from childhood to adult life. *Journal of Child Psychology and Psychiatry, 30,* 23–51.

Rutter, M. (1997). Antisocial behavior: Developmental psychopathology perspectives. In D. M. Stoff, J. Breiling, & J. D. Maser (Eds.), *Handbook of antisocial behavior* (pp. 115–124). New York: Wiley.

Rutter, M., & Quinton, D. (1984). Long-term follow-up of women institutionalized in childhood: Factors promoting good functioning in adult life. *British Journal of Developmental Psychology, 2,* 191–204.

Sameroff, A. J. (1989). Commentary: General systems and the regulation of development. In M. R. Gunnar & E. Thelen (Eds.), *Systems and development: The Minnesota Symposia on Child Psychology* (Vol. 22, pp. 219–230). Hillsdale, NJ: Erlbaum.

Sampson, R. J., & Laub, J. H. (1994). Urban poverty and the family context of delinquency: A new look at structure and process in a classic study. *Child Development, 65,* 523–540.

Sanders, M. R., Dadds, M. R., Johnston, B. M., & Cash, R. (1992). Childhood depression and conduct disorder: I. Behavioral, affective, and cognitive aspects of family problem-solving interactions. *Journal of Abnormal Psychology, 101,* 495–504.

Schlossman, S., & Cairns, R. B. (1991). Problem girls: Observations on past and present. In G. H. Elder Jr., R. D. Park, & J. Modell (Eds.), *Children in time and place: Relations between history and developmental psychology* (pp. 110–130). New York: Cambridge University Press.

Select Committee on Children, Youth, and Families, U.S. House of Representatives. (1990). *No place to call home: Discarded children in America.* Washington, DC: U.S. Government Printing Office.

Shadish, W. R., Montgomery, L. M., Wilson, P., Wilson, M. R., Bright, I., & Okwumabua, T. (1993). Effects of family and marital psychotherapies: A meta-analysis. *Journal of Consulting and Clinical Psychology, 61,* 992–1002.

Shaffer, D., Fisher, P., Piacentini, J., Schwab-Stone, M., & Wicks, J. (1989). *Diagnostic interview schedule for children.* New York: New York State Psychiatric Institute.

Shaw, D. S., & Winslow, E. B. (1997). Precursors and correlates of antisocial behavior from infancy to preschool. In D. M. Stoff, J. Breiling, & J. D. Maser (Eds.), *Handbook of antisocial behavior* (pp. 148–158). New York: Wiley.

Snyder, J. J. (1991). Discipline as a mediator of the impact of maternal stress and mood on child conduct problems. *Development and Psychopathology, 3,* 263–276.

Southam-Gerow, M. A., & Kendall, P. C. (1997). Parent-focused and cognitive–behavioral treatments of antisocial youth. In D. M. Stoff, J. Breiling, & J. D. Maser (Eds.), *Handbook of antisocial behavior* (pp. 384–394). New York: Wiley.

Stoolmiller, M. (1994). Antisocial behavior, delinquent peer association and unsupervised wandering for boys: Growth and change from childhood to early adolescence. *Multivariate Behavioral Research, 29,* 263–288.

Szapocznik, J., Kurtines, W., & Fernandez, T. (1980). Biculturalism and adjustment among Hispanic youths. *International Journal of Intercultural Relations, 4,* 353–375.

Szapocznik, J., Perez-Vidal, A., Brickman, A. L., Foote, F. H., Santisteban, D., Hervis, O., et al. (1988). Engaging adolescent drug abusers and their families in treatment: A strategic structural systems approach. *Journal of Consulting and clinical Psychology, 56,* 552–557.

Szapocznik, J., Scopetta, M. A., Kurtines, W., & Aranalde, M. A. (1978). Theory and practice in matching treatment to the special characteristics and problems of Cuban immigrants. *Journal of Community Psychology, 6,* 112–122.

Taylor, T. K., Eddy, J. M., & Biglan, A. (1999). Interpersonal skills training to reduce aggressive and delinquent behavior. Limited evidence and the need for an evidence-based system of care. *Clinical Child and Family Psychology Review, 2,* 169–182.

Thompson, R. A., & Calkins, S. D. (1996). The double-edged sword: Emotional regulation for children at risk. *Development and Psychopathology, 8,* 163–182.

Thompson, R. W., Smith, G. L., Osgood, D. W., Dowd, T. P., Friman, P. C., & Daly, D. (1996). Residential care: A study of short- and long-term effects. *Children and Youth Services Review, 18,* 139–162.

Thornberry, T. P., & Krohn, M. D. (1997). Peers, drug use, and delinquency. In D. M. Stoff, J. Breiling, & J. D. Maser (Eds.), *Handbook of antisocial behavior* (pp. 218–233). New York: Wiley.

Tolan, P. H., Cromwell, R. E., & Brasswell, M. (1986). Family therapy with delinquents: A critical review of the literature. *Family Process, 25,* 619–650.

Tolan, P. H., & Thomas, P. (1995). The implications of age of onset for delinquency risk: II. Longitudinal data. *Journal of Abnormal Child Psychology, 23,* 157–181.

Trachenberg, S., & Viken, R. J. (1994). Aggressive boys in the classroom: Biased attributions or shared perceptions? *Child Development, 65,* 829–835.

Tremblay, R. E., Pagani-Kurtz, L., Vitaro, F. A., Masse, L. C., & Pihl, R. O. (1995). A bimodal preventive intervention for disruptive kindergarten boys: Its impact through mid-adolescence. *Journal of Consulting and Clinical Psychology, 63,* 560–568.

Tronick, E. Z., Als, H., Adamson, L., Wise, S., & Brazelton, T. B. (1978). The infant's response to entrapment between contradictory messages in face-to-face interaction. *Journal of Child Psychiatry, 17,* 1–13.

Tronick, E. Z., & Gianino, A. F., Jr. (1986). Interactive mismatch and repair: Challenges to infant coping. *Zero to Three, 6*(3), 1–6.

Underwood, M. K. (1995). *Competence in sexual decision-making by African American, female adolescents: The role of peer relations and future plans.* Unpublished manuscript, Reed College, Portland, OR.

Underwood, M. K., Kupersmidt, J. B., & Coie, J. D. (1996). Childhood peer sociometric status and aggression as predictors of adolescent childbearing. *Journal of Research on Adolescence, 6,* 201–223.

U.S. Department of Health and Human Services. (1999). *Mental health: A report of the Surgeon General.* Rockville, MD: Author.

U.S. Department of Health and Human Services. (2000a). Children and mental health. In *Mental health: A report of the Surgeon General* (DHHS

Publication No. DSL 2000-0134-P) (pp. 123–220).Washington, DC: U.S. Government Printing Office.

U.S. Department of Health and Human Services. (2000b). Prevention of violence. In *Mental health: A report of the Surgeon General* (DHHS Publication No. DSL 2000-0134-P) (chapter 5). Washington, DC: U.S. Government Printing Office.

U.S. General Accounting Office. (1994). *Foster care: Parental drug abuse has alarming impact on young children* (GAO/HEHS-94-89). Washington, DC: Author.

Vorrath, H., & Brendtro, L. K. (1985). *Positive peer culture*. Chicago: Aldine.

Wahler, R. G. (1980). The insular mother: Her problems in parent–child treatment. *Journal of Applied Behavior Analysis, 13*, 207–219.

Wahler, R. G., & Dumas, J. E. (1987). Stimulus class determinants of mother–child coercive interchanges in multidistressed families: Assessment and intervention. In J. D. Burchard & S. N. Burchard (Eds.), *Prevention of delinquent behavior* (pp. 190–219). Beverly Hills, CA: Sage.

Wahler, R. G., & Fox, J. J. (1980). Solitary toy play and time out: A family treatment package for children with aggressive and oppositional behavior. *Journal of Applied Behavior Analysis, 13*, 23–39.

Walker, H. M., Colvin, G., & Ramsey, E. (1995). *Antisocial behavior in school: Strategies and best practices*. Pacific Grove, CA: Brooks/Cole.

Walker, H. M., Stieber, S., Ramsey, E., & O'Neill, R. (1993). Fifth grade school adjustment and later arrest rate: A longitudinal study of middle school antisocial boys. *Journal of Child and Family Studies, 2*, 295–315.

Walsh, S. (1999). *Gender differences in the protective effects of planning orientation on the sexual activity and deviant peer influence of at-risk adolescents.* Unpublished doctoral dissertation, University of Oregon, Eugene.

Webster-Stratton, C. (1985). Predictors of treatment outcome in parent training for conduct disordered children. *Behavior Therapy, 16*, 223–243.

Webster-Stratton, C. (1994). Advancing videotape parent training: A comparison study. *Journal of Consulting and Clinical Psychology, 62*, 583–593.

Webster-Stratton, C. (1996). Early-onset conduct problems: Does gender make a difference? *Journal of Consulting and Clinical Psychology, 64*, 540–551.

Wells, K. (1991). Placement of emotionally disturbed children in residential treatment: A review of placement criteria. *American Orthopsychiatric Association, 61*, 339–347.

Westen, D., Ludolph, P., Misle, B., Ruffins, S., & Block, J. (1990). Physical and sexual abuse in adolescent girls with borderline personality disorder. *American Journal of Orthopsychiatry, 60*, 55–66.

Wahler, R. G., & Dumas, J. E. (1986). Maintenance factors in coercive mother–child interactions: The compliance and predictability hypotheses. *Journal of Applied Behavior Analysis, 19,* 207–219.

Whittaker, J. K., & Pecora, P. J. (1984). A research agenda for residential care. In T. Philpot (Ed.), *Group care practice: The challenge of the next decade* (pp. 126–153). Surrey, UK: Community Care/Business Press International.

Willet, J. B., Ayoub, C. C., & Robinson, D. (1991). Using growth modeling to examine systematic differences in growth: An example of change in the functioning of families at risk of maladaptive parenting, child abuse, or neglect. *Journal of Consulting and Clinical Psychology, 59,* 38–47.

Zaidi, L. Y., Schnurr, P., Knutson, J. F., Kriegler, J., Blake, D., Bremmer, D., et al. (1991, November). *Childhood sexual experiences questionnaire* (Addendum to the Assessing Environment–III). Aimes, IA: National Center for PTSD and University of Iowa.

Zanarini, M. C., & Gunderson, J. G. (1997). Differential diagnosis of antisocial and borderline personality disorders. In D. M. Stoff, J. Breiling, & J. D. Maser (Eds.), *Handbook of antisocial behavior* (pp. 83–91). New York: Wiley.

Zimring, F. E. (1981). Kids, groups, and crime: Some implications of a well-known secret. *Journal of Criminal Law and Criminology, 72,* 867–885.

Zoccolillo, M. (1993). Gender and the development of conduct disorder. *Development and Psychopathology, 5,* 65–78.

Zoccolillo, M., Pickles, A., Quinton, D., & Rutter, M. (1992). The outcome of childhood conduct disorder: Implications for defining adult personality disorder and conduct disorder. *Psychological Medicine, 22,* 1–16.

Zoccolillo, M., & Rogers, K. (1991). Characteristics and outcome of hospitalized adolescent girls with conduct disorder. *Journal of the American Academy of Child and Adolescent Psychiatry, 30,* 973–981.

INDEX

separation from, 124
Dependent variables, 103–104
Depression
    maternal, 34, 39, 134
    and parental discipline practice, 10
    in youth, 86, 112
Developmentally delayed youths, 50, 132–133
Developmental progressions, 4
Development of antisocial behavior, 3–16
    and age of onset for juvenile offending, 11–13
    and community-based treatment models, 6
    contextual factors in, 8
    and determination of intervention targets, 13–15
    family processes, role of, 9–10
    individual factors in, 7–8
    and intervention theories, 5–6
    longitudinal studies of, 5
    peer processes, role of, 10–11
    research breakthroughs on, 4
    social interaction processes as factors in, 9–13
"Deviancy training," 11, 27
Deviant peers, 11, 23, 57, 107. See also Delinquent peer association
Difficult temperament, 7
DISC-2 Interview, 122, 123
Discipline practice, 13
    and adult depression/alcoholism, 10
    adult perception of, 99
    and aggression, 9
    and early- vs. late-onset offenders, 12
    and efficacy of MTFC model, 57
    and EIFC model, 135–136
    by family, 30
    in group care vs. MTFC program, 100, 101
    harsh, 7
    parental, 23–24
    and parental stress, 8
    of preschoolers, 131
    and resistance to treatment, 40–41
Discrepancy scores, 99–103
Disdainful facial expressions, 112
Disengagement methods, 72
Dishion, T. J., 10, 11
Disruptive behavior, 7
Dissemination of MTFC model, 141–149
    creating a culture for, 146–148

    examples, 142–143
    potential barriers to, 144–146
    and progression of model, 148–149
    steps for, 143–144
Distraction techniques, 132
Divorce, 114
Dropping out of school, 113
Drug abuse. See Substance use
DSM-IV, 122, 123
Dunedin studies, 111
Dysthymia, 86

Early-adulthood, antisocial behavior in, 6
Early attachment problems, 7
Early childhood
    antisocial behavior in, 5
    interventions in, 42
Early Intervention Foster Care (EIFC), xiii, 66, 129–140
    model of, 130–131
    study results of, 135–140
    targets of, 131–135
"Early-onset" delinquents, 59
EBC. See Elliott Behavior Checklist
Eclectic–behavior management programs, 65
Ecological interview, 98–99
Eddy, J. M., 42
Educational outcomes, 21
Efficacy (of family-based interventions), 35–38
EIFC. See Early Intervention Foster Care
Elliott Behavior Checklist (EBC), 63, 104, 123–124
Emotionally disturbed youths, 49, 110
Emotional problems, 53–55
Emotional reciprocity, 134
Emotion regulation, 7, 133–135
Empowerment, 147
Enhanced training and support (ETS), 55
Environment, 12, 30
    for preschoolers, 132
    reinforcing, for youths, 67
    safe and supportive, 124
    supportive, for MTFC parents, 67
ETS (enhanced training and support), 55
Exclusion, 5, 112
Exposure to risk factors, 5
Expulsion, school, 87
Eye contact, 85
Eye rolling, 112

Face-to-face meetings, 74

ABOUT THE AUTHOR

Patricia Chamberlain, PhD, is a senior research scientist at the Oregon Social Learning Center (OSLC) and the executive director of the OSLC Community Programs. She is also a cofounder of TFC Consultants. After graduating from Ohio University, she began her career as a primary school teacher for children with behavioral and emotional problems in Chicago. She earned a masters degree in special education from Northern Illinois University and worked as an educational specialist at the Children's Memorial Hospital in Chicago (Department of Psychiatry). She then moved to Oregon to enroll in graduate school at the University of Oregon, where she completed her PhD in educational psychology in 1980.

Dr. Chamberlain has been the principal investigator on eight studies funded by the National Institute of Mental Health, the National Institute on Drug Abuse, the U.S. Department of Education, and the Children's Bureau. Her research has focused on the development and testing of community-based prevention and treatment programs for children and teenagers with conduct problems. She has focused on examining methods to strengthen the roles that adults can play to improve youth adjustment in multiple areas including at home, in school, and with peers. In 1983, she founded the Multidimensional Treatment Foster Care (MTFC) model as a community and family-based alternative to placement in training school, residential center, or group care settings. The MTFC program has received numerous awards and recognitions, including being designated as a national Blueprints Model Program, a Center for Substance Abuse Prevention Exemplary Program for Strengthening America's Families, and a U.S. Department of Education Exemplary Program for Safe, Disciplined, and Drug-Free Schools. The MTFC model was also highlighted in two recent U.S. Surgeon General's reports on children's mental health and youth violence prevention. Dr. Chamberlain is currently the lead investigator of a collaborative project with the San Diego Department of Health and Human Services and the Child and Adolescent Services Research Center aimed at improving foster care. She is also conducting a study in collaboration with the Oregon Youth Authority to examine ways to improve services for girls involved in the juvenile justice system.